The Magnificent Barbarians

Little-Told Tales of the Texas Revolution

Bill and Marjorie K. Walraven

Illustrated by John C. Davis Jr.

Eakin Press • Austin, Texas

FIRST EDITION

Published in the United States of America
By Eakin Press, P.O. Drawer 90159, Austin, Texas 78709

Books by Bill Walraven:

History

Corpus Christi: History of A Texas Seaport
El Rincon: A History of Corpus Christi Beach

Humor

Walraven's World or Star (Boarder) and Other Wars
Real Texans Don't Drink Scotch in Their Dr Pepper

Library of Congress Cataloging-in-Publication Data

Walraven, Bill, 1925–
[1st ed]
The magnificent barbarians : little-told tales of the Texas Revolution / Bill and Marjorie K. Walraven ; illustrated by John C. Davis, Jr.
p. cm.
Includes bibliographical references and index.
ISBN 0-89015-873-8 : $18.95
1. Texas–History–Revolution, 1835–1836–Anecdotes.
I. Walraven, Marjorie K. II. Title.
F390.W17 1993
976.4'03 – dc20 92-71462
CIP

To Valerie, Wilson, and Joe, and to Sandy,
for their children and all other future Texans

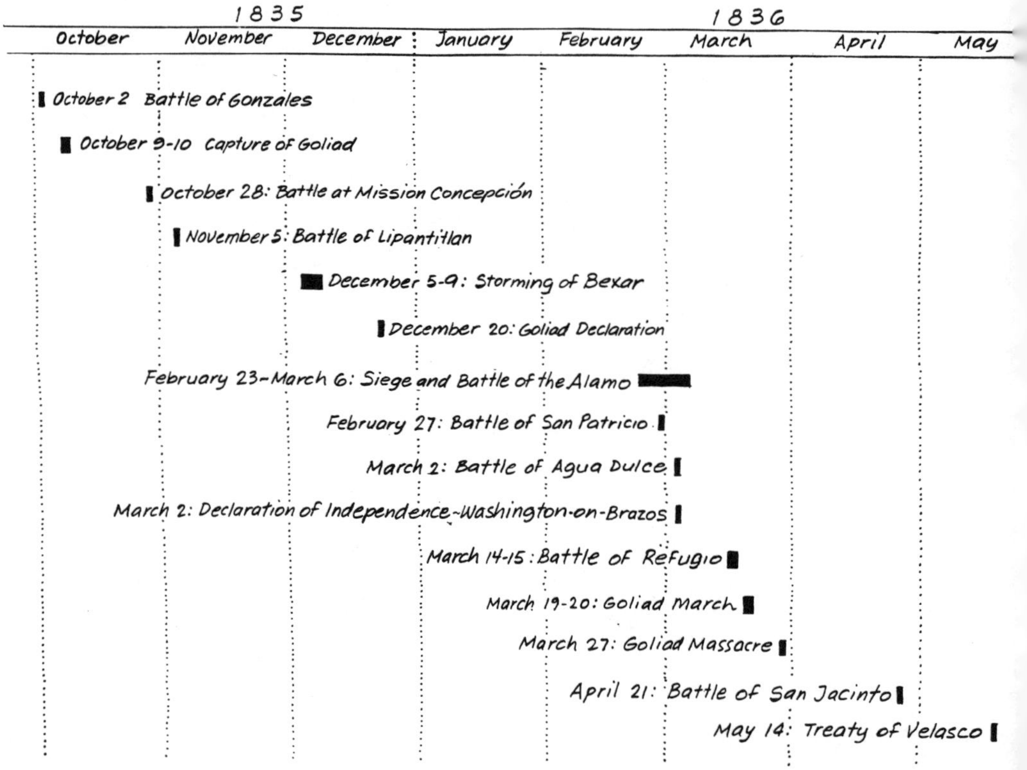
1835
1836
October
November
December
January
February
March
April
May
October 2 Battle of Gonzales
October 9-10 Capture of Goliad
October 28: Battle at Mission Concepción
November 5: Battle of Lipantitlan
December 5-9: Storming of Bexar
December 20: Goliad Declaration
February 23–March 6: Siege and Battle of the Alamo
February 27: Battle of San Patricio
March 2: Battle of Agua Dulce
March 2: Declaration of Independence–Washington-on-Brazos
March 14-15: Battle of Refugio
March 19-20: Goliad March
March 27: Goliad Massacre
April 21: Battle of San Jacinto
May 14: Treaty of Velasco

Contents

Preface

This book was originally planned as a collection of newspaper columns I wrote for *The Corpus Christi Caller-Times* between 1974 and 1989. My purpose in writing them was to show that history can be lively and interesting if it is presented as what it is—the story of people.

In compiling the columns, we discovered that I had sometimes covered the same subjects more than once, often emphasizing different aspects. These we combined and updated.

Space constraints kept the newspaper articles short. Research to flesh them out and verify information led to discovery of other material, some of it previously unpublished, that we decided to include. So what started out as a collection of columns evolved into a different form.

The first chapter deals primarily with the early Spanish explorers, but most of the stories tell of Texians, as the settlers were known throughout the days of the Republic. Some of the material seems chauvinistic, as it supports the view of those Texians as heroes who died fighting for freedom against the tyrannical Antonio López de Santa Anna. Some of the material appears revisionist, as it raises serious questions of covert U.S. Army participation in the Battle of San Jacinto. The book is intended to be neither. History is more complex than "the good guys against the bad guys."

We did not intend to play one group or race against another. Our purpose was to tell of the contributions of all. The first Texian blood spilled in the revolution was that of a black man. Most histories do not credit the some 200 Texians of Mexican descent who participated in the Siege and Storming of Bexar, the Alamo, and San Jacinto. Santa Anna's Mexican soldiers, although ill-equipped, poorly led at times, and badly treated, also fought with great courage.

The people who came from Europe, the United States, and Mexico to become Texians were a rough, tough, and often crude breed. They were sometimes brave to the point of absurdity. Some were motivated by greed. Many came to fight and die for principle. Others came just to fight.

By civilized standards they could be considered barbarian, a term often applied to Sam Houston. But they also left a grand legacy. Their names cover our maps on cities, counties, and streams. They were truly magnificent.

We intentionally excluded footnotes, for we don't claim this to be a "scholarly" work. It is popular history, presented as accurately as possible. We tell stories of the participants, using their own words; the reader can make the judgments.

The story of the 1824 flag was previously printed in *The Alamo Journal*. We thank the management of *The Caller-Times* for permission to use material published in its pages. We thank the partners of Morehead, Dotts & LaPorte advertising agency for letting us use their scanner. We are also indebted to many people who have contributed to the book.

One of the most helpful was the late Bernice Strong, librarian at the Daughters of the Republic of Texas Library at the Alamo, who was anxious to correct the many misconceptions about Texas history.

Charles Long, curator emeritus of the Alamo, has provided many leads and anecdotes over the years.

I have always leaned on friend Dan Kilgore, former president of the Texas State Historical Association and other historical groups, for information, advice, and critical services.

Dr. Terrence Barragy, military historian and history professor at Texas A&I University, has been a useful consultant on military weapons and history.

Galen Greaser, Spanish interpreter at the General Land Office in Austin, was of invaluable help, for he alone seemed able to crack the code of ancient Spanish colloquialisms. Bobby Santiesteban and Doug Howard of the same office were of great assistance in finding the exact location of Camp Sabine.

Patty Murphy, archivist at the Corpus Christi Museum of Science and History, and Tom Kreneck, Special Collections librarian at Corpus Christi State University, have provided excellent materials.

Mrs. Kathleen Huson Maxwell allowed me free rein in the fabulous Dawgwood collection of her father, Hobart Huson, at Refugio.

Kevin R. Young, former chief of historical interpretation at La Bahía and technical adviser on "Alamo. . . The Price of Freedom," has been a valuable resource.

Linda Derry, projects manager for Old Cahawba, directed us to the cemetery near Cahawba, Alabama, where John Walker Baylor is buried.

Others who contributed include Claude D'Unger, partner-in-crime at historical archaeological digs; Gerard Alvarez III, who provided information on the descendants of Panchita Alavez, the Angel of Goliad; and Ray Esparza of San Antonio, who helped with information on his ancestor, Gregorio Esparza.

Thanks also to the staffs at the U.S. Military Academy Archives, the military section of the National Archives, the Perry-Castañeda Library, and the Barker Collection of the University of Texas at Austin, the Texas State Archives, and the Baylor University Library.

There are many others who helped during the twenty years since the columns began. I wish I could remember all of them.

Bill Walraven

ABOUT THE AUTHORS

BILL WALRAVEN, a journalism-history graduate of Texas A&I University in Kingsville, Texas, studied professional writing at the University of Oklahoma. May of his daily columns in the *Corpus Christi Caller-Times* were historical tales, accurate history with a journalistic twist that proved popular with readers. Walraven has also written a history of Corpus Christi and a history of Corpus Christi Beach, as well as two humorous books.

His wife, MAJORIE K. WALRAVEN, a journalism major with an M.A. in history, taught journalism and advised student publications at Mary Carroll High School for twenty-nine years, while working part-time for most of those years as a copy editor for the *Corpus Christi Caller-Times*. She collaborated in consolidating and rewriting the columns and in researching and writing previously unpublished tales.

Introduction

Every acre on earth has been conquered by someone at some time in history. For 350 years Native Americans and the Spanish, French, English, Dutch, and finally the United States contended for North American territory in wars or at the treaty table.

In the early 1800s the drama shifted to the Southwest, where Spain lost out to Mexico. Mexico, already in danger of losing California to Great Britain, was forced to grant Texas independence in 1836. The annexation of Texas led to the U.S.–Mexican War, and Mexico's loss in that war meant that the United States would obtain the territory of the forty-eight contiguous states. This, in turn, brought on the American Civil War, as the nation's acquisition of roughly 500,000 square miles of new land made compromise on the slavery issue impossible.

The key to it all was Texas. And land was the key to its acquisition. The opening of the virgin land to colonization by Americans was the beginning of the end for Hispanic domination.

The early colonists did not worry much about the Mexican government, as long as it left them alone. They were supposed to be Catholic; and the rules, even under the liberal Constitution of 1824, were more restrictive than those of the U.S. Constitution. But land was free. There were no taxes, and no one collected customs fees. In little more than a decade, the newcomers outnumbered the native-born population six to one.

The American frontier spirit began to take over. Public meetings and a voice in government were too strongly ingrained for them to keep quiet. Their town meetings looked like revolutionary gatherings to nervous Mexican rulers, who faced recurring revolutions at home. When Centralists displaced the constitutionalists and ordered more control of the faraway Texians, armies marched and the revolt began.

Many of the colonists did not favor revolution. All they wanted was to farm, raise their families, and have nothing to do with politics. But they were drawn into the maelstrom, either as soldiers or refugees, as massive Mexican armies surged northward. The colonists were in the minority at the Alamo, at Goliad, and at San Jacinto.

Many of the paladins were "foreigners." They came from all over the world, for a variety of reasons. Some had "woman trouble." Others fled from crimes or debt. Most were interested in a new start with land promised for military service. An economic depression in 1819 had sent hundreds of displaced Americans to Texas—lawyers, doctors, merchants, tradesmen, farmers. A surprising number were deserters from the United States Army. Yet they were also fired by idealism. This, combined with rage at the executions and massacres inflicted by Antonio López de Santa Anna, made them a formidable force.

But there was still another group of Texians. In 1836 the population of the state was 35,000 to 50,000. Of this number, 4,200 to 7,000 were native-born citizens of Spanish-Mexican descent. For the most part their role in the struggle against Santa Anna's despotic Centralist government has been overlooked.

The late Hobart Huson of Refugio—attorney, philosopher, general, and historian—was especially critical of the way Texas history has been written and presented in the schools. In 1971 he suggested a new nomenclature, calling the Spanish-Mexican population of the state *Tejanos*. The others would be *Nordics*—American, English, Irish, Scottish, Welsh, French, German, and other ethnic groups. He named the Texas Revolution the "Mexican Federal War in Texas," which originally aimed at restoring the Constitution of 1824. He recommended teaching that the war was an extension of a general uprising throughout Mexico. He called for an exhaustive investigation of all historical matter, allowing the facts to speak for themselves. If this were done, he wrote, Tejanos would be accorded their "rightful place in the radiance of Texas lore."

The Texas Revolution was a joint effort of Nordics and Tejanos to win a revolution against overwhelming odds. Although, as in the American Revolution, there were some Tories, for the most part the Tejano *rancheros* served the Texas Federalist armies as well as the Nordics did and in the same ratio to the population.

If the Tejanos had joined forces with the Centralists, it is very likely that Santa Anna would have been victorious at San Jacinto, and dreams of a free Texas would have been long delayed.

The raging mob of ragged men, Nordic and Tejano, who stormed the barricades at San Jacinto became judges, legislators, and leaders of a new republic and state. Most of them didn't plan it that way, but–for better or worse–they became the fuel for the Manifest Destiny of the United States.

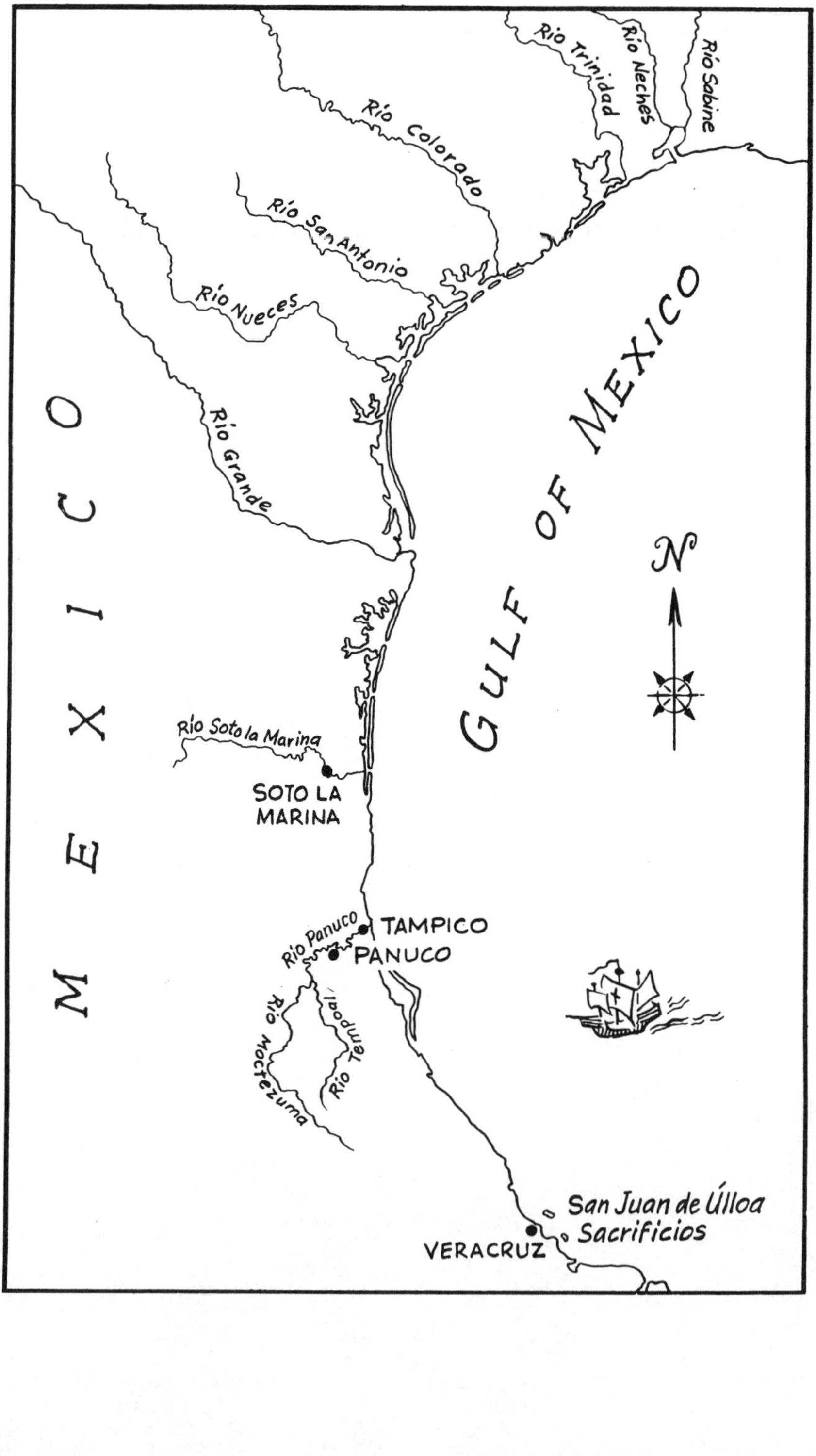

Río Trinidad
Río Neches
Río Sabine
Río Colorado
Río San Antonio
Río Nueces
Río Grande
MEXICO
GULF OF MEXICO
N
Río Soto la Marina
SOTO LA MARINA
TAMPICO
Río Panuco
PANUCO
Río Moctezuma
Río Tempoal
San Juan de Úlloa
Sacrificios
VERACRUZ

[1]

THE PATHFINDERS

The First Europeans

Who was the first European to set foot on Texas soil? Was it Amerigo Vespucci? Alonso Álvarez de Piñeda? Alvar Nuñez Cabeza de Vaca?

The argument will never be settled.

Vespucci drew a map showing a rough outline of the Gulf of Mexico during a 1495 voyage and published it in 1507, Corpus Christi historian Dan Kilgore said. German cartographer Martin Waldseemüller copied the maps. He assumed Vespucci had discovered the new continent and labeled it *America* in his honor. Other Europeans maintained that Vespucci never made the voyage. Waldseemüller omitted the name from subsequent maps, but the damage was done. The original map was widely circulated; and the new land masses, both north and south, were firmly labeled America. No evidence has been found that Vespucci ever set foot on Texas soil.

Twenty-four years after that voyage, in 1519, de Piñeda sailed along the Texas coast under orders from Francisco Garay, Spanish governor of Jamaica. Garay was anxious to find a passage to the Spice Islands and at the same time acquire some of Mexico's gold before Hernán Cortés sacked it all up.

De Piñeda landed at various points, noting rivers, inlets, and the nature of the native population. He made stops around the entire perimeter of the Gulf of Mexico, each time pausing to claim the land for Emperor Charles V, king of Spain. His fleet of four ships carried 270 soldiers. He edged his way into Cortés country and dropped anchor at Vera Cruz.

Cortés took time out from his conquering duties to deal with de Piñeda. He captured a landing party, and the fleet sailed back to the north. De Piñeda sailed up what he called *Río de las Palmas.*

This river is generally believed to be the one known today in Texas as the Rio Grande and in Mexico as the *Río Bravo,* although no proof of that fact exists. Researchers for the Texas Antiquities Committee have found that by the mid-1500s the Rio Grande was labeled *Río Bravo* on most Spanish maps, and the river known today as Soto la Marina was called the River of Palms. In de Piñeda's day, however, the mouth of the Rio Grande was covered with Texana palms, one of the state's few native palms. For that reason, historians have also known it as the River of Palms.

In any event, de Piñeda located a sloping sandy beach to careen his ships so they could be scraped and caulked. Residents of some forty Indian villages watched curiously and appeared to be peaceably inclined. And de Piñeda picked up enough gold trinkets to whet the governor's appetite. He reported back to Garay that the tribesmen were friendly and the land was healthy, fertile, and peaceful. The spot was ideal for a settlement.

With this in mind, in 1520 Garay sent Diego de Antonio Camargo with 150 men, brick, lime, and laborers to build a permanent fort. The settlement was to be named Garay. But the Spaniards behaved as they had elsewhere in the New World. They took food from the natives and ordered them to get more. They did as they wished with the Indian women and likely forced the males into hard labor. When the Indians objected, Camargo blustered and threatened them with his thunderous weapons.

That was a mistake, because the Spaniards were not dealing with a docile people. The Indians were peaceful; but when disturbed, they became warlike and aggressive. They resisted. Camargo decided to march upriver and burn a few villages to teach the heathens a lesson. Suddenly, he was confronted by thousands of warriors. He ordered a retreat.

The fleeing Spaniards lost eighteen men and all eight of their horses before they could clamber aboard the slow-moving ships. The vessels then had to navigate twenty miles of river, all the time surrounded by canoes filled with warriors firing arrows onto the decks, killing and wounding many more soldiers and sailors. One ship went aground and was lost. A second sank before it reached Vera Cruz and the third a few days afterward. The sixty survivors had no choice but to join Cortés. A group of reinforcements dispatched by Garay found only hostile Indians. Some of Garay's men made their way to Vera Cruz. Others were not so fortunate. Later some of their conquistador comrades were horrified to find the hides of some of these men nailed to temple walls, their beards intact, facial features recognizable.

With no word of the disasters, Garay set sail for his new colony in 1523 with an army of 750 officers and men in sixteen ships. He arrived with a charter and with a civil government already appointed, the first in Texas. When they landed, they found nothing but angry Indians and ruins of an encampment. His men went south to Panuco and learned that the territory belonged to Cortés by royal decree. Garay surrendered to Cortés and died soon after as Cortés' "house guest."

Río de las Palmas was forgotten. And whether Garay would have been in Tamaulipas or in Texas does not matter, for it was not to be. It would be more than three centuries before the permanent settlement of Brownsville, Texas, appeared near the mouth of the Rio Grande.

Too bad. Garay would have made a great tourist attraction. It would have been 326 years older than Brownsville; 90 years older than Santa Fe; 162 years older than Ysleta, the oldest city in Texas; and 36 years older than St. Augustine, Florida, the oldest European settlement in the United States.

It pays to be nice to the natives.

Super Seamanship

Lawyers and insurance companies were active in old Spain. When the owners sent supplies to the New World, they shipped them in the oldest, most unseaworthy ships they could find. Some had their hulls badly eaten by saltwater worms. The ships would then be insured for three times their actual worth. Of course, the crew and passengers on the ships didn't know this. Many of them were in the middle of the ocean when they discovered the ploy.

If, however, the owners counted on silver, some gold, spices, skins, oils, and other goods being returned to Spain, they wanted ships in good condition.

Good condition, however, was none too good. Besides prisoners and slaves, passengers returning to Spain included adventurers who had made their fortunes, priests, and others. Most were of high birth, but there were no privileges on these miserable ships. The food was terrible, often served at night so the passengers couldn't see the worms in it.

In rough weather the voyage was torture. "Along the keel, seawater, food scraps, urine and vomit collected in the bilge . . . A storm would put the crew in a frenzied state as they worked to save the ship. The passengers would become a quivering mass of humanity lodged between the decks," one report said.

When the situation became intolerable, the ship was "rummaged," or run aground, and everything removed, scrubbed, washed in vinegar, and reloaded. The passengers complained of the coarseness of the crew and the horrible sanitation. The toilet was a platform along the after rail in plain view of everyone. The joke was when the person sitting there was doused by a wave.

Food was cooked in the forward part of the ship over a fire built in a sand box. Sometimes this caught a ship on fire and burned it to the water line. After seamen discovered the hammock from New World natives, they were probably more comfortable than the passengers, who were crammed into small cabins.

Occasionally the little ships, no more than one hundred feet long with ninety or more people aboard, became becalmed. Food supplies and water were exhausted, and those aboard perished before the winds freshened. Cannon were so crude they were almost as much danger to the gunners as to their targets. The weapons were effective only at very close range. For this reason, the ships' manifests included crossbows, shields, and boarding pikes. Cannon shot included iron and lead balls, as well as round stones. Cannon were loaded with a breach chamber that was almost as likely to blow backward as forward.

The English are generally regarded as the great mariners. But the Spaniards, in their leaky tubs, managed to explore and claim much of the New World.

That took real seamanship.

Cabeza de Vaca

By 1528 the Spanish crown had created the province of Panuco-Victoria Garayana, which extended from Panuco to Florida, with Nuño de Guzmán as governor. Guzmán, who was receiving no gold, started a new industry–slavery. He sent out patrols to capture Indians and sold them, a fact that spread from tribe to tribe across the country. The practice portended disaster for the survivors of the Pánfilo de Narváez expedition.

It was logical that if there was gold in Mexico and gold in South America, there must be gold to the north. Therefore Narváez, with Alvar Nuñez Cabeza de Vaca as his navigator, sailed from Cuba on a voyage that was to culminate in one of the most dramatic sagas of history. Four survivors, after undergoing untold suffering, traversed the southwestern part of North America for six years before finding other Europeans to lead them back to Mexico.

The ships sailed for the *Río de las Palmas*, but spring winds blew them onto the west coast of Florida. Narváez sent the fleet on around the Gulf, planning to march with his cavalry and foot soldiers to Panuco, which he erroneously thought was only a few hundred miles away. The ships missed the mouth of the river, then returned to search for their leader; but he was not to be found. They gave up and returned to Vera Cruz.

Narváez's force had set out to find gold and food but found neither. Disease and hostile natives decimated their number until they decided to try the sea again. More than 200 Spaniards set out from Florida on five crude boats they built to sail across the Gulf of Mexico. One was lost in the Mississippi Delta, and Narváez's vanished at sea. The vessel commanded by Cabeza de Vaca shipwrecked on an island the Spaniards called *Malhado* (Misfortune)—possibly Galveston Island. Another wrecked nearby. Some eighty men were cast ashore more dead than alive.

Karankawas carried the survivors to their village, nursed them, and wailed their sympathy at the strangers' misfortune. Their friendship waned when white man's diseases wiped out half their number.

And there were other problems. In his journal Cabeza de Vaca wrote the following account: "Five Christians, of a mess (quartered) on the coast, came to such extremity that they ate their dead; the body of the last one only was found unconsumed. . . . This produced great commotion among the Indians giving rise to so much censure that had they known it in season to have done so, doubtless they would have destroyed any survivor." The Karankawas are often accused of cannibalism themselves. If they did, indeed, adopt the practice, perhaps they learned it from Spaniards.

Another barge beached far to the south, some say on Padre Island south of present-day Corpus Christi, where Indians of the

Camoles tribe killed all forty-eight castaways, who were too weak to resist.

Most of the survivors on the upper coast perished attempting to go overland to Panuco; but, incredibly, four lived to return to New Spain–Cabeza de Vaca, Alonso del Castillo Maldonado, Andres Dorantes de Carranca, and Estevanico, Dorantes' Moorish slave. They were enslaved by various tribes for six years before they escaped and made their remarkable trek across the country, ending in Sonora in March 1536. Dangerous natives accepted them as medicine men; and de Vaca performed possibly the first surgery in what is now the United States, removing an arrowhead from an Indian's shoulder.

In his report he mentioned finding turquoise, selling trinkets among the Indians, and hearing rumors of cities of fabulous riches. This stimulated conquistador imaginations and led to a 1540 commission to Francisco Vásquez de Coronado to find and conquer the fabled cities. Coronado found only pueblos, hovels, poverty, and failure that led to his premature death.

The same bug bit Hernando de Soto. He searched for gold in Florida, Georgia, North and South Carolina, Tennessee, Alabama, Mississippi, Louisiana, Arkansas, Missouri, Oklahoma, and possibly Kansas. Hogs that escaped from his expedition became ancestors of the razorbacks of Arkansas and East Texas. Various Indian tribes harassed de Soto constantly, likely because he could not resist kidnapping their women and accumulated a harem of about a hundred Indian maidens. His three-year search began in 1539 and ended in 1542, when he died of fever and was buried near the Mississippi. His lieutenant, Luís de Moscoso de Alvarado, continued into and across Central Texas and back to the Mississippi, where he built boats and sailed down the Texas coast to Mexico with half the original 600 men surviving.

The cost was high for these explorers, who did not find the riches Cortés and others claimed to the south. They suffered mightily, and many died of disease and from retribution by natives they antagonized. But they validated the Spanish claim to lands that would endure four centuries of bloody confrontations. And, through their sacrifices, they left an indelible Hispanic heritage over a vast territory of what is now the United States.

A Beach Ordeal

Laughter and happy farewells echoed over the docks as the passengers boarded the caravels. The long wait was over; they were going home. The year was 1554, and most had been in primitive New Spain for several years. Among the group were *conquistadores,* successful settlers who had made their fortunes, others broken by disease, some who had achieved spiritual contentment as missionaries, a few slaves, and several prisoners who were returning to Spain to face trial.

In the midst of the bustling confusion on the pier, Fray Ivan Ferrer of the Order of Saint Dominic had a dark premonition. A number of his fellow missionaries and Vera Cruz citizens and officials who had come to bid farewell heard his loud voice quieten the din: "Woe to those that go to Spain because neither us nor the fleet will get there. We will all die, most of us, and the ones that will remain will experience great difficulties, even though at the end they will die, except for the very few."

The priest said that he himself "will stay hidden in some secluded place and will live some years with good health; but the importance of my trip is to fulfill the will of God."

An uneasy silence followed, for such a disaster was entirely possible. Then, likely, his friends smiled at the dire prediction, for Fray Ferrer was considered eccentric, to say the least. He was a good scholar who had readily learned the native languages, but he had written a mysterious book composed of numerals and symbols that only he could understand. He sent a brief explanation of it to Emperor Charles V, hinting that he knew of happenings among the royal families of Europe and was able to see strange events in the future. This piqued the royal curiosity; and the Crown ordered him back to Spain, directing that no one should delay his coming.

His superior wrote that Ferrer's head was full of dreams and fantasies. The order to send him "can only cause confusion there, misfortune here and shame to the habit he wears. . . . This is a much talked-about, unsavory topic among us here and we trust the situation will be remedied," wrote Friar Andres de Moguer. "I do not regret his departure."

Ferrer's deadly prophecy was recalled by Fray Marcos de Mena, who survived the tragedy foretold by the mystic priest. Mena reported the account to Fray Augustín Dávila Padilla, who also interviewed another survivor of the disaster.

The saga began at San Juan de Ulua, the port of Vera Cruz, as the four vessels, the *Santa María de Yciar, San Esteban, Espiritu Santo,* and *San Andres,* were loaded with cochineal, liquid amber, white sugar, wool, cowhides, and a fortune in gold and silver. It was April 9, 1554, too early for the dreaded hurricane season, which runs from June through October.

The flotilla sailed without incident for twenty days, following the current northward along the Gulf Coast so it could enter Havana from the north. Then, from the east, a sudden storm hit with the fierceness of a hurricane, stirring up fifteen-foot seas and sending the helpless caravels scooting toward the Texas shore. Fray Mena said about 400 were aboard the vessels. The crews threw out anchors in a desperate attempt to halt the mad slide to the beach. Anchors and lines snapped, and three ships piled up on the shore of Padre Island. Anchors held for the *San Andres,* the only ship of the four to remain largely intact. It limped on to Havana, leaving the others to their fate. The three ships piled into the sandy beach near the present-day Port Mansfield Channel, forty-five miles north of the Rio Grande.

Three hundred passengers and crewmen survived by swimming or clinging to boxes and pieces of wood. Among them were Mena, Ferrer, and three other friars. Provisions, including hams, biscuits, and other foodstuffs, a box of crossbows, and swords, washed ashore. Seamen salvaged wood or possibly a small boat from the surf; and one of the captains, Francisco del Huerto, and six other survivors set sail for Vera Cruz. They arrived on June 4, and the normally unyielding bureaucracy moved with amazing speed to send a fleet to recover the lost treasure before others got to it.

Had the survivors stayed with the wreckage and conserved the salvaged food, they might have been rescued. However, as they figured they were only two or three days from Spanish settlements at Panuco, they set out walking, carelessly taking food for only one day. Even with adequate food, survival would have been difficult.

They traveled south for six days and saw no one. On the seventh, they saw about one hundred Indians, heavily armed with bows and arrows, but appearing peaceful. The Indians offered fish and game and built a fire to cook it. Suspicious, the military men remained on watch as the others started to eat. Suddenly, the Indians shot arrows. In retaliation, the Spaniards attacked with arrows from their more powerful crossbows. No Spaniards died, but three Indians were killed.

The march continued. The Spaniards had no shoes, and their clothing was scanty. They were soon sunburned, exhausted, and thirsty. All the time the Indians were charging in to shoot arrows into stragglers. They were emboldened to see that the Spaniards did not have a "harquebus," an ancient firearm. They were much afraid of the noise and fire of the stick with the power of the sun, like lightning from a cloud.

At the *Río Bravo* the Spaniards built rafts. A priest, Diego de la Cruz, thought he was jettisoning his personal belongings, but threw the party's crossbows overboard. Now the war party attacked in earnest. Women and children were particularly vulnerable. Many fell from exhaustion. Two Spaniards were captured, stripped of their clothing, and released. The others removed their clothing, thinking the Indians would then leave them alone. Military men, churchmen, women, and children, all were naked in the sun. The women were sent ahead so their nakedness would not be on view to the men.

"The Indians, amused no doubt at the actions of their marked victims, gathered the clothes with much shouting and dancing, but far from desisting in their pursuit of the poor Spaniards, they redoubled the attacks upon the stragglers and harassed the entire group continually . . . ," Dávila wrote. "No sooner would a mother stop to help a child than an arrow found its mark . . . . If a mother lingered by the side of a dying baby, she soon joined him in death . . . ."

After five days 200 remained alive, half of them seriously wounded. While the men crossed the River of Palms (*Soto la Marina*), the few remaining women and children were killed on the bank. Two priests went inland, attempting to find help from a friendly tribe. They were joined by Francisco Vásquez, a seaman. The friars both died of wounds. Vásquez retreated to the wreck site–a move that was to save his life.

Three other Dominicans and two sailors decided to recross the river, but their canoe was upset by waves created by two large whales swimming toward the Gulf. They built a raft and decided to catch up with the party going south. The first group they found were dead or dying, all punctured by many arrows. The next day they overtook the rest.

The Spaniards straggled on with little to eat or drink. For twenty days they did not see an Indian. They thought they might yet reach the safety of a friendly village.

They were wrong. The Indians had no crops or herds to tend. They could devote their full energies to the game. The sport was to hunt down and kill the unarmed Spaniards. The struggling survivors reached another big river, made a raft, and prepared to cross, elated that their goal was so near. Suddenly, a fleet of hostile Indians in war canoes came down the river. The naked survivors hid in tall reeds.

"Their concealment probably would have succeeded had it not been for an unforeseen circumstance," Dávila's account said. "While crouching quietly in the rushes, they suddenly became aware of millions of ants that stung them with such fury that they were unable to withstand the fire of their stings, preferring to throw themselves upon the merciless Indians who would put an end to their misery."

The Indians attacked, killing practically all the men. The few who made it to the opposite bank were wounded. The bleeding survivors decided to leave those who were unable to travel. Among those who could not go on was Fray Marcos de Mena. His friends buried him in the sand to keep Indians and animals away from his body, leaving his face uncovered so he might breathe until the end.

The friar heard his friends leave. He fainted, but woke briefly and heard the Indians pass by. He awoke later feeling better. The warm sand had stopped the flow of blood from his wounds. Strengthened by his rest, he left his shallow grave and followed the tracks of the others. About a mile down the beach he found them, all dead—except for Ferrer, who had disappeared. Mena sat down among the corpses and wept, then prayed and continued the march.

He walked for four days, looking for Indians all the way, expecting to be killed. He had only foul-tasting clams to eat and nothing to drink. When he stopped to rest on a log, he was covered by sandcrabs attracted by worms in his festering wounds. The crabs seemed to be trying to devour him alive.He stumbled on for several days until he reached the Panuco River. At last he would have water. He tried to drink and found the water salty. It seemed to be the end. He raised his hands to heaven and asked to be relieved of his life of suffering.

Looking up, he was happy to see Indians in a canoe. If they were friendly, he would live. If they were hostile, he would die. He fainted. Later he awoke in the bottom of a canoe. Two friendly Indians took him to Tampico, where seven arrowheads were removed from his body. Earlier he had painfully pulled one from his eye.

It was July when he was rescued, after he had walked for forty days. He lived until 1584, working in the church, but the torturous trek left him a near invalid the rest of his life.

When the single boatload of survivors reached Vera Cruz in June, Capt. Angel de Villafaña was sent to recover the treasure from the sunken ships. Francisco Vásquez greeted him from the wreckage. He was half-starved but alive because of food from the ships, fish and crabs he had been able to catch, and water from holes dug in the beach.

Divers left some 52,000 pounds of precious metals in the sands of Padre Island but recovered some 36,000 pounds. Vásquez received a salvage share and lived many years as a respected citizen in Mexico. But hundreds of lawsuits were filed over the recovered treasure, as shippers and others argued about amounts they claimed to have contributed to the cargo. Many became rich from the fortunes of those who died.

Mena believed that the disaster was punishment for the harsh treatment of Indians by Spaniards interested only in riches. Their retribution was loss of their treasure and death at the hands of the Indians.

As for the mystic Ferrer, the others saw his promise to them fulfilled. Did he die or did he find the "secluded place" he had predicted for himself? Dávila believed he died. Nothing was ever heard from him again. Only God knows if the priest fulfilled His will.

Incredible Journey

The Gulf Coast was not kind to intruders. Just as it did to so many Spaniards, it claimed the lives of most of 114 Englishmen put ashore north of Tampico in 1568. But three, David Ingram, Richard Browne, and Richard Twide, traversed what would become the United States from south to north, ending up in what is now New Brunswick, in a feat that was as spectacular as that of Cabeza de Vaca thirty-five years earlier.

They were seamen aboard one of Capt. John Hawkins' ships. Not yet a famous privateer, Hawkins, with his young cousin Francis Drake, commanded a fleet composed of the *Jesus of Lubeck*, *Minion*, and four smaller ships, *Angel*, *Swallow*, *Judith*, and *William and John*. The Englishmen raided for slaves in Africa and sold them to Spaniards, contrary to orders from the Spanish crown.

In September 1568 Hawkins pulled his fleet, battered by storms and desperately short of water, into the harbor of San Juan de Ulua for repair and refitting. He had three captured ships and one hundred hostages to exchange for this service.

Suddenly, a Spanish fleet appeared. The stalemate was broken when the English agreed to let the Spanish enter the harbor and to release their hostages if they could reprovision in peace. The Spanish commander sent written word that his intentions were peaceful. Hawkins invited him in.

Once inside the harbor, however, the Spaniards refused to honor the agreement. They uncovered their cannon and opened fire on the anchored English ships. It was a duckshoot. Hundreds of English seamen were killed. The incident, dismissed by the Spaniards as chastisement of pirates who had disregarded orders forbidding trade in Spanish territory, was the first step leading to war between England and Spain.

All the ships but two were sunk. The *Minion*, commanded by Hawkins, and the *Judith*, commanded by Drake, managed to make sail and escape, picking up survivors as they went. The ships were overloaded and short of water. Just north of the present site of Tampico, 114 seamen volunteered to be put ashore. The men thought their chances of survival were better on land.

Many were killed by Indians made hostile to whites by the Spanish. Most marched to the south, to be captured by the Spaniards and presumably accorded all the usual amenities reserved for pirates. Twenty-six went north.

What happened to the others is not clear. The Indians must have killed some. Apparently, others stayed and married natives. Hawkins and Drake, furious, vowed to devote their lives to revenge on the Spanish. But Ingram, Browne, and Twide, three ordinary seamen, survived to complete one of the most fantastic journeys ever recorded.

Richard Hakluyt recorded their saga in *The Principall Navigations, Voiages and Discoveries of the English Nation.* They walked up the barrier islands off New Spain, swimming swift currents of rivers and island passes. They met tribe after tribe of hostile Indians. Perhaps they convinced them that they, too, were enemies of the Spaniards. They passed shipwrecks, some still bearing gold and silver treasure they could not carry. They saw many strange people who, no doubt, thought them even stranger. They endured blistering hot and freezing cold and covered all types of terrain.

Ingram had his own name for the Rio Grande–the River of May. The coastal plain he described as "great plaines, as large & as fayre in many places as may be seene, being as plaine as a board." He got some of the animals and plants in the voyage mixed up, recalling the hippopotamus and elephant from an African stop and some plants from South America. He said they traveled more than twelve months and figured they traveled 2,000 miles without stopping more than three or four days at any one place.

He wrote: "The ground & Countrey is most excellent, fertile and pleasant, & specially towards the river of May. For the grass of y rest is not so greene, as it is in these parts, for the other is burnt away with the heate of the Sunne. And as all the Countrey is good and most delicate. . . ."

They found the grass near the water too thick, so they walked on higher ground. Ingram was amazed at the natives' rubbing briers together to make fire and at palm trees which "carieth hayres on the leaues thereof, which reach to the ground, Whereof the Indians doe make ropes and cords for their Cotten beds, and doe vse the same to many other purposes."

He told of a tree that yields sweet sap "which is most excellent drinke. But it wil distemper both your head and body, if you drinke too much thereof, as our strong Wines will doe in these partes. . . . Also they haue a kinde of Graine, the eare whereof is as big as the wrist of a mans arme: the graine is like a flat pease, it maketh very good bread and white." It was the European introduction to corn.

Ingram also told of animals. He described buffalo, which he called "Buffes," as " beasts as big as two Oxen, in length almost twentie foot, hauing long ears like a Blood hound, with long haires about their eares, their hornes be crooked like Rams hornes, their eyes blacke, their haires long, blacke, rough, & shagged as a Goat: The Hides of these beasts are solde very deare, this Beast doeth keepe companie onely by couples, male and female, & doeth alwayes fight with others of the same kinde when they do meete. . . ."

The path of the three is uncertain, but it took them to the Atlantic Ocean. This was almost forty years before the first English colonists landed at Jamestown in 1607 and more than fifty years before the Pilgrims landed at Plymouth.

They drew pictures of ships in the sand, and Indians told them they had seen such ships. They continued on to the St. John River in modern-day New Brunswick, where a French ship that had put in to get water, the *Gangarine*, picked them up and transported them to France. They made their way home to England in 1569. Two weeks later, they "came to Master John Hawkins, who had set them on shore vpon the Baie of Mexico, and vnto eche of them he gaue a reward."

They drew pictures of ships in the sand, and Indians told them they had seen such ships.

That chance encounter on the North American coast was to cost Spain dearly. The tale Ingram told helped stimulate the English to colonize America. And by that encounter the Spaniards made an arch enemy of Sir Francis Drake, who would become rich and famous pillaging Spanish ships and ports. Hawkins and Drake designed and led the fleet that defeated the Spanish Armada twenty years later.

Had those two died in a minor sea battle off Vera Cruz in 1568, the Spanish might have controlled the seas and perhaps the seeds of Anglo culture would never have been planted on the eastern shore of the continent to sprout into the United States of America.

The First Republic

Parades and celebrations in modern-day Texas honor the *Diez y Seis*, the Sixteenth of September, Mexican Independence Day. Although most of the celebrants are Americans of Mexican descent, all Texans can claim a connection with the revolution that won Mexico's independence from Spain.

Miguel Hidalgo y Costilla became the father of Mexican independence on September 16, 1810, when he rang the bells of his church at Dolores and shouted his famous *grito*, "Long live our Lady of Guadalupe! Long live independence! Down with bad government!"

Calling for the expulsion of foreign rulers, he led a ragged army against the well-equipped Spaniards. He was ambushed March 21, 1811, at Acatita de Baján and put to death four months later. And the man who laid the trap for Hidalgo, Ignacio Elizondo, was to play a role in the Mexican Revolution in Texas.

It's not generally recognized, but the same breed of wandering, adventuresome American frontiersmen who won immortality at the Alamo and San Jacinto came to Texas to help free Mexico from Spanish rule. Their motives were not entirely altruistic. They wanted land; and they figured that if they could help the rebels win, they would be entitled to establish Texas as a republic or as a new state in the Union. More of them died in the revolt against Spain than were killed later in the Texas War of Independence. But their deaths created no great stir in the United States, for their cause did not have popular support. A few survived to claim veterans' land grants from the Mexican government.

The story is almost unknown in Texas history, but it is told in *Forgotten Battlefield of the First Texas Revolution: The Battle of Medina, August 18, 1813,* written by Ted Schwarz and edited and annotated by Robert H. Thonhoff, and in *Green Flag Over Texas*, by Dr. Julia Kathryn Garrett.

Another account of the period was published in 1913 by John Warren Hunter. It is "The Autobiography of Carlos Beltran." In the December 1940 issue of *Frontier Times*, Hunter said he translated the manuscript after obtaining it through W.W. Mills, who had served as U.S. consul at Chihuahua, where Beltran died in 1876. According to that manuscript, Beltran was born in Wheeling, Virginia, in 1788. At eighteen he joined an expedition by Aaron Burr, "the object of which no one seemed to know, further than the promise of good pay and adventure without limit."

The one hundred-man party barged down the Ohio and Mississippi rivers, and Burr was arrested when they reached Louisiana. The expedition disintegrated, and Beltran went to Nacogdoches, where the Spaniards threw him in jail on March 1, 1807. After a number of adventures, he took up residence as a tinner and gunsmith in the Spanish frontier outpost of San Antonio de Béjar (pronounced Bay´-har), known to Americans as "Bexar," with the *x* silent.

The revolt started by Father Hidalgo reached San Antonio in

1811 when a retired army captain, Juan Bautista de las Casas, took over the town and announced for Hidalgo. As revolution and counterrevolution swirled across Mexico, Casas was betrayed and executed. His head was then exhibited on a pole near the former Mission San Antonio de Valero. The mission had been converted to a fortress known by the name of a detachment of soldiers quartered there. They, in turn, had been known by the name of the cottonwood trees –*los alamos*–in the part of Coahuila from whence they had come.

In 1813 Don José Bernardo Gutierrez de Lara and Augustus William Magee, a West Point graduate who had resigned his commission, invaded Texas with an army of Americans, native Texans, Europeans, and Indians. The army included a contingent of Americans Gutierrez had recruited in the United States and others he later was to call "ambitious rascals" from the Neutral Ground. This was a lawless no-man's land between Mexico and the United States, bordered by the Sabine River on the west and the Arroyo Hondo to the east, where criminals and renegades from both countries found refuge. Gutierrez offered the recruits a league of land and booty captured from the Spaniards.

On April 6, 1813, under the leadership of Gutierrez, Texas declared its independence from Spain. Gutierrez published the first Mexican constitution for the new republic, creating a president and a junta with seven members appointed by the president. He appointed himself president.

Gutierrez had won this position when the rebel army defeated a Spanish army led by Governor Manuel Salcedo of Texas and Governor Simón Herrera of Nuevo León at the Battle of Rosillo, also called the Battle of Salado, on March 29, 1813, thus capturing San Antonio.

Gunsmith Beltran had managed to stay out of politics until earlier that year, when the Spanish *comandante* demanded that he turn over all his rifles. He refused and was thrown into jail but was freed by the victorious Republicans.

The rebel victory at Rosilla opened the floodgates of the bloodletting that would wash over the Alamo City. One evening a few days after Salcedo and Herrera surrendered, a group of about one hundred armed men took the two governors and other Royalist leaders from their prison in the Alamo and executed them a short distance from town on the banks of the San Antonio River. Accounts of the massacre differ, but historians generally agree that the Royalists were denied the rites of the Church and then their throats were slit with "swords whetted on the soles of the executioners' boots." In *Our Catholic Heritage in Texas*, Dr. Carlos E. Castañeda said, "Their bodies were stripped, and left to be devoured by the coyotes and the buzzards."

Most accounts agree that the leader of the massacre was a captain named Antonio Delgado. According to Beltran's account, Delgado said his father had been executed by the Royalists; the young officer was acquitted after making a spirited defense of his actions. Schwarz quotes a report that claimed Delgado's mother was forced to be present as her husband was beheaded and "by order of Salcedo the blood from the bleeding head of his father was sprinkled over his unfortunate mother."

Gutierrez received the blame for the treachery, though some historians believe a mob carried out the lynching. The executions disgusted the Americans, and many returned home. Castañeda credits another reason for their departure. Gutierrez declined to give them credit for their assistance; and, in the formation of his government, ignored their leaders. Furthermore, he called upon the people of Texas to "free themselves from all foreign domination."

Meanwhile, Elizondo, a former insurgent officer who turned his back on the rebel cause and then betrayed Father Hidalgo, was gathering his forces. Although Gutierrez tried to reconvert him, he refused, writing to the Republican, "I would not consent to it because I am determined that in Hell shalt thou be put, which will be thy last refuge, thy hairs pulled out, thy body burnt and thy ashes scattered, and I denounce thee a coward–nevertheless being a Catholic, I desire thy salvation."

Elizondo and his troops then advanced upon San Antonio. With the help of the remaining Americans, Gutierrez's Republicans caught the Royalists at prayer on Sunday morning, June 20, 1813, and badly defeated them in the Battle of Alazan Creek. Indians who had been promised a bounty killed and scalped the fleeing soldiers and their women, as well as the wounded. Elizondo and some of his troops escaped. Texas was free of Spanish rule–but only briefly.

Factional struggles, largely instigated in the United States, split the rebel movement; and soon Gutierrez was relieved of command. He returned with his family to the United States, where he fought under Andrew Jackson at the Battle of New Orleans.

Meanwhile, the developments in Texas were precipitating a storm from the south. In 1811 a ruthless Spanish officer, Col.

Joaquín de Arredondo, had been sent from Vera Cruz to quell the rebellion in Texas. Because of uncertainties about landing a military force on the Texas coast, he sailed instead to Tampico and established headquarters at Aguayo, capital of Nuevo Santander. In 1812 he fought rebels to the south, in San Luís Potosí. In 1813 he was ready to turn his attention back to Texas. He marched northward, proclaiming that towns that followed the rebels would be consumed in blood and fire.

In San Antonio, Gen. José Álvarez de Toledo took command and renamed his military force the Republican Army of North Mexico. Toledo was a Spanish-born Cuban backed by the Americans but mistrusted by the native-born Tejanos. He divided the army along ethnic lines, with one company to be made up of the American volunteers and another to be made up of Mexicans and Indians. It was an unfortunate decision. Within two weeks after Toledo assumed command, the army was destroyed.

The rebels met Arredondo's Royalists on August 18, in the Battle of Medina, fought in the *encinal* (live oak motts) and hot sands of present-day Atascosa County, some ten miles south of the Medina River and north of the Atascosa River. The Republicans charged when they thought the enemy was retreating. When they were exhausted, they ran into the main force of Arredondo's army. Most of the Americans were killed in the battle. Others were hunted and speared by Spanish cavalry.

Schwarz described the battle as the bloodiest ever fought on Texas soil. Most of the more than 400 Americans and 600 Tejanos and Lipan Indians died. Almost that many of Arredondo's Royalist Spanish Army were also killed. More men died in the Battle of Medina than perished in all the combined sieges and battles of the Revolution of 1835-36.

"Never in the history of this country has there been a major battle with such a disproportionate number of unknown dead and so many unhonored survivors," Schwarz wrote before his death in 1977.

Schwarz's book dispels many myths that have surrounded the battle. Most twentieth-century histories report it at the Medina River instead of Encinal de Medina. Also, the accepted view was that Arredondo drew Toledo into a trap. *Texas History Movies* pictures a lot of little dots chasing some retreating circles into a V that turned into an 0, with Royalists cutting the Republicans down with deadly crossfire. Actually, Toledo's army chased a patrol, met another column, and chased it inadvertently into Arredondo's barricaded camp. The battle lasted four hours in blazing heat. The outcome was in doubt. In fact, one American participant wrote that "... the battery of the enemy was twice silenced by the American rifles, and the singular spectacle presented itself of two armies flying from each other, each thinking itself defeated."

Some accounts say the leader of the Tejanos, Col. Miguel Menchaca, refused to follow Toledo's orders and, with his men, charged into the Royalist main force. One of these was written many years later by Antonio Menchaca, a teenage relative of the revolutionary officer in 1813 and later a hero himself at the Battle of San Jacinto. Miguel Menchaca, a member of the San Antonio aristocracy, was a charismatic leader. His troops followed him gallantly and, even after he was fatally wounded, rallied twice before heavy losses forced them to retreat.

Finally the ragtag Republican army broke and ran. Some turncoats, many of them former Royalist soldiers who had been impressed into the Republican army, butchered the fallen and strung them on trees like quarters of beef to show their loyalty to the king of Spain.

No roster lists the Americans involved. Many who had come to Texas to fight had gone home in disgust. They were replaced by new arrivals who came, fought, and died anonymously, simply disappearing from history. The Royalist dead, buried in a churchyard, were also mostly unnamed recruits, hurriedly assembled along the border.

Arredondo ended the short-lived republic by executing 350 Republican sympathizers and chasing others across the Sabine River. Fewer than ninety made it to Louisiana, as mounted Royalist lancers hunted down stragglers, civilians and rebels alike. One who was shot down, near the Trinity River, was Antonio Delgado, leader at the butchering of Salcedo and Herrera.

Elizondo, sent by Arredondo to mete out retribution to the fleeing rebels, met his own fate after he was attacked by one of his officers who was maddened by the bloodshed. He received saber wounds in the hand and right side and died at the San Marcos River.

Many of the survivors, both Anglo and Tejano, later thought it wise to remain silent about their earlier lives. This was particularly true of the residents of Bexar, who remembered the horrors of Arredondo's revenge. In San Antonio, according to some accounts, the triumphant Spaniard crowded 300 men into a small adobe granary. The next morning, eight had died of suffocation.

Of the survivors, forty were selected to die—three were shot every third day—and the rest were forced into hard labor.

Wives and female relatives of the rebels were crowded into a building called *La Quinta*, where, historians agree, they were forced to grind corn and make tortillas for Arredondo's army. Dolorosa (Sorrowful) Street, by Market Square in modern San Antonio, derived its name from the location of *La Quinta*, which translates either as "the villa, "or "the fifth" or "the fifth one." In an ironic twist, in 1982 the motel chain that took the name La Quinta opened one of its most popular establishments across from Market Square, on Dolorosa Street.

Some accounts indicate that the Spaniards' vengeance was not limited to tortillas. Schwartz quotes John Villars, an American participant in the revolution who was captured and sent as a prisoner to Monterrey, as saying the women "were treated with great brutality, whipped, ravished and maltreated in every possible form . . . ." Their children were turned loose to fend for themselves.

One young Royalist lieutenant found inspiration in Arredondo's ruthlessness. When he returned twenty-three years later as a general determined to crush the Texian revolt, Antonio López de Santa Anna often based his tactical decisions on lessons he had learned at the Battle of Medina. He forgot them a couple of times and was whipped by Sam Houston at San Jacinto and later by Zachary Taylor at Buena Vista.

Beltran, badly wounded in the battle, was saved by his future brother-in-law, who had been captured and raised by Comanches. He took the American to live with Indians until it was safe to return.

Texas was almost depopulated. Republicanism was dead. Strangely, two thousand American volunteers on their way to Texas were recruited by Gen. Andrew Jackson to fight the British in the War of 1812.

Beltran lived the rest of his life with his family in Mexico. Before his death he wrote, "I firmly believe that but for that war with England, the Spanish power in Mexico would have been crushed before the close of 1815, Mexican Independence would have been established and the province of Texas would have passed to the ownership of the United States and the war of 1846 would never have been waged."

In *Green Flag Over Texas*, Dr. Garrett wrote, "Among the States of the Union, Texas can boast that three flags emblematic of liberty and republicanism have waved over her domain: the green flag of 1812-13, the flag of the Republic of Mexico and the flag of the Texas Republic.

". . . .Texas can boast of having been twice a republic. Texas finds three declarations of Independence in the pages of its history: That of April 4, 1813, that of March 2, 1836, and its adopted one, that of July 4, 1776.

"Texas claims not one, but two Liberty Bells—the Mexican Liberty Bell, which hangs in the National Palace, Mexico, D.F., and the United States Liberty Bell in Independence Hall, Philadelphia . . . ."

So you don't have to be a Mexican to kick up your heels on September 16. All Texans can drink a toast to freedom on the *Diez y Seis*.

"GTT"

In early-day Texas, it wasn't considered polite to inquire into another's past, since the past of many of the pioneers involved running away from some scandal or another in the United States. The story that "GTT" scrawled on the door meant one more ne'er-do-well had "gone to Texas" was hardly exaggeration.

In 1827 Noah Smithwick came to Old San Felipe, the town Stephen F. Austin founded as the centerpiece of his colony. Smithwick described an indiscretion in which one such character was awarded "a brand new suit of tar and feathers, . . . escorted through the whole length of the town seated on a rather lean Pegasus and bidden a long adieu at the further end."

The gentleman in question had written a poem lamenting the fate of a woman who, "though posing as the wife of a prominent man, had previously sustained the same relation to an old circus manager, who she deserted without the formality of a divorce when a younger suitor appeared." Before long, that suitor preferred charges against his erstwhile sweetheart so he would be free to court a woman closer to his own age.

This injustice fired the poet's soul with indignation, Smithwick said, and,"the pen being mightier than the sword, the champion of the injured fair, chose the former weapon with which to avenge her wrongs, but unfortunately for him, he neglected to put up his shield when entering the arena."

Smithwick said he did not recall all the verses, "nor would their publication be admissible, but the . . . following will . . . establish their character. They were headed 'Mrs W—–s' Lament':

'The United States, as we understand

Took sick and did vomit the dregs of the land
Her murderers, bankrupts and rogues you may see
All congregated in San Felipe.'

"There followed a long string of names including those of the most prominent men in the place, together with the cause which impelled them to emigrate. There was literally more truth than poetry in the argument. . . ."

Smithwick didn't name names, but a number of Texas heroes stepped onto the stage of history because of their problems with women. Among them were Sam Houston, William Barret Travis, and likely a great many others. Both Travis and Houston left their wives, but neither would dishonor himself by revealing the reasons.

And many of the revolutionaries had been kicked out of this school or that. Some who claimed to be West Point men were expelled or withdrew from the Academy. James Walker Fannin left after two years. James Butler Bonham was ejected from a military academy for leading a protest riot against poor food. Houston in his early days flunked out of school. Travis was expelled from one academy. Davy Crockett ran away from home and school.

At times it seems a sport for some authors to tear down these heroes and their compatriots. It's not difficult to do, for the folks who came to this country were rough, tough people. They had to be or they would not have survived. And they were not always sterling characters. So it's easy to make them out to be villains.

Jim Bowie, revisionists say, was a slave trader and land swindler. It is true that he was a slave smuggler and an Indian fighter who worked with pirate Jean Laffite to circumvent the law. He and many others were land speculators.

In *Duel of Eagles* Jeff Long dwelt on the "prestige, power, and wealth" Bowie gained when he married Ursula, "the beautiful teenage daughter of Governor Veramendi." Long said of the marriage, "his motives were less romantic than fiscal." Yet Antonio Menchaca, who was there, wrote that in 1835, two years after his wife's death in a cholera epidemic, Bowie cried when he spoke of it. Bowie was a Mexican citizen who, in partnership with his father-in-law, started a cotton mill in Saltillo. He was among the first to resist the tyranny of the Centralist government and was one of those who resisted an order by Sam Houston to blow up the Alamo and retreat.

Ben Milam, who led the fight for San Antonio and was killed as the Texians captured it, had also been in the illegal slave trade. Most of the settlers who came to Texas were "land grabbers," as were nearly all the pioneers who went west. Land was always an attraction. And if it could be had free, it was much more so.

An especially popular theory, which revisionists emphasize, is that the revolution occurred because immigrants came to Texas to make it into slave-holding territory and eventually a slave state.

Many of the early settlers were from the South and brought their slaves with them. But Southern aristocrats did not leave their comfortable homes for the rude and dangerous accommodations of 1820s Texas to spread their way of life. They did it because an 1819 economic depression in the United States had spelled financial ruin for many of them. Texas offered a new start.

In 1836 the majority were not wealthy and did not own slaves. And the large land- and slave-holders were largely absent from the battles. In *The Day of San Jacinto,* Frank X. Tolbert quoted a speech by William H. Wharton:

"In glancing over the list [of those who fought in the Battle of San Jacinto] I am surprised and mortified to find that very few men of property had any part in the perils of that glorious day [April 21, 1836]. I do not see on the roster a single one of the wealthy merchants of Matagorda or the opulent planters of Old Caney . . . . The planters were taking care of their cattle and slaves and the merchants were minding their goods. . . ."

No doubt historians can find other scandals–some quite juicy–to report, for these people were humans with human failings. Many of them came to Texas because they were rebels, and it was natural they should seek out a rebellion. Had they been peaceful souls who stayed home and plowed the fields, we would not have the saga of Texas to celebrate.

[2]

Rumblings of Revolt

Background

What did John Quincy Adams have in common with Andrew Jackson and Sam Houston?

When they looked at the setting sun, all three could see California in the golden glow, part of a nation stretching from sea to sea. Each contributed his part to make the dream a reality.

From the days of Jamestown and Plymouth Rock, European settlers followed the sun across the North American continent. In 1965, in *The Oxford History of the American People*, Samuel Eliot Morison said that "the vital stake in all wars and diplomatic maneuverings since 1700 was the American West." Although no one came up with the grandiose title *Manifest Destiny* until 1845, Washington statesmen–and/or politicians–had dreams of westward expansion from the first days of the republic.

Even Thomas Jefferson was not immune. As vice-president, Jefferson had met with Philip Nolan, an American adventurer who came to Texas ostensibly to hunt mustangs. Jefferson had written Nolan to inquire about the wild horses "in the country West of the Mississippi." However, Nolan had been described to Jefferson as "a man, who will at all times have it in his Power to render important service to the U.S. . . ." In view of that description, it's possible that the two had subjects more serious than horses to discuss. It's also possible that Nolan contributed to the vision of Texas found in the following passage from a letter Jefferson wrote to President James Monroe in May 1820:

"I confess to you I am not sorry for the non-ratification of the Spanish (1819 Adams-Onís) treaty. . . . To us the Province of Techas will be the richest state of our Union, without any exception. Its southern part will make more sugar than we can consume, and the Red River on the north, is the most luxurious country on earth. . . . The treaty has had the valuable effect of strengthening our title to the Techas, because the cession of the Floridas, in exchange for Techas, imports an acknowledgment of our right to it. This province, moreover, the Floridas and possibly Cuba, will join us on the acknowledgment of their independence. . . ."

The letter was reprinted by Mattie Austin Hatcher, archivist at the University of Texas, in *The Opening of Texas to Foreign Settlement, 1801-1821.* It is interesting to note that Jefferson prefaced his statements about Texas by saying, "These texts of truth relieve me from the floating falsehoods of the public papers."

In 1821 empresario Moses Austin, a former resident of Spanish territory, was trying to recoup a fortune he had lost in the Panic of 1819 by establishing colonies of Americans in Spanish Texas. A new liberal government was in control in Spain; and the Spanish governor granted Austin's request, at least partially in the belief that such colonists would be loyal to that government and thereby help Spain hold its New World territory. Americans and Europeans would be encouraged to settle on the dangerous northern frontier, where few Mexicans were willing to live.

Before Austin's dream could be achieved, he had died and Mexico had won its independence; however, the new republic permitted Stephen F. Austin to fulfill his father's plans. After many delays he established 300 families in Texas in 1823. One reason Mexico approved the request was that the colonists would serve as a buffer between Mexican settlements and hostile Indians.

In a speech made in Kentucky in March 1836, the younger Austin said, "But a few years back Texas was a wilderness, the home of the uncivilized and wandering Comanche and other tribes of Indians, who waged a constant and ruinous warfare against the Spanish settlements. These settlements at that time were limited to the small towns of Bexar (commonly called San

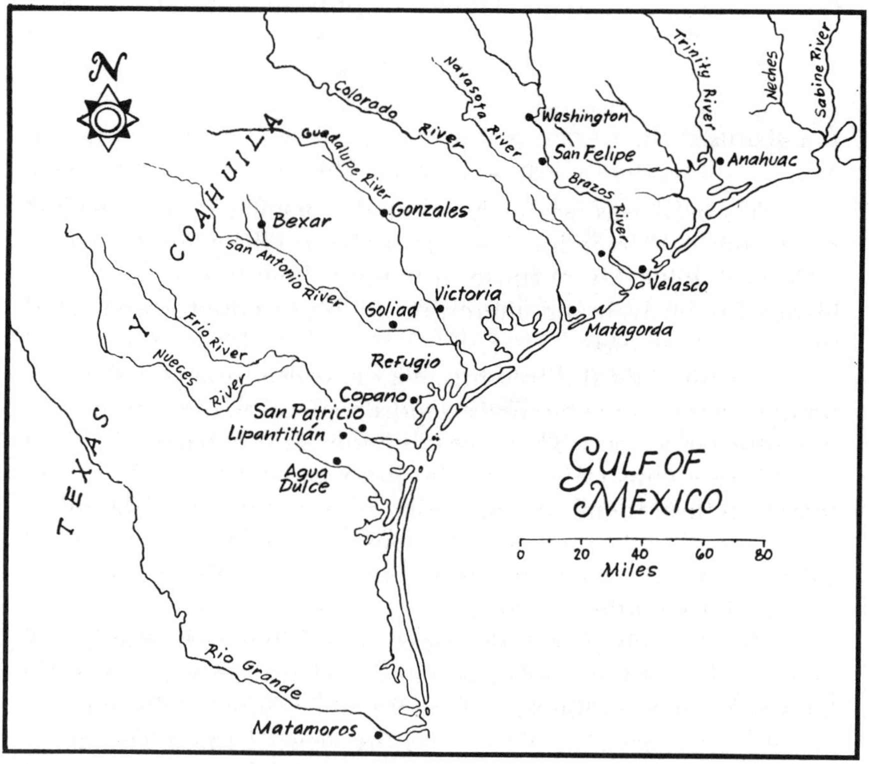

Antonio) and Goliad. . . .The incursions of the Indians also extended beyond the Rio Bravo del Norte, and desolated that part of the country.

"In order to restrain these savages and bring them into subjection, the Government opened Texas for settlement. . . ."

At that time the United States, not yet fully established as a federal republic, was generally considered a union of sovereign entities. The name of the nation was commonly written "united States." Many settlers who went west thought of themselves not as "Americans," but as "Pennsylvanians" or "Virginians" or "Tennesseans." Thirty years later this dedication to states' rights, a concept scorned in modern times by its association with racism, was one of the factors that led many of these same frontiersmen and their Southern kin into the ill-fated attempt at secession.

In the 1820s most of those who became citizens of the Mexican state of *Texas y Coahuila* left their old homes for a new allegiance. In 1824 Mexico adopted a constitution that divided power between the states and the federal government. While it was similar to the U.S. Constitution, there were differences. Roman Catholicism was the official religion. The trial by jury section was short of the American model, and civil authority was subordinate to military. The document, however, guaranteed other freedoms and contained a provision that would let Texas become a separate state when the population reached a prescribed number. Most of the Texians expected to remain in a democratic Federalist Mexico.

But turbulence plagued the young republic, and the liberal constitution was not long in effect. In 1830 Anastacio Bustamante seized control in a coup and set up a military dictatorship. In Texas, Austin consistently sought to avoid antagonizing the government; and the Texians, far to the north, at first were relatively untouched by the strife. When brothers Hayden and Benjamin Edwards tried to establish an independent state of "Fredonia" in 1826, Austin and other colonists had been quick to put them down. But the Fredonian Revolt planted seeds of distrust, and Mexican suspicions increased that Texas colonists secretly wanted to join the United States.

To the Mexicans the uprising seemed a continuation of a conspiracy started in 1825, when U.S. President John Quincy Adams sent Joel R. Poinsett to Mexico to buy Texas. Andrew Jackson continued the negotiations and upped the offer from $1 million to $5 million in 1829. Poinsett's mission failed. His sole accomplishment was bringing to the United States the Christmas flower that bears his name.

In 1830, under Bustamante, the distrust resulted in passage of decrees that prohibited further immigration from the United States, ordered collection of duties, and provided for garrisoning Mexican troops in Texas. The Mexicans were distressed in 1832 and 1833, when Texians started holding conventions and consultations to air their grievances. To the colonists this was the democratic way. But it stirred thoughts of treason in Mexico, where leaders expected revolution when protests were voiced in "pronouncements" (revolutionary statements of aim).

Despite the friction, Austin was again able to smooth over an open rupture of affairs in 1832, when Mexican officials jailed hotheaded William Barret Travis and another attorney, Patrick Churchill Jack, for harassing Col. John David Bradburn, customs director at Anahuac. The colonists considered Bradburn unreasonable and tyrannical. Friends of Travis and Jack raised troops at Velasco to go to their aid. After Mexican authorities refused them permission to leave, they took the Mexican fort on June 26, 1832, in the first preliminary battle of the revolution. Seven of the Texians were killed and twenty-seven wounded, while fifty-two Mexicans were killed and seventy wounded. The Texians allowed the defeated force to return to Mexico.

In July, Col. José Antonio Mexía arrived with 400 additional troops. Austin convinced him that the Velasco affair had been an expression of support for Gen. Antonio López de Santa Anna, who was jousting with Bustamante for control of the government. Colonists at Brazoria received Mexía and Austin with speeches and a cannon salute and entertained them with a "Santa Ana dinner and ball." The Mexican force sailed away.

But the trouble was just beginning. Across Mexico a controversy about the structure of the government, similar to the controversy fomenting in the United States, was growing. The terminology was different. In the United States the term *Federalist* evokes thoughts of support for the central government. In Mexico it stood for those favoring the states, as opposed to Centralists—backers, obviously, of the national government. And north of the border, the tragedy of slavery would obscure the issue of a constitutional question. But in both nations the result of the controversy was the same: bloody civil war.

As 1832 ended, Bustamante retired into exile. Santa Anna was elected president and, professing liberalism, proclaimed the Plan of Vera Cruz, the first provision of which was the restoration of the Constitution of 1824. Federalist generals supported the new hero, and the government of Texas–Coahuila declared in his favor. A town of Santa Anna (in present-day Jackson County, Texas) was named in his honor. Encouraged by the apparent victory, the colonists continued to hold conventions, framing a proposed state constitution.

Instead of taking office as scheduled in 1833, Santa Anna stepped aside and let Vice-president Valentín Gómez Farías assume the office of president. That same year Austin journeyed across the country to the Mexican capital. He got the 1830 anti-immigration law rescinded, but failed to get Texas separated from Coahuila. Frustrated, he wrote letters urging that state leaders go ahead and form a *de facto* government without waiting for congressional action. The letters came to the attention of Mexican officials in January 1834. Austin was arrested in Saltillo on his way home, returned to the capital, and placed in solitary confinement in the former prison of the Inquisition. He remained in custody for nineteen months.

In the meantime Farías made radical moves against the church, the army, and the wealthy class. Those powerful groups strongly opposed the reforms and turned to Santa Anna as their savior. In April 1834 he took office with full support of the conservatives, who now consented to a dictatorship. He threw aside his cloak of liberalism and set about establishing a strong central government. He renounced the Federalists' democratic principles and abolished the congress and state and local governments.

By October of that year, Santa Anna had installed a complete Centralist government. When the state of Zacatecas revolted, he ruthlessly crushed the opposition, annihilating an army of 5,000 Zacatecas state troops in the spring of 1835.

In Texas the colonists had won many concessions from the Coahuila–Texas government, such as religious toleration, a form of trial by jury, and the right to use English to conduct public business. In Coahuila both Saltillo and Monclova claimed the state capital. The national government approved Monclova. A rival government was formed at Saltillo. The Saltillo government was critical of Santa Anna, who sent his brother-in-law, Gen. Martín Perfecto de Cós, to take it over in April 1835.

Historian Rupert Richardson wrote that corrupt collaboration with land promoters by the state government had made the colonists so fed up with it that they didn't see the consequences of Santa Anna's elimination of constitutional government or what he might do as absolute dictator. Most preferred to stay out of the fight.

"Yet," Richardson wrote, "there was a small but active war party in Texas. Opposed to them was a peace party, likewise small, active, and persistent. The great majority of the people stood between these two extreme groups, indifferent at first but finding their complacent attitude more and more untenable as the currents of revolution swirled about them. Developments in the summer of 1835 favored the war party."

By this time the settlers had organized committees of safety and correspondence. Their stated purpose was to organize the militia for defense against the Indians, but they also served to spread word of what was happening around the state. They got a clue from letters taken from a courier at San Felipe that the Mexicans had plans to beef up the garrison at Anahuac. In response, representatives of the War Party at San Felipe authorized Travis to capture the Anahuac fort. He raised thirty troops and forced the garrison to surrender in a rerun of the action at the same site three years earlier. The Mexican prisoners were paroled.

Most of the colonists rejected the action by Travis and the War Party. On June 28, 1835, the people took a vote in nearby Columbia and condemned it, pledging their loyalty to Mexico. Many favored a soft approach to the central government—especially while their leader, Austin, remained a prisoner.

By the end of the summer of 1835 the call went out for a consultation for representatives from all over the state to meet on October 15 at Washington-on-the-Brazos. Among those who sought the meeting was Lorenzo de Zavala, former Mexican congressman, senator, governor of the state of Mexico, and Mexican minister to France. De Zavala, a staunch Federalist, had recently come to Texas after breaking with Santa Anna over the dictator's betrayal of constitutional government.

Such unrest in the Texas–Coahuila colony alarmed the Mexican government. On September 20 General Cós landed at Copano on the Texas coast with 500 to 600 troops to reinforce garrisons at Goliad and Bexar. Shortly after landing, Cós ordered that leading troublemakers be turned over to military tribunals for punishment and that all artillery possessed by the colonists be seized.

The colonists passed additional resolutions assuring Cós of their loyalty to Mexico. Cós replied by demanding de Zavala's arrest and soon expanded the list to include Francis W. Johnson, a land speculator; Robert M. Williamson, a judge and outspoken advocate of independence; Travis; Samuel Williams, Austin's secretary and confidant; War Party members Moseley Baker and John Henry Moore; and two native-born Federalist leaders, José M.J. Carbajal and Juan Manuel Zambrano.

The Anglo-Saxon view of justice would not allow the Texians to turn any of their own over to a military court without the right to a fair trial. Cós could not believe those who would so defy the government could be loyal to it. In August he declared in a letter: "The constitution by which all Mexicans may be governed is the constitution which the colonists of Texas must obey, no matter on what principles it may be formed."

The Texas town of Santa Anna changed its name to Texana.

Meanwhile, Austin had been released from prison in a general amnesty proclaimed when Santa Anna became dictator.

Austin returned to Texas in September 1835 and began privately to urge friends in the United States to send men and supplies for the struggle he now saw as inevitable. For the most part, Texas had steered clear of Mexican politics and revolutions. Now it could not avoid the Federalist–Centralist clash.

Take One Cannon

The Smithsonian Institution reports that countries traditionally gave their worst pieces of ordnance to their colonies. The loaner cannon from the Mexican government to the Texas town of Gonzales was no exception. According to Noah Smithwick, who was a gunsmith, the Gonzales cannon had been spiked and the spike driven out. He figured the Magee–Gutierrez expedition had spiked the old cannon in 1813. It apparently had been used in Mexico's revolution against Spain, in the battles of Rosillo, Alazan, and Medina. Later it was used at the presidio at Bexar. In 1831 the Bexar garrison sent the old cannon to Gonzales for protection against Indian attacks.

Worn out as it was, the cannon became a symbol when Col. Domingo de Ugartechea, commander at Bexar, followed orders from General Cós and sent a detachment of cavalry to Gonzales to pick it up in late September 1835. In response to the noises of revolt from the Texas colonists, President Santa Anna was getting ready to march.

On September 29 the Texians buried the cannon in a peach orchard. Ugartechea ordered Lt. Francisco Castañeda and a hundred troops to march on Gonzales and seize the weapon. Gonzales Alcalde Andrew Ponton declined the formal demand for the cannon, concluding "only through force will we yield." By this time 160 defenders had gathered; and some had dug up the cannon, polished, loaded and primed it, and mounted it on oxcart wheels.

John Henry Moore took command of the rapidly growing force at Gonzales. He had first come to Texas in 1818. The story says he ran away from college in Tennessee to keep from having to study Latin, but his father made him go back. He returned in 1821 as one of Stephen F. Austin's Old Three Hundred, became prominent in colonial affairs, and served as one of the Texian leaders during the Gonzales encounter. He said the ladies of the town made a flag with a replica of the cannon on a white background and the words "Come and take it."

Battle lines were drawn on the banks of the Guadalupe

River. Skirmishers advanced, and the cannon fired a blast. The outnumbered Mexicans retreated to San Antonio.

Smithwick repaired the touchhole damage and put the cannon in top trim, and it was ready for further battle. So were the Texians. They elected Stephen F. Austin commander and decided to advance to Bexar. In October he led the march to San Antonio with the army's prize cannon, drawn by two "long-horned Texas steers," bringing up the rear.

Later Smithwick wrote: "Our pride in our artillery soon began to wane. . . . Sometimes, when the forward column opened a rather wide gap, we prodded up the oxen with our lances (the only use that was ever made of them) until they broke into a trot and the old trucks bumped and screeched along at a lively gait until the gap was closed. But rapid locomotion was not congenial to them. They protested by groans and shrieks and at length began to smoke. We poured on water, but our way lay across a high prairie where no water was obtainable and our supply was limited to the contents of our gourds, a quantity totally inadequate to quench their insatiable thirst. We tried tallow, the only lubricator at hand, but that failed. . .and finally . . . the old cannon was abandoned in disgrace at Sandy Creek before we got halfway to San Antonio."

Another account says that when the men dumped the cannon on the creek bank, they chopped up the wooden wheels, put them on top of the cannon, and set them afire, so the site would look like an Indian campsite.

A flood in 1936 uncovered a small iron cannon on the west bank of Sandies Creek near Gonzales. It lay in the town post office unnoticed for thirty-two years, used as a doorstop, then was sold and exhibited at a gun show in 1979.

Dr. Patrick J. Wagner of Shiner bought it and discovered it had been spiked and bushed. Testing showed the breach had been reinforced. He said scientific tests proved the cannon is, indeed, the "Come and take it" cannon. It was exhibited at The Star of the Republic Museum at Washington-on-the Brazos for three months in 1981.

However, Dr. Wagner's cannon weighs only sixty-nine pounds. Some say that the Texians would not have abandoned a cannon that small, for it would have been easy to carry on back of a horse or mule. And the caliber and type of the cannon have been a matter of dispute.

Miles Bennett, whose father fought at Gonzales, said Dick

Chisholm and John Sowell, both blacksmiths, had prepared the cannon, "a brass six-pounder," cut up pieces of chain, and forged them into cannon balls. Smithwick, who did not arrive at Gonzales until the day after the battle, said it was an iron six-pounder. Sion R. Bostick, after manning a cannon at the Siege of Bexar, said, "We had but one little old cannon, the one we had at Gonzalez, which was about a four-pounder." He neglected to mention the brass cannon captured in the Battle of Concepción.

Historians also disagree. John Henry Brown said the cannon was a four-pounder, but Mary Austin Holley, Henry Stuart Foote, William Kennedy, Henderson Yoakum, and George Bancroft all called it a six-pounder.

In any event, somebody thought it would be a good idea to kick off the Sesquicentennial celebration in 1986 by firing the little 21.5-inch-cannon. The ceremony was scheduled for the Alamo at noon October 2, 1985, to mark the 150-year anniversary of the opening shots of the revolution.

Experts had measured the amount of powder it should use in a little confetti bag. But the bag would not clear a little bottleneck in the barrel, Wagner said. So his Eagle Scout son, Jason, with assistance of bystanders who turned the cannon on end, poured in powder free-lance, poked in paper wadding, and tamped it down with a broomstick.

Gonzales Mayor Carroll Wylie was afraid it was going to blow up. When it went off, he was sure it had. Alamo officials agreed. The explosion was the loudest noise they had ever heard. A second cannon, a replica of the Twin Sisters used at the Battle of San Jacinto and about twice the size of the little cannon, was not nearly so loud. Workers in the department store across the street thought something had blown up.

Before that ceremony, the last time the ancient, rust-pitted cannon had been fired likely was 1835.

"This year it was fired twice," Dr. Wagner quipped in 1985, "the first and last time. In its day, it scared hell out of the Indians and the Mexicans. And now it has scared a bunch of us."

Whether his cannon is the "Come and take it" cannon or not, it made the Sesquicentennial kickoff a resounding success.

La Bahía

Fortress La Bahía at Goliad has witnessed more history and more bloodshed than almost any other structure in Texas. Its roots extended into soil soaked by the blood of inhabitants of

Rene Robert Cavelier, Sieur de La Salle's Fort St. Louis, who were murdered by Carancahua Indians in 1689.

The mission of *Nuestra Señora del Espiritu Santo de Zuniga* and the presidio of *Nuestra Señora de Loreto* were built on top of the French ruins on Garcitas Creek in 1722. Together they were called La Bahía, meaning the bay or the harbor, because they were located on Espiritu Santo Bay, now Matagorda Bay. They retained the name even after being moved twice, once in 1726 to a point on the Guadalupe River near Victoria, now called Mission Valley, then in 1749 to their present site on the south bank of the San Antonio River. Texians spelled La Bahía as they heard it and called it "Labadie." The site, chosen because of its defensible hilltop position, was accessible to the coast. For this reason, it became a key location in Spanish colonial wars and other conflicts, for whoever held it controlled the supply lines to Bexar and other crucial locations.

In response to a petition from the people of La Bahía, in 1829 the Coahuila–Texas legislature changed the name of the settlement to Goliad, created from an anagram made from the surname of Father Miguel Hidalgo, hero of the Mexican Revolution. The *H*, silent in Spanish, was omitted.

In 1835 Gen. Martín Perfecto de Cós made a tactical blunder after he arrived in Texas to deal with the Nordic population. He marched to Bexar, leaving La Bahía, the guardian of the coast and his supply lines, lightly guarded. It was too good a chance for the aroused Texians to pass up. George Morse Collinsworth and some fifty men set out on another historic siege of the old fortress.

Collinsworth, born in Missouri in 1810, had come to Brazoria in 1831. He participated in the Battle of Velasco in June 1832. In early October, three days after colonists at Gonzales fired their "Come and take it" cannon at Mexican Army Lt. Francisco Castañeda, Collinsworth was raising a troop at Matagorda. His plan was to capture the fortress and get supplies and a cache of payroll cash it was rumored Cós had stored there–and possibly to capture Cós himself. On October 6 Collinsworth left Matagorda with twenty volunteers. At Victoria they were joined by twenty-nine others, including Capt. Philip Dimmitt and thirty mounted Federalist *rancheros* under José Antonio Padilla, Sylvestre DeLeon, José María Jesús Carbajal, and Victoria Alcalde Placido Benavides.

Their cry was for individual freedom–not for independence. At this point, arrivals from the United States still joined the established colonists in expecting to defend democracy within the Mexican Republic. Thus, this compact dated October 9, 1835, was signed in the town of Guadaloupe Victoria, present-day Victoria, Texas:

> The volunteers under the command of Capt. George M. Collinsworth, being about to take up the line of march for Goliad, and to give the population of that town protection against military domination, deem it duty which they owe to themselves, to their fellow soldiers embodied else where in the same patriotic cause, but more especially to the citizens of Guadaloupe Victoria, to declare in a clear and unequivocal manner, their united and unalterable resolution to give ample and complete protection to the citizens of this town, and to those also of every other which they may entertain—requiring only, that, the citizens of said towns stand firm to the Republican institutions of the Govt. of Mexico and of Coahuila & Texas under Constitution of 1824; and for the redemption of this resolution, we pledge our lives, our property, and our sacred honour.

Sixty-six volunteers signed the document.

The little army marched all day, reaching Goliad at about 11:00 P.M. on October 9. Along the trail they found Col. Ben Milam hiding in the brush. Milam was an American who had fought for Mexican independence from Spain. In 1835 he had been imprisoned in Monterrey with other supporters of the Federalist cause. Friendly guards allowed him to go to the river to bathe when he wished, and on a dark night he had seized the opportunity and escaped. Now he was anxious for revenge on the Centralists.

Federalist sympathizers from town told them Cós had departed, leaving only a skeleton force in charge of the fortress. Lt. Col. Francisco Sandoval, Capt. Manuel Sabriego, and Ensign Antonio de la Garza were in command of fifty troops.

Bill Neyland, who led the drive to restore La Bahía in the 1960s, told this story about that battle:

There was a walkway over the wall that led to Madam Garcia's emporium and bordello, where the troops could have a midnight toddy and all the comforts of home. A guard was posted at the catwalk.

"Milam told the others, now joined by men from Refugio, Victoria, and other points, they could get into the fort without bloodshed. They knocked on the door. The madam offered 24 hours service. Inside, they bound the madam and her girls. Two of the men put on dresses and waved to the guard. The guard investigated the come-on and was tied up, too," Neyland related. "Then they entered the fort, knocked on the commandant's door. They held a pistol at his head and ordered his troops to stack their arms."

Other accounts say the Federalist townspeople supported the Texians. They did rig a dance outside the walls and invite the Mexican officers to attend. But the Mexicans saw through the ruse and departed early. The accounts don't say if unwashed revolutionaries wearing dresses caused them to leave.

In any event, the Federalists chopped down the presidio door and captured Sandoval, but there was a battle of nearly an hour that ended when the Centralists ran out of ammunition. In the brief fighting, three Mexican privates were killed and seven wounded. Twenty-one were captured and about twenty escaped. One Texian was wounded.

Thus the old presidio basked in the light of history once more, but one of its darkest days was in the making.

Death of a Friendly Foe

James McGloin's Irish was up. The Mexican *comandante* first asked to "borrow" his cannon. He refused. The *comandante* then demanded that he give up the cannon or pay the consequences.

McGloin sent word back to 1st Lt. Nicolás Rodriguez: "You can't have it. This is private property. I bought it with my own money for protection against hostile Indians or anyone else who is a threat to San Patricio."

The little two-pounder wasn't much of a cannon, but it made a lot of noise. Lieutenant Rodriguez had heard that Texians under George Collinsworth, who had recently captured La Bahía, were preparing to attack his Fort Lipantitlán, across the Nueces River and five miles upstream from the village of San Patricio.

"Bring me that cannon," Rodriguez told his men, "and lash McGloin to it. He needs to be taught a lesson." He knew that the Irish empresario was sympathetic to the liberal Constitution of 1824, the same cause the rebels, calling themselves the Federal Army of Texas, were backing.

Rodriguez was not acting from philosophical malice. When Texian militia had attacked La Bahía fifty miles to the east, three members of the garrison had been killed and seven wounded.

Some twenty presidial soldiers and Lt. Joseia M. Valdez escaped during the battle and made their way to Lipantitlán. Contingents at Refugio and El Copano, retreating before the Texian onslaught, also swelled the Mexican ranks.

The Texians had captured Rodriguez's superior, Lt. Col. Francisco Sandoval, and Sandoval's second in command, Capt. Manuel Sabriego, at La Bahía and sent them to San Felipe, where Federalists tried to convert them. Sandoval was paroled. Sabriego, a professed Federalist in 1832, seemed easily persuaded. He was released and fled to Mexico. He later said he feared to return to his Goliad home because rumors had been spread that he had furnished Indians firearms to use in attacks on the Texians. However, he soon returned under cover and served effectively as a spy and guerrilla leader for the invading Centralist army.

Fort Lipantitlán had been established as a customs station and a defense against Indians. McGloin described it as "a simple embankment of earth, lined within by fence rails to hold the dirt in place. . . . [It] would have answered tolerably well, perhaps, for a second-rate hog pen."

Since 1830, when McGloin and John McMullen founded San Patricio, relations between the garrison soldiers and the Irish immigrants had been cordial. One young officer, 2nd Lt. Marcelino Garcia, was a close friend of McGloin and also of John J. Linn, a Victoria trader and merchant.

After capturing Goliad, the Texians sent two young Irish colonists from Refugio, John Williams and John O'Toole, with dispatches asking the *ayuntamiento* (town council) and principal men of San Patricio to declare for the rebel cause and send reinforcements to Goliad. Hobart Huson wrote, "These two Irish lads dropped into the hornet's nest of Fort Lipantitlan; were captured, fettered, and required to work on the fortifications, and soon after were sent to Mexico in chains. This incident laid the predicate for the Lipantitlán Expedition."

Philip Dimmitt, commander of the Goliad garrison, feared attacks from Rodriguez's forces. Also, the Mexican presence protected the supply lines from the coast and overland to Bexar. Dimmitt decided to eliminate it with a surprise raid by troops under Capt. Ira Westover. "Reducing this post [Lipantitlán]," Dimmitt said, "will give security to the frontier, supply us with some important means of defense, strike a panic and encourage the counter revolution in the interior. . . ." He ordered Westover to burn the garrison; bring captured arms, ammunition, and horses back to Goliad; and take all Mexican officers prisoner, but Rodriguez received word of the assault plan from spies at Goliad.

Faced with an immediate threat, Rodriguez needed the cannon for additional firepower. He was in no mood to negotiate. He would have McGloin tied to his cannon, and it would be a hard, rough ride, equal to several severe beatings. The soldiers grabbed McGloin and started to manhandle him, but Lieutenant Garcia interceded. Through a compromise, the local *ayuntamiento* took possession of the cannon and turned it over to the Mexicans.

In *The History of Nueces County,* Dan Kilgore wrote that Westover left Goliad with thirty men October 31. They went down the road to Refugio, where, other sources say, he added as many as forty men recruited by Col. James Power. To avoid Mexican scouts, the mounted force traveled east of the main road to a ranch on the Nueces a few miles below San Patricio. There they learned that Rodriguez had moved up the Goliad road to intercept them.

Rodriguez had approached Goliad the same day Westover left. After his spies warned him of the impending attack on the fort, he hurried back to Lipantitlán, but did not find the Texians. "In his perplexity," Kilgore said, "Rodriguez turned back to Goliad with most of his fighting force, . . . sixty of his own men and ten Irishmen from San Patricio. Westover learned that Lipantitlán was not garrisoned, and pushed on by forced marches to the fort."

They arrived at the crossing near Lipantitlán at sundown November 3 but found the river flooded. They got a canoe from San Patricio and crossed after nightfall. After posting guards, Westover had his men surround the fort. He planned to attack the next morning, but two Irishmen from the village walked by and one, James O'Reilly, offered to go in and persuade the soldiers to surrender. By 11:00 P.M. they had agreed, on condition that prisoners be released on parole.

The Texians burned several buildings and freed several Irish prisoners. Some Irishmen who had been pressed into military duty there decided to throw in with the Texians. Residents of the colony were split. Nine, including Thomas Henry, the *alcalde,* were reported to be Santa Anna supporters. Others backed the Constitution of 1824.

The Texians captured McGloin's cannon, another, a four-pounder, and a number of muskets. With the river at flood stage, they jettisoned the two cannon in the river since they lacked draft animals to pull them. Half of the contingent had recrossed the river when the Rodriguez force attacked. The Texians, protected by trees and the riverbank, inflicted casualties on the Mexicans, who advanced across an open field. The sole Texian casualty was William Bracken, who lost three fingers on his right hand.

Dimmitt was angry that Westover had paroled the captured Mexican troops, that he had not brought the cannon back to Goliad, and that the Mexican garrison had not been permanently eradicated, even though the *jacales* and adobe huts there had been burned. He believed the mission had failed. Huson pointed out that Dimmitt did not realize that "the expedition thwarted an impending attack to recapture Goliad. Had the Federalist attack been delayed for a few days, reinforcements from Mexico would have arrived, and the blow would have fallen. The expedition also interrupted a channel of communications between Mexico and the beleaguered General Cos (at Bexar) at a vital point in Texas History. . . . General Austin and the leaders boasted the victory, and its news was toasted in the press of the United States." It has not been accorded the same importance in the annals of history.

In the Battle of Lipantitlán, the Mexicans suffered seven killed, fourteen wounded, and seven missing. They withdrew, but Nicolás Rodriguez later returned as a valuable scout and adviser to Gen. José Urréa on his victorious sweep up the Texas coast. Before the Mexicans retreated, however, they brought their wounded into San Patricio under a flag of truce, since they had no doctor. The Irish alcalde and sheriff suffered minor injuries. Lieutenant Garcia was mortally wounded.

John J. Linn, who accompanied the men from Goliad, said, "Lt. Marcelino Garcia was a particular friend of this author who did all that was possible to mitigate his excruciating pains the few hours that his lamp of life was permitted to burn. He presented me the horse that had borne him through the battle."

Irish lore says a ghostly lady in green, García's beautiful fiancée, appeared at the dying officer's bedside to comfort him in his final moments. According to the legend, her visits continued after her lover's burial, stopping at the exact time of her death in Mexico City.

The Texians buried the young lieutenant with full military honors.

"With his last breath," Linn said, "Lt. Garcia deplored the unhappy relations existing between Texas and the mother country in consequence of Santa Anna's ambitious purposes. He was opposed to the schemes of the wily and unreliable president-general, and at heart was a sympathizer with the Texans; but, being an officer of the regular service, had no option in the premises."

The First To Fall

The night was quiet and fog boiled over the San Antonio River, hiding Mission Concepción 500 yards to the east. The Mexican army probably was on the move out of San Antonio, Col. James Bowie knew, but he had no idea where they were. He dispatched a lookout to climb the bell tower of the abandoned mission and stationed outposts on the ground as the troops made camp in the river bottom.

At morning on October 28, 1835, the pickets stumbled into camp, two of them wounded. There were scattered shots and the noise of marching men, cavalry, and Spanish profanity as artillerymen flayed balky animals. The Texians, with Bowie and Maj. James Fannin in joint command, prepared for an attack. Gen. Stephen F. Austin was still ten miles away at Mission Espada with the main force of 500 men.

Bowie drew up plans for defense, dispersing men around a curve in the river, exposing the approaching Mexicans to a crossfire. He had the men clear away bushes and vines near the riverbank, which was five to six feet high, and cut steps for footholds with enough room for them to pass each other.

The fog lifted, and General Cós' troops were surprised to find they had almost surrounded the band of Texians they had set out to find. Almost immediately, the Mexicans fired their cannon. Noah Smithwick noted that the Texians, with deliberate calm, ate the pecans that grapeshot brought down from the trees. The Mexican infantry charged.

The Texians, with long-barreled Kentucky rifles, fired from the cover of the bank and trees, downing a row of Mexicans with each volley. Their battle plan allowed the men "to ascend the bluff, discharge their rifles, and fall back to reload. . . each man retiring under the cover of the hill and timber to give place to others while he reloaded," Bowie reported.

The assault was turned back. It came again, faltered, and fell back, the ground littered with dead and wounded. The Mexicans moved to the left to try to outflank Fannin. Bowie ordered some of the men to reinforce the other position, cautioning them to stay behind the embankment. In their enthusiasm some dashed across the open field, exposed to enemy fire. A Mexican cannon roared once. Several Texians were wounded—only one seriously: Richard "Big Dick" Andrews, who fell with a hole in his side.

Others picked off the cannoneers before they could fire again. Now the Texians charged. The Mexicans fled back toward San Antonio, many of them throwing down their weapons as they retreated. The battle was over in half an hour. The first real clash of the Texas Revolution ended in a victory for the Texians. Ninety-two men had defeated 500, and the first Texian to die in the revolution had been mortally wounded.

Smithwick said Andrews knew of the victory. He asked Andrews if he was hurt badly.

"Yes, Smith. I am killed. Lay me down."

Smithwick put something under Andrews' head and continued the charge. They were burying the big Texian under a pecan tree when a priest from town brought out a column to retrieve the sixty dead Mexicans and the wounded.

Dick Andrews had been in Texas longer than Austin, operating a trading post near Richmond since 1818. He and three brothers had come from Georgia to Texas. All were Indian fighters. His brother Micah had his thumb shot off at Concepción. It still pained him at San Jacinto, where he could not be restrained from taking revenge for his former captain, Fannin, and for his brother.

In 1913 a laborer turning soil with a spade unearthed a skeleton near Mission Concepción. It was determined to be a Caucasian of immense size. The fact that Andrews was more than six feet four inches tall and of big bone structure identified him.

On the 100th anniversary of the battle, a historical marker was placed at Concepción honoring the first Texian killed in the revolution. Descendants asked that he be buried in Milam Square alongside his comrade Ben Milam.

Dick Andrews was a gentle, jovial man. His companions grieved for him. But most Texans have never heard of the gentle giant.

Ben Milam's Last Fight

Mention the Storming of Bexar, and an informed Texan might recall the story of a ragged Ben Milam stirring up the bored group of Americans besieging San Antonio in December 1835 with the cry, "Who will go into San Antonio with Old Ben Milam?"

That cry set in motion a battle that became an army textbook on urban warfare. Even so, the story of the historic battle that set up the Battle of the Alamo three months later remains largely unknown.

As the Siege of Bexar wore on in November 1835, the attackers were quarreling among themselves. By this time, American volunteers outnumbered the Texas colonists. Many of the settlers had gone home to take care of their farms. The expected arrival of a twelve-pound cannon gave them a standard excuse: "I'm gonna go see if I can help 'em move that cannon."

Some left because they lacked winter clothing. But the final straw had been an order from the provisional government for the Texian army to call off any plans of attack and retreat to Goliad. The Americans, on the other hand, had no other place to go. They stayed and fought alongside the contingent of Tejanos, many of whom lived in or near Bexar. Some 150 women in town had husbands or sons off somewhere with the Federalist army. Tejano leaders at the siege included Juan N. Seguín and his officers, Salvador and Manuel T. Flores, Juan M. and José M. Zambrano, and Lt. José A. Rendón and Lt. Sylvestre de Leon and their troop.

During the siege, the attackers had no ammunition for their cannon, one of which they had captured from the Mexicans the previous month at the Battle of Concepción. Local citizens obliged by returning cannonballs that had been shot into town.

The rebel army finally decided it was hopeless to assault the bastion and decided to march to Goliad the next day. That night a man appeared and convinced them they could capture the city. The slightly built Mexican was Jesús Cuellar, a lieutenant in General Cós' army, known as "Comanche" because he had been kidnapped by the Indians as a child and lived with them for several years. He slipped from the Alamo fortress during the night and asked to be taken to Col. Edward Burleson. He told Burleson, within hearing of the volunteers, that Cós' supplies were low. The fort, he said, was far from impregnable. There was much dissatisfaction. Food was scarce, there had been desertions, and sympathy for the Federalist cause was strong. He would lead them into the city, and the town could be taken.

Burleson was still determined to follow the orders to retreat, but Milam was convinced of Cuellar's sincerity. In addition, John W. Smith, a surveyor who had been held prisoner in town along with merchant Samuel Maverick, had drawn an accurate map of the city and its defenses. The Texians drew a plan of attack, apparently with Cuellar's connivance.

Col. William G. Cooke, who became one of the commanders, later claimed credit for getting the Americans moving. Milam, shot to death outside the Veramendi Palace on the third day of the battle, didn't survive to dispute Cooke's claim. Most witnesses, however, say it was Milam.

Stephen Franklin Sparks, who was there, said, "We arrived at General Ed Burleson's camp about 1 o'clock one morning and went to what they called the brush fence where all who wanted to fight could get arms. We drove the squad of Mexicans that came to meet us across the river and went into camp. Colonel Ben Milam and Frank Johnson walked out and made a mark on the ground and said, 'Who will follow old Ben Milam into San Antonio? Those who will, cross to my side.'

"My captain and his company were the first to cross the line and history tells the result."

In a 1905 speech, Sparks said Milam "took a stick and made a long mark and asked those who would fight to follow him. Some three hundred men declined to cross. They came and shook our hands, bade us goodbye and told us it was suicide–that we would all be killed and would not last until breakfast."

Sparks, Alphonso Steele, and William Physick Zuber, the last surviving veterans of the Battle of San Jacinto, frequently met and told war stories at functions of the Texas Veterans Association. Zuber was the author of the legend that William Barret Travis drew a line in the dirt of the Alamo compound and ended a long formal speech: "I now want every man who is determined to stay here and die with me to come over the line. Who will be first? March!"

Zuber attributed this story to Moses Rose, the only defender to abandon the Alamo late in the siege, as a story Rose told to Zuber's parents shortly after his escape from the Alamo. The account was published in the *Texas Almanac* in 1872, some thirty-six years after the battle. In 1888 Mrs. Anna M.J. Pennybacker's book, *A New History of Texas for Schools, Also for Teachers Preparing for Examinations,* introduced the legend of Travis and the line to schoolchildren so dramatically it became a permanent part of Texas lore. In view of the close relationship between Sparks and Zuber, it is only fair to wonder if Milam's stick was not the father of Travis' sword.

Cuellar acted at the behest of José María Gonzalez, a Federalist colonel who had been his commander. Gonzalez had previously told Stephen F. Austin he believed he could convince 200 to 250 cavalrymen formerly under his command to desert to the

Ben Milam "took a stick and made a long mark and asked those who would fight to follow him."

Federalist cause.

On December 9 the provisional government voted Colonel Gonzalez $500 for use toward this end. He distributed leaflets within San Antonio, exhorting Cós' troops to desert and join the fight for freedom. His efforts succeeded: Some 250 cavalrymen sent out to escort reinforcements simply did not come back. They returned to Mexico.

Just before dawn on December 5, 1835, Cuellar helped lead the attack, quickly infiltrating before the sentries were aware of the Texians' presence. In the battle the Americans and the local Federalists fought from house to house and room to room, using crowbars to dig holes in the adobe brick walls and drive the defenders out. Many of the rooms held frightened civilians, who were generally sympathetic to the Federalist cause. The local women cooked for the Americans and brought them water from the river until Mexican soldiers started shooting at them. The house-to-house technique was used later by Gen. Zachary Taylor's troops at the Battle of Monterrey in the Mexican War and as recently as World War II in house-to-house warfare in European cities.

Describing one scene, Sparks wrote: "A man named Sylvestre got a hammer and running through the Mexicans right up to their cannon and spiked them and wheeled and ran back to us. As he jumped into the door of the house we had just taken, he turned his head and they shot him in the eye, but did not kill him. This same man was the first to leap over Santa Anna's breastworks at San Jacinto. The conspicuous bravery of this man deserves a place in history."

The man likely was James Sylvestre, who appears on rosters of troops in both battles.

Desertions of the cavalry troops had left others in the Mexican garrison despondent. They felt defeat was imminent. A rumor that General Cós was dead spread quickly, and the defenders were disconsolate. They were even more despondent when reinforcements under Colonel Ugartechea arrived in chains. They were criminals, and more than one hundred of them could not be trusted with firearms. Mutiny and insubordination became rampant. Officers were afraid of their men. Cós himself was roughed up by the unruly convicts. All the while the Americans and Tejanos pressed the attack.

The amazing accuracy of the American long rifles dumbfounded the defenders, who soon learned that to light a cigarette at night meant almost certain death. Still the courageous Mexicans put up stiff resistance. Finally, faced with a breakdown in discipline, desertions, and treason, Cós surrendered on December 9. The Mexican soldiers were paroled on condition they not fight again. A number were allowed to keep their arms for protection against Indians, and some 250 of them marched south with Colonel Gonzalez to join 200 other Federalists near the Rio Grande. Unfortunately, they were soundly defeated by a superior Centralist army before they could join the revolt in Texas.

Historian Hobart Huson noted that the convict riots were not mentioned in official Texian reports, but the terms of capitulation included one clause "that the General take the convicts brought by Col. Ugartechea beyond the Rio Grande."

Meanwhile, Generalissimo Antonio López de Santa Anna was convincing Federalists in Mexico that the colonists were not interested in the Mexican Constitution of 1824, that they were in Texas only to annex the province to the United States. Some were, no doubt, and Santa Anna's actions convinced many of the others that accommodation with Mexico was impossible. The Texas section of the Federalist Revolution changed its direction, and soon even the most ardent doves were shouting for independence. Unfortunately, their victory at the Storming of Bexar gave them a bad case of overconfidence, a condition that would cost them dearly at the Alamo and at Goliad.

Some of their Tejano allies turned neutral or marched with Santa Anna when the Mexican army returned to Texas. But Jesús Cuellar, who later played a role in the Battle of Goliad, and José María Gonzalez, fully committed to the Federalist cause in a sovereign Mexico, had made their indelible imprints on the history of two nations.

Philip Dimmitt

In the small chapel of Goliad's Fortress La Bahía–*Presidio de Nuestra Señora de Loreto de la Bahía*–you can almost feel the flow of history about you. The grounds of the little fortress have been stained with the blood of the fallen in numerous sieges, attacks, and battles.

Undoubtedly, some Spanish troops were attacked there by hostile Indians from time to time. Then came a succession of revolutionaries and American adventurers. Augustus William Magee and José Bernardo Maximiliano Gutierrez de Lara, with their army of Americans and Mexican Republicans, captured the fort in February 1813. Magee became ill, died, and was buried in the presidio. His place was taken by Sam Kemper, who soundly defeated the Royalists. Later the Republican army was nearly exterminated by Gen. Joaquín de Arredondo at the Battle of Medina.

In June 1817 troops under Henry Perry attempted to capture troops of Col. Ignácio Pérez at La Bahía. Instead Perry was beaten on the grounds where Col. James Fannin and his men were later captured. Perry, wounded, committed suicide. In 1819 an expedition that declared for Texas independence under James Long appeared at La Bahía. Long's 300 men were crushed by 500 Spanish troops under Pérez.

When Texian Federalist forces captured the fort on October 9-10, 1835, three of the Mexican defenders were killed. Later Fannin's men were imprisoned in this windowless chapel before they were marched out and shot on Palm Sunday of 1836.

But La Bahía marks the site of another noteworthy event in Texas history–the signing of the Goliad Declaration of Independence, which preceded the recognized Declaration of March 2, 1836, by almost three months.

Before December 1835, many of the Texians strongly supported the Constitution of 1824, asking only that it be changed to sever Texas from Coahuila and make each of them a separate state within the Mexican Republic. Among these Texians were members of the La Bahía garrison, commanded by Philip Dimmitt, another Texas hero who has been largely overlooked.

Born in 1801 in Kentucky, Dimmitt came to Texas in 1822 as a frontier trader. He learned Spanish and developed many friends in Mexico and among the ruling class of Spanish/Mexican Texians. He married María Luísa Lazo in 1828 and became a successful merchant, with import warehouses at Dimmitt's Landing on the east bank of the Lavaca River.

Historian Hobart Huson, in his *Captain Phillip Dimmitt's Commandancy of Goliad October 15, 1835–January 17, 1836*, described him as "strong, sturdy, bronzed from frequent long exposures to the sun. A total stranger to fear, he was brave without swagger or braggadocio. He was stoical and intellectually and morally honest, and had the courage of his convictions. He was a stern disciplinarian, blunt and undiplomatic–a natural leader of men."

The Texians elected him captain after they seized the fortress. With only fifty men, the garrison stood in the way of possible Mexican invasions from the sea or from Fort Lipantitlán to the south on the Nueces River. Through his knowledge of native ways and customs, Dimmitt was able to supply troops besieging General Cós at Bexar. He sent out the raiding party under Ira Westover that captured Fort Lipantitlán and defeated Mexican forces on November 5, 1835.

He incurred the wrath of Dr. James Grant and F.W. Johnson, two prominent land speculators, when he refused to recognize Augustín Viesca, the deposed Federalist governor of Texas–Coahuila, as governor of Texas. They complained loudly to Gen. Stephen F. Austin. Goliad residents also complained that Dimmitt had pressed their property, in spite of the fact that he had contributed the merchandise from his warehouses to the cause. Austin tried to dismiss him, but Dimmitt's troops, who had elected him, sent a petition demanding that the order be rescinded.

Dimmitt led a contingent to San Antonio, where they participated in the Storming of Bexar. Unfortunately, Johnson wrote the battle reports and omitted the names of Dimmitt and most of his men, as well as Jim Bowie's and those of the Tejanos who had helped capture the city. In addition to the dispute over Viesca, there could have been another reason for such an omission: Johnson felt emnity toward another ambitious man seeking to command the Texian army, Sam Houston, who was a friend of both Bowie and Dimmitt.

After San Antonio was captured, it became obvious that the Texians would receive little support from other revolutionaries in Mexico. In addition, some of the former Tejano Federalists were switching to Santa Anna's Centralist position. Dimmitt returned to Goliad convinced there was no hope for the liberal cause, that independence was the only answer to the Texas problems. As armies started marching northward to massacre or drive out disloyal colonists, he urged a strong declaration of independence. So, on December 20, 1835, the motley bunch of Americans, Tejanos, English, Scots, French, Irish, and others declared Texas to be a free nation.

Ira Ingram, a Freemason from Vermont, drew up the document and set it up dramatically under candles on an altar of the fortress' little chapel. It was signed by ninety-two members of the garrison. Each came forth in a formal ceremony. Ingram felt the chapel would show the dedication and fervor of the men and add to the significance of the document, as they knew their signatures were death warrants if they were captured by the Centralists. At the signing, they raised several flags, among them the first flag of independence–depicting a bloody, severed arm grasping a sword, signifying a fight to the death.

The document they signed warned of a war of extermination by the central government. It declared Texas should be a free and sovereign state. It also hit at those who would barter the gains won by the army with capitulation; those who would be served by and not serve their country; politicians who sought emolument without serving, "swarming like flies around the body politic."

So it was not strange that the General Council rejected the declaration, attacking the signers with as much vigor as it did the dictator in Mexico. However, copies had been distributed widely, and they served its intended purpose of forcing the council to action.

Early in January 1836, Dr. James Grant with some 160 men arrived in Goliad on an ill-fated trip to invade Matamoros, just across the Rio Grande from present-day Brownsville, Texas. They challenged Dimmitt to take down his flag and proceeded to strip La Bahía of supplies and horses.

Disgusted, Dimmitt's men voted to disband. Some went to the Alamo with James Bowie, and others went later with Dimmitt. Many died there or in the Goliad Massacre. Some who survived the war became prominent in the new nation.

José Miguel Aldrete, born near La Bahía, fought in the siege of Goliad and Bexar. He furnished supplies to the Texas Army and later became a judge in Refugio County .

William S. Brown, designer of the bloody-arm flag, reportedly died in the Goliad Massacre. However, a William S. Brown also served later as an officer in the Texas Navy.

Elkanah Brush, member of the Lipantitlán and Goliad expeditions, served in the first Texas Congress.

José María Jesús Carbajal, prominent as a surveyor in Austin's Colony, had laid out the town of Victoria. He led a force that defeated a Mexican Centralist army near Mier in 1839, fought against the United States in the Mexican War and against the French in 1862. He became governor of the Mexican states of Tamaulipas and San Luís Potosí.

John Dunn operated a store in Refugio before arrival of other Irish colonists. He had sounded the alarm when General Cós landed at Copano, and he carried the declaration to San Felipe. He later held congressional and county posts and was a businessman, schoolteacher, and rancher.

Nova Scotian John James attempted to save government archives during the revolutionary battle at Refugio, but was captured and put to death.

Walter Lambert, nephew of empresario James Power, fought at Lipantitlán, Goliad, and San Jacinto and was guide for the "Horse Marines," who captured three loaded Mexican schooners in Copano Bay–all at the age of fifteen.

Thomas O'Connor at seventeen was at Goliad and San Jacinto. He would own more than 500,000 acres in seven counties.

Dimmitt and his aide, Lt. Benjamin J. Noble, left the Alamo

to reconnoiter for Col. William Barret Travis as the Mexican army arrived. As they returned, they found they were cut off by a large number of Mexican troops and set out for Victoria. Sam Houston had ordered Dimmitt to recruit men at Victoria and meet him at Gonzales.

Hobart Huson wrote: "Dimmitt appears to have left Bexar with the firm intention of raising as many volunteers as possible to go to the relief of the beleaguered Alamo. It now seems probably that many of the men whom he took with him to San Antonio in January, 1836, were left in the Alamo, and that he deemed it a sacred duty to extricate them."

Dimmitt had twenty-five men when he neared Gonzales on March 17, but by this time the Alamo had fallen. Houston's force had retreated on the night of March 13, and the Mexican army was already in Gonzales. In a brief skirmish the Texians killed a dozen Mexicans on the bank of Kerr's Creek. They then abandoned their horses, escaped down the Guadalupe River, and marched four days without food. Dimmitt helped remove refugees from Matagorda, appeared at Galveston with sixty volunteers on April 20–still trying to rejoin Houston's army–and arrived with two cannon at San Jacinto April 22, the day after the Texians won the war's decisive battle.

Huson says the tragedy of the Alamo and the loss of many of his former comrades there appear to have affected Dimmitt "deeply and lastingly. He named one of his sons 'Alamo.' "

After the war, he resumed his trading vocation. One of his competitors was Col. H.L. Kinney, founder of the city of Corpus Christi. In July 1841 a troop of Mexican soldiers raided the area. From Kinney they received food and brandy. They kidnapped Dimmitt. As a result, Kinney and his partner were arraigned on a charge of treason for complicity in the kidnapping. Since no witnesses appeared at their trial in Austin to testify, they were found not guilty.

To the Mexicans, Dimmitt's crimes were raising the flag of independence and selling goods to Mexicans who afterwards smuggled them into Mexico. He died in captivity while being taken to Monterrey. Apparently, historians' views of Dimmitt have been dimmed by the fact that he had left the Alamo. In his own day he was held in high esteem, and many cried for a punitive raid into Mexico after his death.

Huson saluted him with the "heraldic motto: SEMPER FIDELIS."

Philip Dimmitt is another hero who deserves an honored place in Texas history.

A Texas Villain

It was a rotten way to wake up. Someone was ripping the walls apart. Bugles were sounding. There were shouts of "Viva Santa Anna! Death to the Americans!"

Freezing rain lashed into the crude hut when suddenly dozens of muskets flashed, filling the room with thunder and clouds of gunpowder, some of it still burning. There were screams of men suddenly awake, startled as they lay wounded or dying. It was February 27, 1836, and the revolution had returned to South Texas.

The Texians had controlled the territory for two months, since General Cós and his troops, defeated in the Storming of Bexar, had been sent back across the Rio Grande. In Mexico Santa Anna had temporarily relinquished the presidency but retained his role as *generalissimo*. Now he ordered his forces north, determined to oust the American invaders and crush other rebels as he had those in Zacatecas.

In late 1835, when many Texians still considered the struggle part of the larger Federalist Revolution that had raged in Mexico, a number of people thought a quick invasion of Matamoros might draw help from Federalists in the Mexican interior. However, Sam Houston, Stephen F. Austin, Governor Henry Smith, and Goliad commander Philip Dimmitt, who probably had given birth to the invasion idea, all changed their minds and opposed it. Nevertheless, Dr. James Grant and Col. F.W. Johnson went on with plans to organize such an expedition.

Most conventional Texas histories portray Santa Anna as the villain of the revolution, but Grant is another who might qualify for the title. From ulterior motives having nothing to do with patriotism for either Texas or Mexico, and with the help of Johnson, he was responsible for:

- The destruction of the provisional government.
- The creation of chaos in the Texian army, which resulted in appointment of four commanders at the same time.
- The deadly weakening of the garrison at the Alamo by taking away 200 men and vitally needed supplies.

The rustling of foodstuffs, cannon and all the horses from

the Goliad garrison, which would later render that bastion practically helpless.

Grant, a Scotsman who was never a Texas citizen, had huge land holdings in the state of *Coahuila y Texas*. With dreams of a personal empire, he began to drum up enthusiasm for the invasion among volunteers from the United States after the successful Storming of Bexar. He drew visions of plunder, warm climates, fandangos, female companionship, and adventure. The lure was irresistible.

He sold Johnson, at that time the commander of the Alamo, on the idea, which wasn't difficult, as Johnson was also heavily involved in land speculation. He also convinced the General Council of Texas, which named him and Johnson to head the expedition. Subsequently, the council also named James Fannin, while Governor Smith was appointing Houston, to head the same army. As a result, Smith disbanded the council and the council impeached Smith and nobody knew who commanded the army. Houston gave up and went to parley with the Cherokees.

From the Alamo, Grant and Johnson gathered up most of the gunpowder, small arms, shot, medicine, and even the blankets for the sick. The expedition set out on January 1, 1836, for Goliad. There, on January 5, they found Dimmitt's Flag of Independence flying over La Bahía. After the threat of battle between Grant's men and the garrison troops, Dimmitt lowered his flag.

Grant, described as an abrasive, overbearing man, confiscated the scant supply of foodstuffs from the garrison and took its entire herd of horses, leaving none for scouting, foraging, dispatch, or means of returning home. Then the expedition, swelled by volunteers along the way, advanced to Refugio, where Houston talked some 300 of them into abandoning the project—warning that if the Texians split their forces, the Mexican army would defeat them one after the other. But the damage was done. Col. William Barret Travis would be short of gunpowder and shot, and Fannin's retreat would be severely hampered by lack of horsepower.

By the time the expedition reached San Patricio, the force had dwindled to around sixty men. They rounded up one hundred horses from area *rancheros*, and Johnson took the horses and thirty-four men—seven of them Tejanos—back to San Patricio. Grant and twenty-five men—including three Tejanos—went south for more horses.

As the Texians did exactly what Sam Houston had told them

not to do, Mexican Gen. José Urréa's force marched into the teeth of a cold, wet South Texas norther. Several lightly clad Central American Indian conscripts froze to death in camp about where the King Ranch Headquarters is located today, near Kingsville, Texas, forty miles southwest of Corpus Christi. In his report Urréa said that after his men crossed the Nueces River, his dragoons were so cold they could not feel their horses and dismounted with great difficulty.

Among the native Texas population Urréa had spies who had accurately informed him as to the strength of the Texas forces. Johnson was not the efficient commander he had been three months before, when he took over after Ben Milam fell and led the Texians who drove the Mexican army from San Antonio. Although he knew Urréa was marching northward from Matamoros as Santa Anna moved toward San Antonio, he posted no pickets at San Patricio—no sentry to fire the alarm. His little band, sound asleep, was totally surprised when Urréa's men attacked.

Capt. Thomas K. Pearson fired his musket and ordered his men to do the same. This was a fatal mistake, because the Mexicans set the thatch roof ablaze and the Texians tried to surrender. It was too late. Seven were killed, cut down by bullets and lances as they stepped outside. A few in another hut managed to surrender. Johnson, barefoot, and three others sneaked out the back of their hut during the excitement and escaped to Refugio. Johnson kept going and lived to write a history of Texas.

Those who were captured were tied up. They were joined by three companions taken at a corral a mile away, where three others had been surprised in their sleep and killed. One man got away. Then Urréa sent his spies to locate Grant and tell him all was well in San Patricio.

On March 2, the same day that the Texas Declaration of Independence was being signed at Washington-on-the-Brazos, Urréa's dragoons surprised Grant's party of twenty-six at El Puerto de las Cuates crossing of Agua Dulce Creek, on the present-day La Puerta Ranch, twenty-five miles west of Corpus Christi in Nueces County. Grant fled. He fired two shots at a Mexican lieutenant, who thrust a lance through his back. Twelve of his men were also killed, seven captured, and six escaped.

Santa Anna, laying siege to the Alamo, was elated by Urréa's victories. He ordered the prisoners shot, but Urréa instead sent them to Matamoros.

Mexican casualties in the two South Texas battles were light.

At San Patricio two men were killed and one wounded. At Agua Dulce, a bullet grazed one horse. On the Texian side a total of twenty-three men had been killed and seventeen captured. Grant was dead and Johnson was gone, but in the confusion, eleven men had escaped to spread the alarm of invasion up the country. Among them was Placido Benavides, who has been called the Paul Revere of Texas.

Independence Declared

It was a cold and blustery March 2, but it wasn't uncomfortable in Noah Byars' blacksmith shop at Washington-on-the-Brazos. Cloth stretched over the openings served as windows, and the delegates bundled up against the cold, wearing all the clothes they had. Their bodies warmed the room.

It wasn't a very good meeting place; but Washington Town was only a collection of shacks, and the uncompleted barn was the best structure around. Owners Byars and Peter M. Mercer made the most of it. They soaked the government of Texas $170 for three months' rent, a considerable sum in those days.

Two flags flew over the makeshift capitol. One was the bloody-arm flag of independence. The other, designed by Sarah Dodson, was composed of three equal-size panels of blue, white, and red, with a lone white star in the blue panel.

Inside, there was a sense of urgency among the fifty-nine delegates. The temporary government had argued and bickered. The confusion had spread across Texas, and the people were unprepared for war. Now the Mexican army was on the move, and they had much to do.

Lorenzo de Zavala, noted for his long orations, rose and began, "Mr. President, an eminent Roman statesman once said–"

Thomas J. Rusk interrupted, "It behooves this convention to give less thought to dead Romans and more attention to live Mexicans."

His point was well taken, for as they talked, Gen. José Urréa's troops were ambushing Dr. James Grant's force near present-day Agua Dulce. Placido Benavides, *alcalde* of Victoria, escaped to warn James Fannin, now in command at Goliad, then the rest of Texas of the Mexican invasion.

As Santa Anna's main army was approaching, William Barret Travis was pleading for aid at the Alamo. The defenders there and the Bexar citizens had sent Samuel Maverick and three others to represent them at the convention.

Placido Benavides escaped the Mexican ambush at Agua Dulce and rode hard all the way to Goliad to warn James Fannin and colonists along the way of Gen. José Urréa's advance.

Texas had avoided the issue earlier. Now the delegates knew with certainty that independence was the first issue of business. A committee headed by George C. Childress was named to prepare a declaration.

Childress, who had arrived from Nashville weeks before, was said to have brought a copy of the document in his saddlebags. It was ready the morning of March 2 and immediately approved. He patterned the document after Thomas Jefferson's model. It begins, "When a government has ceased to protect the lives, liberty and property of the people from whom its legitimate powers are derived . . . ." Among the grievances listed are the abandonment of the Federal Republican Constitution, the forcible change of the government to central military despotism, jailing of agents of petitions, and mercenary armies sent forth to force new government at bayonet point.

The Anglo-Americans had colonized Texas under promise of a written constitution. Now Santa Anna offered the alternative of leaving their homes or submitting to his discretion. Other accusations against Mexico included not providing trial by jury and a system of public education; placing military over civil power; dissolving the state of Coahuila and Texas; demanding surrender of citizens; making piratical attacks on commerce; denying the right of free worship; demanding surrender of arms needed for protection; invading the country by sea and land; inciting Indians to massacre citizens; and maintaining a weak, corrupt, and tyrannical government.

Childress also proposed that a flag with a single star be adopted as the emblem of the Republic. The declaration was approved on March 2, but it was March 3 before five handwritten copies could be prepared for signing.

Ellen N. Murry, editor of *Star of the Republic Museum Notes* at Washington-on-the-Brazos in 1986, said all five of the original copies disappeared during the hectic retreat from the Mexican army. However, one copy was discovered in 1896 in the U.S. Department of State, where it had been deposited in 1836 by William H. Wharton. It is now in the Texas State Archives.

On March 15 news of the fall of the Alamo created havoc among the population. Terrified, people clogged the roads fleeing to safety. The delegates worked on. Late on March 16 they completed the constitution and at 4:00 A.M. on March 17 elected an *ad interim* government to replace one that had become paralyzed with dissension. Then they adjourned, some to join Sam Houston's army and others to join their families in the Runaway Scrape.

Murry pointed out that only two of the signers were native Texans. They were José Antonio Navarro and José Francisco Ruiz, both born in Bexar. David G. Burnet was named president, and Lorenzo de Zavala, vice-president. Sam Houston was there, but as a delegate from Refugio. In his home district at Nacogdoches, he had been beaten 610–55 for a seat in the convention.

Among the signers were natives of five countries and twelve different U.S. states. Ten had been in Texas more than six years. Price Carson had been in Texas eight days when the convention started. Forty of the fifty-nine were under forty years of age. Among their number were lawyers, doctors, merchants, farmers, soldiers, congressmen, judges, and governors. Two delegates had fought in the War of 1812, one in the Mexican Revolution, and seven had been involved in earlier battles of the Texas Revolution. All were literate, and several were highly educated.

At least twenty-two of the fifty-nine signers were members of the Masonic Order. Three delegates left Texas after signing. Several later met violent deaths. Secretary of the Texas Navy Samuel Rhoads Fisher was shot and killed by Albert G. Newton. Thomas Rusk, George Childress, James Collinsworth, and James Woods all committed suicide. Robert Potter, later an Indian fighter and congressman, was murdered at his home during the Regulator–Moderator Feud in 1842.

Operating under discomfort and extreme pressure, the delegates did a remarkable job when it needed to be done. The cruel deadline in that little blacksmith's shop hammered out a pretty good product.

[3]

Bexar

Fall of the Alamo

The mystique of the Alamo continues to grow, with new theories and new interpretations. There are the debunkers, who glory in half-truths, and there are those who would crown the heroes with halos.

Few escaped the waves of half-frozen Mexican troops that dark March morning; and, until years later, it did not occur to many to question those who did. So the same basic information about that battle, much of it from reports of Mexican witnesses, has been rehashed, stirred, and served again with viewpoints drawn from the particular prejudice of the author.

The facts are that some 183 men, for whatever reason, fought to the death in the Alamo after Gen. Sam Houston, on January 17, 1836, ordered it blown up and abandoned. Some now say those men died only for messianism, the Americans' belief that it was their God-given mission to conquer the North American continent. Some think they came for the promise of land and possible booty. The pure of heart believe they were interested only in risking their lives to free the land of a tyrant's stranglehold.

Did they fight for the liberal Mexican Constitution of 1824, or were they there to capture territory for the expansion of the United States? Did they come to increase the voting power of the slave states? Or were they there because that's where the fighting was?

It's hard to sort out an answer. Describing the Texians at the beginning of the revolt, Noah Smithwick said, "I can not remember that there was any distinct understanding as to the position we were to assume toward Mexico. Some were for independence; some for the constitution of 1824; and some for anything, just so it was a row."

Most of those who thought the war might put money in their pockets followed Dr. James Grant when he left the Alamo on New Year's Day 1836, calling for an invasion of Matamoros, where, he said, Federalists from northern Mexico would join them. By February, however, the men in the Alamo, like others across Texas, had abandoned hope that their cause would be joined by that liberal movement. They all died; but, for the most part, they were not frontier sharpshooters. They were professional men: lawyers, doctors, clerks, merchants, preachers, carpenters, surveyors, farmers, bricklayers, plasterers, painters, blacksmiths, teachers, sailors. One was a hatter, and one called himself "an aristocrat."

They came from Tennessee, Pennsylvania, North Carolina, New York, Georgia, Connecticut, Alabama, England, Massachusetts, Scotland, Arkansas, Rhode Island, Ireland, Ohio, Mississippi, South Carolina, Virginia, Kentucky, Maryland, Germany, Missouri, Vermont, Wales, Louisiana, Illinois, Denmark, France–and Texas. But all became Texians in their sacrifice, and the Texas mystique was born.

The lack of first-hand accounts and the tendency of storytellers to employ dramatic license have added myth and mystery to mystique. The celebrated feud between William Barret Travis and Jim Bowie is a case in point.

In his 1976 biography *William Barret Travis*, Archie P. McDonald, professor of history at Stephen F. Austin State University, made a man of flesh out of the stone statue of the Alamo commander. McDonald traced Travis' life back to his birthplace in Edgefield County, South Carolina. Along the way, he debunked a lot of myths.

William Barret's father was Mark Travis. As Mark was somewhat of a rounder, questions later circulated about William Barret's legitimacy, but they were probably unfounded.

Mark's brother Alexander was a devout preacher who established Baptist churches all over Alabama. Barret greatly admired his uncle, who in turn contributed greatly to his nephew's education. Young Barret attended a frontier academy and read law until he was admitted to the bar at age twenty. Things started well for him. He married and had a son and another child on the way. Then the marriage, like Sam Houston's, ended under a cloud. Travis suddenly left for Texas.

Romanticized histories say the magnet of liberty drew him west. One version says he left in a huff because a vandal lopped off his horse's tail. Most of the accounts leave the impression that his wife, Rosanna, was unfaithful. His brothers believed that. Hers didn't. Travis suspected that the child she was to bear in 1831 was not his.

Whatever the reason, he left in a hurry. The basic legend is that he killed a man suspected of carrying on with Rosanna, but the story is as varied as the tellers. One claims he stood up in a dramatic courtroom scene and confessed before fleeing. Another says he confessed to save a slave from being wrongly convicted. He appealed to the judge's Masonic friendship and was allowed to escape.

In a simpler story Travis confronted a riverboat gambler and accused him of fooling around with Rosanna while Travis practiced law across the Alabama River. Travis shot him down and left because he felt the incident would hurt his law practice. A family friend reported that Travis shot the man, summoned his servant, Joe, and rode away on his big black horse with no ceremony. (Joe would survive the massacre at the Alamo.) Rosanna obtained a divorce and remarried.

In any event, Travis began a law practice in Texas and soon began rocking the boat of Mexican–Texas politics. He was jailed, captured the fort at Anahuac, and generally made himself well known to the Mexican government. He was fiery and aggressive, one of the strong early advocates of independence, a fact that put a price on his head.

He wasn't lonely. After his divorce from Rosanna, he courted another woman. In the meantime, he kept a diary of his sexual conquests. By 1834 there were fifty-nine entries.

In his brief life Travis had been an Alabama militia officer, an experienced trial lawyer, and a newspaper editor. Like most of his contemporaries, he was an opportunist. He became a member of the colonial assembly, and, when the Mexican invasion threatened, a colonel of cavalry and a recruiter. At the Alamo he, like Davy Crockett, hoped for glory that would benefit him politically.

Travis took part in several skirmishes during the Siege of Bexar and returned to San Antonio February 3, 1836. Shortly thereafter Col. James Neill, commander of the Regular troops at the Alamo, left and named Travis to succeed him. Popular histories have played up the resulting conflict between Travis and James Bowie, leader of the Volunteers.

Hollywood accounts have portrayed Travis as a pompous, hot-headed dandy who arrived at the Alamo in time to argue with Bowie, then die in a flame of glory. The 1960 John Wayne movie, *The Alamo,* cast Wayne as Crockett, Richard Widmark as Bowie, and an English actor, Laurence Harvey, as Travis. Walter Lord, for one, attributes the picture of Travis as a fop, egotistical and something of a prig, to Amelia Williams and her dissertation, "A Critical Study of the Siege of the Alamo and the Personnel of Its Defenders." He said Williams did not like Travis and quotes a letter she wrote saying Travis had a "mean streak" because he did not share credit with Bowie in his final letters. However, in her manuscript Williams describes Travis in glowing terms:

> Travis was preeminently the good soldier, for while it is probable that no man in Texas did more than he did to initiate the revolution, certainly none fought more bravely, served more faithfully, or died more heroically.
>
> . . . In person he was about six feet tall and weighed around 175 pounds, being inclined to be sinewy and raw-boned. His complexion was fair and ruddy; hair auburn, crisp—almost curly; eyes blue-grey; beard reddish; chin, broad and dimpled; forehead, high and white. With intimates the young man was genial, often jolly, but he was given to reverie, and toward mere acquaintances he often appeared stern. His temper was quick and only fairly well controlled, and when aroused, his eyes flashed defiance, his form seemed to grow taller and more commanding, but his courteous, courtly manner was never laid aside and this fact, even in moments of anger, saved the man from abruptness. Travis was a man of charming personality. He had the power of making friends with various classes and degrees of men. Toward women and children his attitude was that of true courtesy. Indeed, the contemporary writers. . . always wrote, "the gallant Travis," and gallant in its best and truest meaning describes him.

The disparate portrayals that show Bowie as the gallant Western hero and Travis as an arrogant dandy are inaccurate. If Travis had been a fake, he could not have commanded frontiersmen. A product of the frontier, he had grown up on it and dealt with it. Known to his contemporaries as "Buck," he was a demanding commander, unafraid to use his authority.

True, the Volunteers were not happy with Travis' appointment; and he, feeling "awkwardly situated," called for an election, which Bowie won by an overwhelming margin. Some use these facts to support the negative view of Travis' personality. In 1985 Tom W. Gläser wrote in *Alamo Images,* "Travis' supercilious attitude apparently alienated much of the garrison."

But other factors were involved. For one, Travis was just twenty-six, rather young to give orders to the forty-two-year-old Bowie. Also, Volunteer forces traditionally distrust the Regular military, and the Volunteers at the Alamo were reluctant to take orders from anyone. Dr. John Sutherland, who left San Antonio as a courier after the Mexican army arrived, provided one of the last eyewitness accounts of the Alamo defenders. Amelia Williams quoted Sutherland as saying, "In truth, the Texian Volunteer, like most other Volunteer soldiers . . . was pretty much his own commander, save when near conflict with the enemy compelled them, in self defense, to choose and obey a leader."

Furthermore, Bowie was drunk most of the time; and his popularity was related to his drunken, permissive style. With Bowie in charge, the Volunteers felt no military constraints and also drank as much as they wanted. Such behavior was especially obnoxious to Travis. Although he apparently was not averse to social drinking, he had headed the temperance union at Claiborne, Alabama, when practicing law there. The rowdiness of Bowie and his Volunteers must have angered the Regular officer.

J.J. Baugh, the Alamo post adjutant, reported to Governor Henry Smith that Bowie "availing himself of his popularity among the Volunteers, seemed anxious to arrogate him to the entire control." He tried to forcibly prevent local citizens from leaving Bexar. On February 13, ten days before the arrival of Mexican troops in San Antonio, Baugh wrote that Bowie had ordered the release of all prisoners, civil and military, and that (Erasmo) Seguín, acting as civil judge, ordered one prisoner remanded to jail. Bowie became enraged and demanded that the prisoner be set free. He sent for his troops and "they immediately paraded in the square, under arms, in a tumultuous manner. Bowie himself and many of his men being drunk, which has been the case ever since he has been in command," Baugh wrote.

Travis objected to the release of a prisoner that a court-martial had convicted of mutiny. After the prisoners were released, Travis protested, to no avail. He angrily marched his Regulars off toward the Medina River, removing his men from temptation and avoiding an open clash with Bowie. He also wrote to Smith, complaining about Bowie and saying he did not want any man's drunkenness to become his responsibility. Meanwhile Bowie, who was stricken with a lung illness, sobered up and apologized for his conduct. On February 14 they wrote a joint letter, telling Smith they had agreed to a dual command.

Another factor contributing to a negative image of Travis is the belief that he was, as Paul Andrew Hutton put it, "viciously anti-Mexican." The strongest evidence of that feeling is the letter in which he wrote, "The citizens of [Bexar] are all our enemies except those who have joined us heretofore; we have but three Mexicans now in the fort: those who have not joined us in this extremity, should be declared public enemies, and their property should aid in paying the expenses of the war."

Travis wrote that letter, to Governor Henry Smith and Gen. Sam Houston, on March 3, 1836, in a fortress under siege by the Mexican army. He wrote it the same day that James Bonham returned with word that James Fannin and his men would not be coming to the aid of the Alamo.

In an earlier letter Travis spoke of getting along well with inhabitants of San Antonio. Archie McDonald, in his biography of the Texian leader, said Travis tried to visit with Bexar citizens "it could be suspected, for intelligence purposes; but some of his interaction was also genuine friendship, despite the fact that he is often reported as being anti-Mexican. Like most Texians, he found much in the Latin culture that was attractive. . . and he did have friends who were Mexican. He often stopped by the residence of J.M. Rodriquez as he made the daily trips from the fort to town; and, although it must be assumed that their conversations were dominated by military and political topics, Rodriquez at least did not feel like a man who was being abused."

As Santa Anna's army approached San Antonio, Travis did become irate at the lack of support from the *Bejarenos*, the local citizens. In his anger he didn't consider their memories of the holocaust their parents and grandparents had endured in 1813 after the earlier revolt was crushed by another vengeful army from the south.

When the Mexican force entered the town plaza on February 23, the Texians fired their eighteen-pounder. It announced the start of hostilities, but hit no one. A white flag appeared, and Bowie thought Santa Anna was offering a parley. He sent a subordinate, Green Jameson, with a message in Spanish, apparently written by Juan Seguín, asking if terms were being offered.

The message was headed "Commander of the Federal Army of Texas" and ended with "God and the Mexican Federation." Bowie's signature shows his illness and also the reversal in his commitment. In a bold, uneven hand he crossed out "Federal" in the heading, drew a line through "Mexican Federation" and changed it to "God and Texas." Except for Seguín and his followers, there was no longer support for 1824 among the Alamo defenders.

Irked that Bowie had not consulted him, Travis sent his own messenger. The Mexicans refused to talk to either. Thereafter, as Bowie became sicker, Travis alone signed the messages that would ensure his immortality.

At this point, Travis had no intention of dying. He had not gone to the Alamo to be a martyr. Many of the Mexican troops were ill-equipped and ill-trained. With more men and supplies, he believed, he could drive the Mexicans back across the Rio Grande. And if the 200 men Francis W. Johnson and James Grant had taken from the Alamo had returned, joined by James W. Fannin and his 380 men from Goliad and the 1,200 in Sam Houston's army, the battle might have been different.

Not until the final two days was it obvious that—except for thirty-two Volunteers from Gonzales—no help was coming and the defenders had martyrdom forced on them. One of Santa Anna's staff officers wrote that the attack schedule was stepped up because the Mexican general heard that the men in the Alamo were thinking about sneaking out.

Did Travis really draw the line in the dirt with his sword? Probably not, but it makes no difference, for it is an accepted part of Texas lore. Susanna Dickinson, the only known adult Nordic survivor, said that about 10:00 P.M. the night before the final attack Travis gave anyone the option of leaving; however, she did not mention the line. A man named Ross left, she said. She could not spell.

That man is known to history as Louis or Moses Rose, who allegedly told the sword story to William P. Zuber's parents. Unfairly branded by later critics as a coward, Rose was not the only man who left the Alamo. Apparently there was no animosity against him at the time, for the revolutionaries were an informal lot, coming and going pretty much as they pleased. He later took up residence in East Texas and Louisiana, operated a butcher shop, and was treated like any other citizen. Although he later

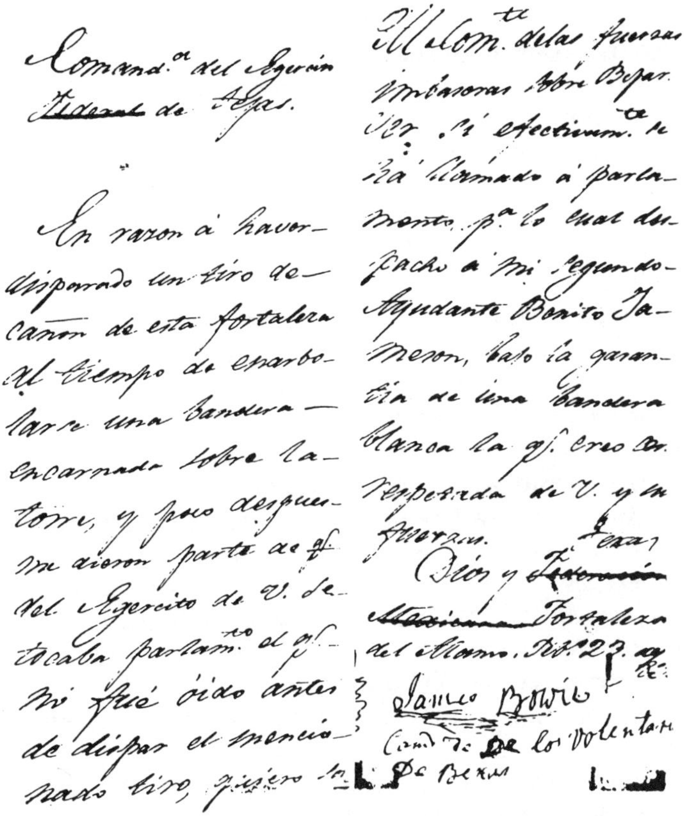
Comand.te del Ejercito Federal de Tejas.

En razon á haver disparado un tiro de cañon de esta fortaleza al tiempo de enarbolarse una bandera encarnada sobre la torre, y poco despues me dieron parte de q.e del Egercito de V. se tocaba parlam.to el q.e á mi fué oido antes de dispar el mencionado tiro, quisiera

Al Com.te de las fuerzas invasoras sobre Bexar.

Sr. Si efectivam.te se ha llamado á parlamento p.a lo cual despacho á mi segundo Ayudante Benito Jameson, bajo la garantia de una bandera blanca la q.e creo ser respetada de V. y su fuerzas.

Dios y Texas
Fortaleza del Alamo, Feb.o 23

James Bowie
Comd.te de los Volentarios de Bexar

Bowie's signature was shaky, but his sentiments were clear.

became a symbol for the massive guilt Texans felt because they allowed the heroes of the Alamo to perish, Rose should have been rewarded for having good sense.

After the Mexican siege began, some men left to protect their families. One of these was Antonio Menchaca, who served with distinction at San Jacinto. Nat Lewis, a merchant, wasted no time leaving town when the Mexican army arrived. He reportedly said, "I am a businessman. I am not a soldier." However, he later served as a scout for the Texian army and was involved in a couple of pitched battles near Gonzales, along with Capt. Philip Dimmitt and his lieutenant, Benjamin Noble, who had left the Alamo at the same time. They recruited seventeen men and fought their way through the Mexican army to reach the coast. Noble was sent as a courier to Houston and was at San Jacinto. Probably others left too. There was no stigma in leaving. Sometimes Travis had no takers when he called for volunteer couriers. Those there thought it more dangerous to go than to stay.

The final attack came in predawn darkness after pickets were surprised, allowing the Mexicans to approach the walls undetected. Baugh gave the alarm as Mexican soldiers, carrying scaling ladders, rushed the walls. Travis awoke and shouted, "Hurrah, my boys! Come on, boys! The Mexicans are upon us, and give them hell!" He added in Spanish, "*¡No rendirse, muchachos!*" —"Don't surrender, boys!"

In a dark suit, he looked more like a preacher than a commander. He is often pictured in uniform. Although he had ordered one, it had not arrived when he left San Felipe for Bexar. He did bring a flag, but no description of it exists.

Apparently Travis was one of the first casualties of the battle, struck in the head with a single bullet as he fired his shotgun down at the charging troops. His young slave, Joe, was beside him. Joe reported that Travis fell down the earthen slope. Dazed, he plunged his saber through a Mexican officer, and they both died. Joe retreated to the barracks, where he fired some shots at the attackers before he was captured. Later he was released and accompanied Susanna Dickinson, the widow of Capt. Almeron Dickinson, and her baby to Gonzales, where Sam Houston was forming his army.

Bexar Alcalde Francisco Antonio Ruiz showed General Santa Anna the bodies of the various Texian officers, including Travis. In his written report, Ruiz said, "On the north battery of the fortress convent, lay the lifeless body of Col. Travis on the gun carriage, shot only through the forehead."

Amelia Williams said, "Twice the attacking forces applied their scaling ladders to the walls, but were twice beaten back. Their third attempt was successful. This came at daybreak; and just as the Mexicans broke over the walls Travis fell, shot through the forehead as he stood behind his now useless cannon and made ready to fire his rifle."

Travis' contemporary, Noah Smithwick, said, "Bill Travis . . . was a good fighter; but, had not the qualities necessary to a commander, else he never would have allowed himself to be penned up in the Alamo."

In a 1971 study of Texas nationalism, Mark Nackman suggested that Travis had "suicidal impulses," a viewpoint sometimes used to explain the decision to remain at the mission fortress. However, the other commanders were at least as responsible as

Travis for that decision. Neill did not want to give up the artillery. In a January 23, 1836, letter to the governor and council, he wrote, "If teams could be obtained here by any means to remove the cannon and Public Property I would immediately destroy the fortifications and abandon the place. . . ."

And Bowie had said the men would "rather die in these ditches than give them up to the enemy."

A report that Travis shot himself may be another reason for his less-than-macho Hollywood portrayals. In a footnote Amelia Williams cited the report of two messengers, Anselmo Borgarra and Andres Bercena, who said Travis had shot himself as the Mexicans poured over the walls. She quoted Ruiz and told of Travis' friend Andrew Briscoe, who said in New Orleans, "The brave and gallant Travis, to prevent his falling into the hands of the enemy, shot himself."

She also gave Joe's account, but in a footnote said, "I am inclined to think that Joe's story is too circumstantial and that Ruiz's statement is more nearly accurate. The fact that Travis's only wound was a pistol shot through the head, together with all the attending circumstances, makes the report carried by [the two messengers] seem very plausible."

As Alamo and Goliad expert Kevin R. Young and other historians have pointed out, Ruiz did not mention a pistol. Neither did any other first-hand source. Mexican Col. José Enríque de la Peña, who was a participant in the battle, gave a very different version. In his diary he said Travis "would take a few steps and stop, turning his proud face toward us to discharge his shots; he fought like a true soldier. Finally he died, but he died after having traded his life very dearly. None of his men died with greater heroism. . . ."

The exact number of casualties in the battle will never be known. In *A Time To Stand*, Walter Lord said the best estimate for the number of Texians is 183. As to Mexican casualties, he pointed out that nineteen different sources give nineteen different figures, ranging from 65 killed and 233 wounded to 2,000 killed and 300 wounded. Using information from two contemporary sources, Reuben Potter and Dr. Joseph Barnard, Lord put the best estimate at around 600 killed and wounded.

Charles Long, longtime curator of the Alamo and Alamo Museum, pointed out that there were quite a few more survivors than is generally believed.

"People usually think only of Mrs. Dickinson, her daughter and the slave, Joe," he said. "But there were fifteen others, mostly women and children."

Mexican army reports mention ten or so other women and children as survivors. One man, Brigido Guerrero, survived by convincing the Mexicans he was a prisoner of the Texians.

"I consider the couriers who left during the siege survivors," Long said. "There were at least sixteen of these."

James Butler Bonham carried two messages out, then rushed back to die in the final assault. Another young man listed among the dead was the courier who carried the last message to Gen. Sam Houston. He was Henry Warnell, twenty-four, who had arrived the year before from Arkansas, where his wife had died. He left his infant son, John, with friends. Warnell had worked for Edward Burleson. Court records describe him as a small man, weighing less than 118 pounds, "blue-eyed, red-headed, freckled and an incessant tobacco chewer. He had a reputation in Arkansas as a good jockey and a great hunter."

On February 28 Travis called for volunteers for courier duty. When no one answered, Travis said, "I shall have to command the service of someone if I get no volunteers." The young jockey agreed to go. As he sped away from the fortress, he was struck by Mexican fire. He remained in the saddle and made his way to Houston on March 4. His condition worsened, and he died a few weeks later at Port Lavaca–an Alamo casualty.

Long also told the story of Asa Walker. Walker and a companion, William Gant, left Tennessee together. At Gonzales, Walker heard Travis' plea for help. His friend was away, so he took the friend's rifle and coat and left this note:

"Mr. Gant, I take the responsibility of taking your overcoat and gun–your gun they would have anyhow, and I might as well have it as anyone else. If I live to return, I will satisfy you for all. If I die, I leave you my clothes to do the best you can with. You can sell them for something. If you overtake me, you can take your rifle and I will trust to chance . . . . Forgive the presumption and remember your friend at heart. A. Walker." He also left an IOU for $35.87 he had borrowed for the trip from Tennessee.

Walker died with the thirty-one other Gonzales volunteers who fought their way into the Alamo shortly before it fell. Gant, who fought at San Jacinto, claimed and received Walker's land bounty toward payment of the debt, which totaled up to $97.87. Republic of Texas land was so cheap then that the 4,000 acres was short of paying it off. Gant died in 1840, before he could take possession of the land.

One poignant Alamo myth that did not come from Hollywood is the tale of the two Bowie children. For some unknown reason, Amelia Williams appears to have invented them.

Jim Bowie, she said, was "consistently courteous, sympathetic, kind and affectionate" toward the prominent Mexican families of San Antonio. Almost all of those families were connected by blood or marriage with Ursula María de Veramendi, the bride he married on April 22, 1831. Williams called their marriage "a real romance," but said, "his domestic happiness was brief.... While on [a visit to her father's family in Monclova in 1833] Mrs. Bowie, *her two infant children*, her father, her mother, and several other members of the family, died of cholera, all within three days' time."

In her original text Williams attributed the information to a letter from José Antonio Navarro to Samuel M. Williams, dated September 26, 1833. In a footnote she quoted the letter as saying, "When I told you my fears of the cholera it looks as if I had a sad premonition, because my brother-in-law, Veramendi, my sister Josepha, his wife, and Ursula Bowie, died unexpectedly in Monclova."

When her dissertation was reprinted in the *Southwestern Historical Quarterly* in 1935, the footnote read: "my brother-in-law, Veramendi, my sister Josepha, his wife and Ursula Bowie and her children died unexpectedly ...."

A photocopy, obtained from the Rosenberg Library in Galveston, shows that the original letter reads *Mi hermano Veramendi, mi hermana Josefa su esposa y Ursulita de Bowie han muerto en una manera inaudita en Monclova.*

A typed copy of the letter shows the word after *manera* as *mandita*, which Williams apparently interpreted as "unexpectedly." The word actually is *inaudita*, "helplessly"; but, either way, there is no mention of children. Searches of church and census records and other sources, including the burial records at Monclova, have failed to verify that any children were born to James and Ursula Bowie.

Every year a simple yet impressive memorial service honors the Alamo heroes. The program opens with a color and honor guard and includes the roll call of the heroes and the states and nations they represented.

"We know little about so many of them," Long said. "They left home, were here a short while, and they died. But every year we find out something about a few more of them."

He told how the flag of the state of Vermont joined the memorial parade in 1982. "There were nineteen men we didn't know where they came from. Now there are eighteen," he said. "We have learned that Miles DeForest Andross was from Vermont. His family was active in the American Revolution . . . ."

After the battle Borgarra and Barcena rushed to Gonzales to tell of the disaster. The news was so distressing that Houston had the two jailed to try to keep the word from spreading. It didn't work.

Mexican officers credited the overwhelming victories at San Antonio and later at Goliad for Santa Anna's indifference and his defeat at San Jacinto. The conventional modern belief is that the Alamo bought time for Sam Houston to raise the army that defeated Santa Anna some six weeks later. But the truth is that the Alamo siege delayed the projected Mexican advance by no more than two days. And as Sam Houston retreated from Gonzales to the Colorado to the Brazos to Harrisburg, his army of some 1,200 shrank by about 400 men. Twice as many men in Houston's command "lit a shuck" as died in the Alamo. It was cold, rivers were flooding, looters and worse were about, and many went to protect their families. Others simply felt they might be safer elsewhere.

There was no reason for the Alamo battle. No less an expert than Mexican Gen. Vicente Filisola wrote later, "On our opinion, the blood of our soldiers as well as that of the enemy was shed in vain, for the mere gratification of the inconsiderate, puerile and guilty vanity of reconquering Bexar by force of arms, and through a bloody contest . . . .

"The massacres of the Alamo . . . convinced the rebels that no peaceable settlement could be expected, and that they must conquer, or die, or abandon the fruits of ten years of sweat and labor, together with their fondest hopes for the future."

He was right. The Texians and those who favored their cause knew that they must conquer or die.

Travis' plea for help, which began, "To the people of Texas and all Americans in the world, fellow citizens and compatriots" and ended "I shall never surrender or retreat. . . . Victory or Death!" sounds melodramatic to modern ears. But in those different times it made the Alamo something more than the defeat of an obscure outpost in an obscure war. That plea was published all over the United States. It was too late to help Travis, but the massacre ignited the anger of America and Europe.

The fate of Travis and Bowie and their men, and the massacre of an army of volunteers at Goliad, caused a shock wave across the United States, stirring patriotism, pride, and anger. From all over the nation, volunteers answered the cry of recruiters. Had San Jacinto been lost, too, Texas would have been freed anyway. Blood of friends and kinsmen spilled in Texas made it so.

Col. James Neill

The Alamo generates far more questions than answers:

Why did the Texians and American adventurers remain in the Alamo when they knew they were vastly outnumbered?

Did Sam Houston really order the fortress destroyed?

And why did Col. James Neill leave his command there?

John R. Knaggs, author of *The Bugles Are Silent* (1977), wrote that Colonel Neill played a larger role in the defense of the Alamo than is generally recognized. Neill was appointed lieutenant colonel of artillery in late 1835. He commanded a company of artillery at the Siege of Bexar and was ordered by Gen. Sam Houston to take command of the military district of Bexar. On January 17 Houston sent James Bowie with orders to Neill to destroy the Alamo and retreat to Gonzales. But he didn't.

Knaggs wrote:

> I found solid evidence that the original strategic decision to fortify the Alamo was made by James Neill–not by James Bowie and or William Barret Travis, as is widely believed. . . . He reported that only eighty effective men remained [following the Storming of Bexar], divided between garrisons at the Alamo and near San Fernando Church . . . he decided to combine them in the Alamo.
>
> The Texians had captured twenty-four artillery pieces, eighteen of which were operational and Neill made the decision to fortify the Alamo . . . [because] he had no means to transport the artillery and it would be foolhardy, indeed, to abandon that much firepower–by far the most concentrated at any location during the Texas Revolution. According to reports at the time, sickness in his family caused Neill to be relieved . . . .

Knaggs enclosed a copy of an 1839 testament in which Neill said he had named Green Jameson engineer to design the fortifications and Jameson apparently died on March 6, 1836. A portion of fortifications had been done by Mexican General Cós, whose troops had built ramps of earth and stones so heavy that a cannon could be hoisted to the rooftops.

Knaggs said that a great-great-great-grandson of Neill's, Monte Tomerlin of San Antonio, claimed to have found indications that Neill might have left the Alamo in a quiet quest for badly needed funds to ease the burdens on his tattered troops. If that was his mission, he would not have announced publicly that he would return carrying thousands of dollars in cash.

Neill, a veteran artillery officer, had fought in the War of 1812. He believed such a highly concentrated collection of artillery could successfully defend the fort.

"Travis or Bowie could have altered the course of events, and I suspect they would if that artillery had not been there," Knaggs wrote. "Though desperate, their situation was not hopeless. That much artillery firing grapeshot from high vantage points was a substantial equalizer to being vastly outnumbered.

"My research convinced me that the Alamo artillery was adequate for its portion of the defense, but more riflemen were badly needed. With at least two hundred more–which Fannin could have provided–the Alamo defenders might well have achieved a stalemate."

Neill was seriously wounded in a skirmish the day before the Battle of San Jacinto and relinquished his artillery command to George Washington Hockley. He died in Navarro County in 1845.

A Tejano Alamo Hero

The saga of Gregorio Esparza is more dramatic than fiction.

Esparza was one of the heroes of the Alamo. He and others in the company of Juan N. Seguín had cast their lot with the Nordic Texians earlier when they ousted General Cós and his troops after the Storming of Bexar. Esparza's brother Francisco was one of those banished soldiers, and there was no love lost between the two. They had long differed politically. Gregorio favored the democratic Constitution of 1824. Francisco sided with President Santa Anna's Centralists.

As Santa Anna's army approached San Antonio, Gregorio prepared to send his family to Nacogdoches with the family of his friend, John W. Smith. However, the Mexicans arrived before the wagon did. Esparza's son Enrique, eight years old in 1836, recalled in a 1907 interview how his father and Smith hurried their families to the Alamo. The doors were barred, but they entered through a window (the same one, Alamo curator Charles Long said, Moses Rose left by).

There was no shortage of food or water during the siege. A

well had been dug in the church so there was no need to draw water from the exposed ditch outside. Cattle provided food. Enrique Esparza said Santa Anna declared a three-day armistice during the thirteen-day siege to let the Texians deliberate on surrendering. Bowie, he said, told those who wanted to leave to go. Some did. Travis sent others out as messengers to get help.

It was dark when the end came after a sudden eruption of cannon fire followed by a swarm of Mexicans firing and slashing.

"By my side was an American boy," Esparza said. "He was about my own age. As they reached us, he rose to his feet. He had been sleeping, but like myself, he had been rudely awakened . . . he stood calmly and drew his blanket across his shoulder. He was unarmed. They slew him where he stood, and his corpse fell over me. My father's body was lying near the cannon he tended."

Gregorio had been shot through the chest and stabbed in the side by a sword. He lay in a small room off the chapel.

"My mother [holding] my baby sister was kneeling beside [the body]. My brothers and I were close to her. I clutched her garments. Behind her was the only man who escaped and was permitted to surrender. His name was Brigido Guerrero . . . ." Guerrero, spared after he convinced Santa Anna he was a captured Mexican soldier who had tried to escape, had told the men in the Alamo the meaning of Mexican bugle calls.

Women and children were taken before Santa Anna, who gave each woman a blanket and two silver pesos. Francisco Esparza asked General Cós if he could remove his brother and not burn him with the others. Thus Gregorio Esparza escaped cremation and was buried in Campo Santo—Milam Square today.

His heirs later had difficulty getting Texas land bounties due for his service at the Alamo. Twice in 1857 the Court of Claims rejected their application without comment. A new commission approved it in 1860. Some of the bounty, Esparza Ranch near Pleasanton, with its own church, flourished for many years.

Gregorio Esparza, long overlooked as an Alamo hero, now has a school named for him in San Antonio. A portrait showing him firing a cannon from the roof hangs in the Alamo chapel.

His credentials as a Texan are the best.

How Did Davy Die?

Corpus Christi historian Dan Kilgore is sort of stuck with Davy Crockett. Every time somebody writes about Crockett, Dan is brought into it.

Some years ago Dan made a speech entitled "How Did Davy Die?" That didn't stir up too much fuss. But when Texas A&M University Press published the talk as a book in 1978, the wire services picked it up, and Dan became a clay pigeon for all those who thought he was sullying the reputation of a Texas hero.

According to the Hollywood account, Davy went down swinging, leaving a pile of dead Mexicans before he cashed in his chips. All Dan did was to quote the many sources, most of them Mexican soldiers, who said Davy and five or six others were overcome and captured after Mexican Gen. Manuel Castrillón interceded, then asked Gen. Antonio López de Santa Anna to spare them. Santa Anna became enraged that his orders to kill all the interlopers had not been obeyed, and they were slain on the spot.

People from all over let Dan know they were unhappy that anyone would say David Crockett was a quitter who surrendered. But in 1986 Kilgore traveled to Tennessee to a David Crockett memorial ceremony and returned with his scalp intact.

Alamo Images, published in 1985 by Southern Methodist University Press, recounts the furor Kilgore raised and points out that the press in the nineteenth century commonly reported Davy's surrender as an example of Santa Anna's barbarity. As early as July 1836, just four months after the battle, Stephen F. Austin's cousin, Mary Austin Holley, wrote the following description in her book *Texas*:

"A desperate contest ensued, in which prodigies of valor were wrought by this Spartan band, which garrisoned the fort until daylight, when only seven of them were found alive. These seven cried for quarter, but were told there was no mercy for them. Of this number were Col. David Crockett, Mr. Benton, and the gallant Col. Bonham of South Carolina. When their demand for quarter was refused, they continued fighting until all were butchered."

In November 1986, *Texas Monthly* printed an article entitled "Davy Crockett, Still King of the Wild Frontier, and a hell of a nice guy besides," by history professor Paul Andrew Hutton.

Crockett never really succeeded in much except creating a legend. He became a legend while he lived, largely because of his frontier image and background. He was a successful hunter but not much of a soldier. He was a great campaigner, for he stood for the rights of the common man. He was a successful politician but not much of a congressman because he was too honest and refused to cater to wealthy backers. As a result, he became an enemy of Andrew Jackson, a powerful force in Tennessee.

Santa Anna became enraged that his orders to kill all the interlopers had not been obeyed, and they were slain on the spot.

In one campaign an opponent smiled a lot, so Davy outdid him by telling how he himself had grinned raccoons out of trees. A Washington play, designed as a parody of Crockett, became a hit. In the end the caricature of Crockett wearing a coonskin hat—which he did not wear—became legendary; and Crockett began to dress and act the part—when he was campaigning.

The Whigs thought they could use his backwoods image to oppose Jackson. There was talk of Crockett for president. But he could never be controlled. Defeated in politics, he went to Texas, where he saw the prospect of free land and unlimited political possibilities. He went at a time when it seemed the Mexicans would not come back.

But once in the Alamo he became the victim of Crockett the legend. He could do no other than stand for the cause of freedom. Mexican soldiers reported that Crockett told Santa Anna he was a tourist who had taken refuge in the Alamo. When his explanation failed, he faced death without complaint and became a super legend. Walt Disney and Fess Parker made him a twentieth-century celebrity.

"That he who so represented the spirit of democracy should perish at the orders of a despot who cared for nothing but his own ambition is somehow fitting," Hutton wrote. "It was a fine close to a magnificent career, and it secured a glorious immortality for Crockett that a successful political career in Texas never could have."

The truth, like that found by Dan Kilgore, can never tarnish a real hero.

The 1824 Flag

Contrary to what has become a general belief, the flag atop the Alamo walls on March 6, 1836, was almost certainly not the Flag of the Mexican Constitution of 1824.

Historians have argued that the 1824 banner flew over the battle on two assumptions: (1) Texas had not declared its independence when the battle started; and (2) the Federalist symbol would possibly elicit support from some of Santa Anna's followers. Quite likely their conclusion is incorrect.

Reuben Marmaduke Potter is generally credited with being the first to offer the flag of 1824 thesis when he wrote in 1860, "It is a fact not often remembered that Travis and his band fell under the Mexican Federal Flag of 1824 instead of the Lone Star of Texas, although Independence, unknown to them, had been declared by the new convention four days before at Washington on the Brazos. They died for a Republic whose existence they never knew."

However, the 1824 flag story may have an even earlier source. Joseph Hefter, an authority on Mexican history, originally published *The Siege and Taking of the Alamo* for Gen. Miguel A. Sanchez Lamego, Mexican military historian. In the English translation of the book, he quoted British historian William Kennedy in *Texas* (New York, 1844), Vol. II, pages 180–181: "It must be kept well in mind that Texas Independence had not yet been declared, and that the defenders of the Alamo fought under the Mexican Federal flag of 1824." George Bancroft quoted the same source. Note the similarity between Kennedy's comment and Potter's. The passage does not appear in Kennedy's first edition, published in 1841 in London.

Regardless of the originator of the 1824 theory, others followed suit. Amelia Williams said, "[Henderson] Yoakum, Potter, H.A. McArdle and other more recent students agree that the Alamo flag was the Mexican tricolor with the numerals 1824 on the white bar . . . .This flag was almost certainly the one used at the Alamo."

J. Frank Dobie in *No Help for the Alamo,* said, "Contrary to popular belief, the Texans did not fly a Lone Star, but a tricolored green, white and red Mexican flag with 1824 stitched across the white stripe."

Historian John Henry Brown, who wrote *History of Texas,* agreed. An 1885 painting by French artist Jean Louis Theodore Gentilz shows the 1824 flag, twenty-five years after the Potter myth was planted.

However, current thinking does not favor the flag. In *A Time To Stand,* Walter Lord said, "Texas stopped fighting for the Constitution of 1824 long before the Alamo . . . early in 1836 popular opinion swung violently and overwhelmingly for independence . . . . Down came the old 1824 flags."

True, the defenders did not know that the declaration of independence had been signed, but they had sent two delegates, Sam Maverick and Jesse Badgett, to represent them at the convention and sign just such a declaration. Maverick and Badgett signed the March 2 document, as did the two Bexar delegates, José Francisco Ruiz and José Antonio Navarro.

On March 3 Travis wrote to Jesse Grimes: "Let the Convention go on and make a declaration of independence; and we will understand what we are fighting for. If independence is not declared, I shall lay down my arms and so will the men under my command. But under the flag of independence, we are ready to peril our lives a hundred times a day. . . . I am determined to perish in the defence of this place, and my bones shall reproach my country for her neglect. With 500 men more, I will visit vengeance on the enemies of Texas . . . ."

Travis had brought his own flag to the Alamo. So did Davy Crockett and probably others, but there is no record as to what they looked like.

The history of the 1824 flag begins with Philip Dimmitt, while he was commander of fortress La Bahía. On October 27, 1835, he wrote to Stephen F. Austin, "I have had a flag made–the colours and their arrangement the same as the old one–with the words and figures, 'Constitution of 1824' displayed on the white in the centre."

At this time Dimmitt and Austin were both supporters of the Constitution of 1824. Dimmitt suggested the flag as he proposed an invasion of Matamoros, where he believed Mexican Federalists would join the cause. Dimmitt probably carried his banner to San Antonio, where he and his men participated in the Storming of Bexar. He knew that 200–250 cavalrymen in Gen. Martín Perfecto de Cós' command had served under Col. José María Gonzalez and were sympathetic to the liberal cause.

However, something he saw in that battle changed Dimmitt's mind. He returned to Goliad firmly convinced that any further liaison with Federalists in Mexico was hopeless, for they were nationalists first and were changing sides to combat the American invaders. Dimmitt said it would be victory or death—no quarter.

It's highly likely Dimmitt left the red, white, and green banner at the Alamo, for back at Goliad he constructed the first flag of independence, using the bloody arm holding a sword. That was the flag raised over La Bahía in conjunction with the signing of the premature Declaration of Independence there on December 20, 1835. Dimmitt borrowed the bloody-arm symbol from a flag one of his men, Capt. William S. Brown, had designed and carried on the march to Bexar. At San Antonio Gen. Stephen F. Austin, still the loyal Federalist, ordered Brown not to display the flag.

Though he credited Dimmitt with creating the 1824 flag, Refugio historian Hobart Huson assumed it was used by the defenders of the Alamo when it fell. This impression may have been created by the fact that the red, white, and green flag probably flew over the Alamo as late as December 30, just before Dr. James Grant embarked on his ill-fated Matamoros expedition.

A young German volunteer who joined Grant on that venture, Herman Ehrenberg, wrote that shortly before the departure, "We still considered Texas and Mexico as one . . . three colors floated over the church."

When Grant stripped the Alamo of blankets, powder, and other supplies that would be vitally missed two months later, he would have also taken the 1824 flag. Grant was not in favor of independence. He was more interested in regaining his land holdings in Mexico than in a revolt for patriotic reasons. On January 10, 1836, Col. F.W. Johnson wrote of the expedition, "The Federal Volunteer army of Texas . . . under the command of Francis W. Johnson . . . march under the flag of 1-8-2-4."

When the volunteers reached Goliad, Grant was incensed at Dimmitt's flag of independence. Dimmitt lowered his flag only after armed confrontation was threatened. A report by Irish empresario James McGloin described the clash and quoted Johnson and Grant as "stating that they were Federalists and would stand for the Constitution of 1824."

When the expedition reached Refugio, Sam Houston harangued the troops and convinced all but about sixty of the 300–

400 that a Matamoros invasion was not a good idea. Johnson and Grant continued on to San Patricio. After the Texian force was decimated in the actions there February 27 and at Agua Dulce March 2, Gen. José Urréa sent the Texians his troops had captured to Matamoros.

Potter, who was in Matamoros, talked to the prisoners and worked to gain their release. In 1878 he wrote that by the end of February 1836, Grant "was probably the only armed Texan who still harbored any hope for the Constitution of 1824 or any wish to prolong the union with Mexico." He also said that Grant's men "had been taken under the flag of 1824."

Since Grant was on a horse-hunting expedition, it is unlikely that he had a flag when he was ambushed. He would have left it at San Patricio, where Johnson and the other contingent waited for him.

General Urréa's report said, "The enemy was attacked at half past three in the morning in the midst of the rain, and although forty men within the fort defended themselves resolutely, the door was forced at dawn, sixteen being killed and twenty-four being taken prisoners. The town and the rest of the inhabitants did not suffer the least damage. *I captured a flag* and all kinds of arms and ammunition."

Urréa did not describe the flag he captured. A "Constitution of 1824" flag would have enraged General Santa Anna. It would have been even more unpopular among the Centralist regime than among the Texians.

Ironically, the fact that Johnson and Grant marched under the banner of the Constitution of 1824 could well have saved the lives of their captured followers. Santa Anna had ordered his generals to execute all prisoners; but Urréa, instead, sent these to Matamoros. He had been a Federalist before the invasion of Texas, and the flag was tangible proof of support for the Federalist cause.

[4]

Death in the Springtime

Fannin's Indecision

When you think of heroes of the Texas Revolution, you usually don't think of James Walker Fannin, Jr. He fought bravely, even when badly wounded, but—unlike Travis, Bowie, and the other heroes of the Alamo—Fannin didn't go out fighting. He is known to history as the indecisive commander of the men who surrendered to Gen. José Urréa on March 20, 1836, at the Battle of Coleto Creek and who were executed a week later.

The Alamo left no survivors, but thirty or so of the Texian prisoners lived to tell what happened at La Bahía, or "Labadie," as they called it. A number wrote accounts, and they all tell very nearly the same story.

Early in the war the volunteers elected Fannin chief. They seemed to think anyone who attended West Point could lead, but Fannin had dropped out. Even so, he was successful in recruiting troops in the United States and getting Americans to supply munitions and supplies.

He did well enough at Gonzales. And his ideas were sound at the Battle of Concepción, although his desire to hog the glory foreshadowed the ego clashes that would later plague the Texians. At Concepción, Fannin held a joint command with Bowie. However, when he sent in his battle report, he signed it, "James Fannin, Commanding," and listed Bowie as "aide de camp." Two days later Bowie offered his resignation, but nothing came of it.

Fannin wanted to invade Matamoros, but Sam Houston didn't approve and withdrew, leaving Fannin in command at Goliad. Houston was worried that his army would splinter and allow the Mexican army to defeat pockets of resistance.

And that's exactly what happened. Grant and Johnson and their men were lost, and Fannin wavered. William Barret Travis was begging for assistance at the Alamo. Fannin had started out with 320 men, but his wagons broke down and he returned to Goliad. Jesús Cuellar, the former Mexican army lieutenant known as "Comanche" who had led Ben Milam's men into San Antonio, had been offered the command in the Texian army that later went to Juan Seguín. Being a deserter, Cuellar really didn't want publicity, but he continued to work for the Federalist cause and shortly accepted a captaincy. He was with Fannin at La Bahía.

Cuellar offered to tell General Urréa that Fannin was preparing a march to San Patricio and to suggest a place where the Mexicans could set up an ambush. Urréa wasn't ready to take the word of a deserter, but Cuellar's brother, Salvador, vouched for him and Urréa arranged for the "ambush."

Cuellar had succeeded in getting Urréa to divide the Mexican army into two groups, setting up an "ambush" in a poor defensive position at a place called Arroyo de las Ratas. Had Fannin attacked the Mexicans at this time, likely he could have defeated Urréa's men in two separate actions and then been in position to reinforce Sam Houston's army. Fannin hesitated. Urréa got fresh spy reports, called the ambush off, and consolidated his army once more.

Historian Hobart Huson said, "Fannin had changed his mind and brought Captain Cuellar's brave efforts to naught."

Jesús "Comanche" Cuellar dropped from Texas history. He apparently saw he had failed, stole away, and was heard no more in Texas. One report said he died in Saltillo several years later. It was a shame, for he already had helped shape Texas history by contributing to the Storming of Bexar when the American volunteers were about to give up. Had Fannin heeded his advice, both Fannin and Cuellar might today be enshrined along with other Texas heroes. But Fannin vacillated and the opportunity passed.

Col. Fannin decided to fortify La Bahía, which he called Fort Defiance.

Houston ordered him to retreat and leave his heavy artillery behind, but Fannin decided to fortify La Bahía, which he called Fort Defiance. Engineer John Sowers Brooks rigged a large number of muskets to fire in sequence like a machine gun. All was in readiness. Once more Fannin was indecisive. Finally, he decided to retreat.

In *Rise of the Lone Star, a Story Told by Its Pioneers,* Laura Steele told the story of John Cash, the youngest warrior in Fannin's company. Steele was a niece of John Crittenden Duval, one of the survivors of the Goliad Massacre. Her account quotes Duval: "One Texas woman, Mother Cash, was with us. She had refused to leave Goliad when danger threatened and was now with our army."

Mrs. Cash was the wife of George W. Cash, a Goliad merchant who had taken part in the capture of the fortress in October 1835 and became a member of Fannin's force.

"She traveled in a cart," Duval said. "While the fighting was going on, a boy, Hal Ripley, son of General Ripley of the War of 1812, climbed onto the cart to fire at the enemy. He was wounded and called to Mother Cash to help him down."

British historian William Kennedy wrote that Ripley, "a youth of eighteen or nineteen . . . had his thigh broken. . . . Mrs. Cash, at his request, helped him into her cart, and fixed a prop for him to lean against, and a rest for his rifle; while in that situation, he was seen to bring down four Mexicans before he received another wound, which broke his right arm; he immediately exclaimed to Mrs. C., 'You may take me down now, mother; I have done my share; they have paid exactly two for one on account of both balls in me.'

"Such was the spirit that animated every man among the assailed save two, who had run under a cart early in the engagement, and covered up their heads. One of them was familiarly called Black Hawk, as he professed to be a very fire-eater—but his courage was all in his tongue."

In his account, Duval noted that Fannin had frittered away an entire day before retreating, as his small cavalry contingent jousted with the mounted Mexican soldiers. Neither side damaged the other, and the horses were badly winded by the dashes back and forth in front of the fortress. Before Fannin finally ordered the retreat, oxen were left unwatered, unfed, and in harness all night. Strangely, most of his men were city-bred and didn't know how to handle livestock. The next day the animals were uncontrollable.

The army crossed the San Antonio River and entered a wide prairie. The men warned Fannin to continue to the wooded area where they would have forage, water, and a defensible position. But an overloaded munitions wagon lost a wheel, and he ordered a halt so that the oxen could be fed. General Urréa, who had been unprepared to attack, now had time to move to the offensive, surrounding the Texians.

The Texians fought off numerous infantry and cavalry assaults on March 19, but the next morning the situation was desperate. They had left food and water behind in favor of muskets and extra cannon. Many men were wounded and suffering greatly from lack of water, George Cash among them. He had been struck in the head by a musket ball but remained conscious.

Abel Morgan, a Texian who survived the massacre as a nurse, told of standing near Cash when he was hit: "The ball cut the size of it out of his head, but it did not kill him."

Later in the battle, Morgan said, "I went into the square [the defense perimeter] to get some more cartridges and to see if Cash was dead, but he had revived as the film of the brain was not broken, but I was much mortified to see so many fine fellows laid down there with their blankets spread over them."

Fannin could not have chosen a worse spot for a defensive battle. It was in the open and gave the enemy the advantage of the high ground, greatly reducing the effectiveness of the Texian artillery. In addition, the artillery commander was dead, two cannoneers and the chief engineer wounded. And there was no water for swabbing the field pieces to keep fresh powder from igniting when it was loaded.

During a lull in the fighting, Mrs. Cash could stand the pleadings of the wounded men no longer. Accompanied by her son, John, who was only fourteen, but had done a full day's fighting the previous day, she walked across the prairie between the two armies to ask to be allowed to bring them water. Seeing a woman in the field, both sides held their fire.

At her request, she was directed to General Urréa, who received her sympathetically. A Mexican officer who had served in the Goliad garrison and knew the Cashes introduced her. She made her request, but Urréa did not seem to notice. Instead, he looked pointedly at young John Cash's shot pouch and powder horn. It was obvious the youth had not been playing games.

Duval's account said the general "looked sternly at the boy and said, 'Woman, why bring a child into battle?' At which the boy replied, 'I am here fighting for my rights for Texas. We mean to get our rights or die.' "

Kennedy says the conversation was interrupted by the raising of a white flag as a token of the Texians' surrender. The stiff wind from a norther blowing at the time immediately tore the flag into three pieces. At this point the general turned his attention to terms of surrender.

Steele thought that young Cash was executed with his father, young Henry Ripley, and the others. However, Hobart Huson reported that Urréa apparently sent the mother and son on their way.

John Cash seethed for revenge. When Texians marched south to punish Mexico for raiding San Antonio and other South Texas towns, he enlisted in Ewen Cameron's Company on November 12, 1842, and was captured in an attack on Mier. After an ill-fated escape attempt, Santa Anna ordered every tenth prisoner executed. To determine the condemned, the Mexicans placed 174 beans, 157 white, seventeen black, in a crock covered with a handkerchief and forced the Texians to draw. John Cash was among the unfortunate seventeen who drew the black beans. His last words were, "Well, they murdered my father with Colonel Fannin, and they are about to murder me." Thus the fighting youth who escaped his father's fate at Goliad met an identical death seven years later.

Fannin, executed with his men a week after the surrender, has been condemned by historians because of his weak leadership, indecisiveness, and poor judgment. In the introduction to *Alamo Images, Changing Perceptions of a Texas Experience,* Paul Andrew Hutton called him inept and timid and said, "Texas has . . . raised monuments to the cowardly Fannin . . . ."

Actually, the monument at La Bahía is not to Fannin alone, but also to the men who died with him. He obviously failed as a military commander, but no contemporary account calls him a coward. In "Some Few Notes Upon a Part of the Texan War," Dr. Jack Shackelford, one of those who had urged the commander not to halt in the open prairie, wrote: "That [Fannin] was deficient in that *caution* which a prudent officer should always evince, must be admitted; but that he was a brave, gallant, and intrepid officer, none who knew him can doubt."

Fannin died bravely; and his decisions, unfortunate as they were, were influenced by concern for settlers and for his men. He received a message from Sam Houston to blow up La Bahía, dump his surplus cannon in the river, and fall back to Victoria on March 13 or 14, but part of the blame for the delay of the retreat until March 19 must be shared by Capt. Amon Butler King, a Kentuckian who did not obey orders. King, by his independent actions, held up the retreat and caused the death of his followers.

Fannin had sent King and forty to fifty men under his command to Refugio to evacuate several colonist families who lacked transport. Included were women, at least one of them pregnant, and children. As King escorted carts carrying the refugees about March 11, he was attacked by about a hundred native *rancheros* and Karankawa Indians under Capt. Carlos de la Garza. The caravan made it to the mission in Refugio, and King sent word to Fannin to send reinforcements.

Lt. Col. William Ward of the Georgia Battalion came to the rescue with 120 to 150 men. After a forced march of twenty-seven miles in a cold, drizzling rain on March 13, they arrived in Refugio and drove some 200 attackers away.

The Texians rested, then attacked the Mexican camp, routing the Mexicans and killing twenty-five, including an officer. The next morning Captain King demanded that he be placed in command of all the troops, despite the fact that Ward was a lieutenant colonel. Ward was prepared to escort the carts back to Goliad when King left on a venture to punish the Texas Mexicans who opposed him. He went up and down the river, burning ranches, wasting time that was far more valuable than he realized.

When he returned to the Refugio mission, he was surprised to find it surrounded by Gen. José Urréa's full army of some 1,500 men. In the church were 120 of Ward's party. The Mexicans made several charges on the church and suffered heavy losses. Some were Central American Indians who spoke no Spanish and could not understand the orders of their officers. King's men took shelter in the woods, where they repulsed attacks, inflicting heavy casualties.

On March 14 Mexican cannon shot began hitting the church. Captain de la Garza's Victoriana Guardes patrolled between Refugio and Goliad, killing all but two of the Texian messengers. One, with a message telling of Fannin's order to retreat, was allowed to go through.

The Texians, low on ammunition, fired only when they had a clear shot. There were four Mexican assaults. During the night, Ward's men slipped out of the church, leaving their wounded behind. On the morning of March 15, Urréa found that the soldiers had departed. His men bayoneted the wounded. The women were not molested. They had hidden one of the wounded, and Urréa, at their pleading, spared his life.

King's thirty-five men got their powder wet as they crossed the Mission River and were easily captured. A German officer in Urréa's command spared two Germans, and Urréa let Lewis Ayers live because his wife was pregnant. The others he ordered shot and lanced at the urging of the irate Tories whose ranches had been burned. Texas Mexican loyalists rounded up some members of Ward's command as stragglers. The others surrendered near Victoria and were executed with Fannin's men on March 27. Thus, Fannin lost a sizable portion of his army and valuable time in which he could have retreated to a more defensible position. Fannin was indecisive, but he might have succeeded in his retreat if the headstrong Captain King had carried out his duties as he had been ordered to do.

Two Who Survived

> . . . . The Mexican soldiers, barely three steps away, leveled their muskets at our chests and we found ourselves in terrible surprise. . . . With threatening gestures and drawn sword, the chief of the murderers for the second time commanded in a brusque tone: "Kneel down!"

> A second volley thundered over to us from another direction and a confused cry . . . accompanied it. This startled our comrades out of their stark astonishment. . . .New life animated them, their eyes flashed and they cried out:
>
> "Comrades!. . .Hear our brothers cry! It is their last one! . . . the last hour for the Greys has come! Therefore–Comrades!"
>
> A fearful crash interrupted him. . . .Then all was quiet. A thick smoke slowly rolled toward the San Antonio. The blood of my lieutenant spurted on my clothing and around me the last convulsions of agony shook the bodies of my friends. Beside me Mattern and Curtman were fighting death. I saw no more. I jumped up quickly, and concealed by the black smoke of the powder, rushed down the hedge to the river. I shouted, "The Republic of Texas forever!" and jumped in.

The description is of Palm Sunday, March 27, 1836, when nearly 400 Texian prisoners were marched out of La Bahía at Goliad to be executed in the final drama of the Battle of Coleto Creek or *Encinal de Perdido* , as the Mexicans called it. A number of the prisoners who had surrendered the previous Sunday survived the massacre. When the firing squads shot, some feigned death, then ran. Most of these were cut down by Mexican dragoons with long lances. But a few, like Herman Ehrenberg, who wrote that description, managed to reach the river and escape.

Another who lived to tell his story was John Crittenden Duval, the twenty-year-old son of Florida Governor William Pope Duval. His older brother, killed in the massacre, was Capt. Burr H. Duval, for whom Duval County, Texas, is named.

The younger Duval wrote:

> A Mexican officer came to us and ordered us to get ready for a march. He told us we were to be liberated on "parole," and that arrangements had been made to send us to New Orleans on board vessels then at Copano.
>
> This, you may be sure, was joyful news to us, and we lost no time in making preparations to leave our uncomfortable quarters . . . . We were formed in three divisions and marched out under a strong guard. As we passed by some Mexican women, who were standing near the main entrance to the fort, I heard them say, "pobrecitos" (poor little fellows), but the incident at that time made but little impression on my mind.
>
> One of our divisions was taken down the road leading to the lower ford of the river, one upon the road to San Patricio, and the division to which my company was attached along the

> road leading to San Antonio. . . . It occurred to me that this division of our men into three squads, and marching us off in three directions, was rather a singular manoeuvre, but still I had no suspicion of the foul play intended us.
>
> When about half a mile above town, a halt was made and the guard on the side next to the river filed around to the opposite side. Hardly had this manoeuvre been executed when I heard a heavy firing of musketry in the direction taken by the other two divisions. Someone exclaimed, "Boys, they are going to shoot us!" and at the same instant I heard the clicking of musket locks all along the Mexican line. I turned to look, and as I did so, the Mexicans fired upon us, killing probably one hundred out of one hundred fifty men in the division.
>
> We were in double file, and I was in the rear rank. The man in front of me was shot dead, and in falling, he knocked me down. I did not get up for a moment, and when I rose to my feet, I found that the whole Mexican line had charged over me, and were in hot pursuit of those who had not been shot and who were fleeing toward the river about five hundred yards distant. . . .

He broke free and swam the river amidst a swarm of musket balls. After days of wandering, he found he had been circling and had returned to Goliad. Then he had a brush with a panther, another with Indians, nearly drowned in a swollen river, narrowly escaped a prairie fire, and was frightened by bears before May 2, when he learned of the victory at San Jacinto.

Duval went on to earn an engineering degree in the East and return to Texas as a surveyor. He accumulated vast tracts of land but was never wealthy because he gave away everything he had. His generosity was widely known. He participated in the Mexican War and became a companion of Bigfoot Wallace, about whom he wrote a book. He also wrote an autobiography titled *Early Times in Texas*, in which, historians say, his imagination often took precedence over fact. In all his writings he never mentioned his brother. The last survivor of the few who escaped the massacre, he died January 15, 1897, in Fort Worth at age eighty.

Ehrenberg also told of his experiences, in *With Milam and Fannin*. A seventeen-year-old German immigrant at the time of the battle, he had come to Texas possibly because he had participated in liberal student revolts in Germany. He landed in New York and made his way to New Orleans, where he joined the New Orleans Greys, a volunteer company formed there to fight for

Texas independence.

He gave a good description of the land and events of the revolution. He told of the bombardment of the Alamo during the Siege of Bexar and of his participation in the Storming of San Antonio in December 1835. He joined the forces of F.W. Johnson, when Johnson planned to capture Matamoros. But he listened to Gen. Sam Houston's speeches opposing the idea and therefore was at Goliad when Johnson's men were killed or captured at San Patricio and Dr. James Grant was ambushed and killed near Agua Dulce.

Houston told the men to expect no aid from Federalists in Mexico nor from Mexican citizens in Texas, for many had already joined Santa Anna while others hid, idle in the forests, to watch the conflict. Texians, he said, "should sever that link that binds us to that rusty chain of the Mexican Confederation."

Ehrenberg's account tells of the raising of a new flag, a blue banner with a golden star, over La Bahía. However, a sudden storm brought the flagpole and the flag to the ground. This was in fact an evil omen, but "what state, just springing into life, will not have to battle against reverses for the sake of independence?" he asked.

He was in the rear guard in Fannin's retreat and brought news that the Mexican cavalry approached. He wrote: "Fannin, our commander, was a gallant and spirited warrior, but . . . where he should act with independence, understanding, and decision, he was totally unfit. Instead of trying to reach the forest one mile away for the sake of our safety, where the Americans and the Texans are invincible, he decided to offer battle on an unfavorable, open terrain."

Ehrenberg told of the slaughter of hundreds of Mexicans early in the Goliad battle, then the suffering of the wounded Texians in the square on the open prairie with no water for drinking or cooling their cannon.

He and the other Greys objected to Fannin's decision to surrender. "Had he forgotten Tampico, San Patricio, and our brothers in the Alamo?" they asked. They wanted to fight their way through the Mexican army to the woods and hope for reinforcements. But outnumbered and without water, Fannin surrendered his 360 or so men.

After his escape at La Bahía, Ehrenberg was recaptured, but he was released after Santa Anna's defeat at San Jacinto. He returned to Germany and published the account of his American adventures. Ehrenberg received a degree in engineering, returned to the United States, fought against the Mexicans in the Mexican War, founded several mining companies, and mapped much of California, as well as the land known as the Gadsden Purchase that the United States bought from Mexico. In 1866, as he returned from California to Arizona, he was murdered by the keeper of a stagecoach way station, apparently for his money.

Thus ended the amazing life of Herman Ehrenberg, Texas hero.

A Soldier's Wish

His last letter was dated March 10, 1836, Fort Defiance, Goliad.

When his parents heard of the March 27 massacre of James Fannin and his command, they feared the worst, for their son, Capt. John Sowers Brooks, was Fannin's aide-de-camp.

In that last letter he wrote:

"We have had no bread for several days, Am nearly naked, without shoes and without money. We suffer much, and as soon as Bexar falls, we will be surrounded by six thousand infernal Mexicans. But we are resolved to die under the walls rather than surrender . . . . Independence has probably been declared. We are in a critical situation. I will die like a soldier."

Though barely twenty-one, Brooks was one of the few professional soldiers among the nearly 500 volunteers. The Virginian, well-educated, had worked in a newspaper office as a writer and printer before embarking on a military career. He had served as a Marine aboard the USS *Constitution* for two years, then obtained a discharge in August 1835.

His task at Goliad was to drill the raw recruits and strengthen the fort as engineer. He built a rack with more than a hundred muskets on it that could be fired from a single fuse.

Earlier he had written to his brother: "The people of [Texas] have established a provisional government, which . . . will be followed by a declaration of independence. The Mexicans have embodied troops, which are now marching upon the colonists. Col. Austin is a prisoner in the City of Mexico . . . . My services as a drillmaster would be valuable; and in the event of a war, I am sanguine enough to believe that I will soon entitle myself to a commission."

By November he saw Texas through the eyes of an idealist. He told his father, "There is something in the cause of the Texians that comes home to the heart of every true American. Its near similarity to the glorious struggle of our own ancestors in '76 must produce a sympathy for them . . .to join the holy crusade against priestly tyranny and military despotism."

In December he was in Velasco. "The die is cast. I am over the Rubicon and my fate is now inseparably connected with that of Texas," he wrote. "I have resolved to stand by her to the last and in a word, to sink or swim with her. Our cause is good and at the worst, we can but die in defense of this little altar which we have erected to liberty in the wilds of Texas."

In all his letters he speaks of dying as if he had a premonition. He tells of dispatches from San Antonio, where some 150 men were prepared to die. He expected Fannin's force to join them, saying, "We have resolved to do our duty and to perish under the walls of the Alamo, if stern necessity requires it. We are but poorly prepared."

He told of how oxen strayed during the night, causing the relief column to Bexar to turn back, and of F.W. Johnson's defeat at San Patricio.

"Each party seems to understand that no quarters are to be given or expected," he wrote on March 2.

He learned of the death of James Grant and his men. In the final letter he said, "We are hourly anticipating an attack and preparing for it. We are short of provisions. . . . I have just returned from a weary and unsuccessful march in pursuit of a party of Mexicans."

The family's next letters were from survivors of the massacre who said Brooks received a severe thigh wound. On Palm Sunday, March 27, he was dragged from his hospital bed and shot in the street outside La Bahía.

His fears had been realized, but he was denied the honor of dying like a soldier.

The Angel of Goliad

The Angel of Goliad, whose compassion saved a number of unfortunates from execution at La Bahía in 1836, did not disappear into the mists of history. Francisca "Panchita" Alavez, the only recognized Mexican heroine in the Texas Revolution, did not die alone and forgotten after she was abandoned by her husband in Mexico, as many histories have suggested. She came back to Texas with her children and is buried on the famous King Ranch, where her son worked for Capt. Richard King. She has many descendants in Texas and other parts of the United States.

Hers is one of the mysteries connected with the Battle of Coleto Creek and the massacre a week later. Another is the controversy over what promises Mexican Gen. José Urréa made to James Walker Fannin when he signed the document of surrender.

This much is known: The Texians near Goliad were surrounded on an open plain, greatly outnumbered and without water. Urréa's artillery arrived to punish them from long range. Sixty or seventy had been badly wounded, ten were dead, and nearly all the others had some scratch or minor wound.

Andrew Boyle, a young Irishman, gave one account of the surrender. Boyle was spared by Mexican Gen. Francisco Garay because Boyle's sister had been kind to the general and asked that her brother be well treated if he fell into Mexican hands. Boyle wrote:

> After firing a shot which passed over our heads, [the Mexican army] hoisted a white flag. A consultation of officers was held, at which it was concluded to capitulate, as preferable to attempting to prolong a hopeless struggle. Our wounded men were on our hands . . . we had no means of caring for them, and Col. Fannin strongly expressed his determination not to abandon them.
>
> Two officers from each army then met in parley and agreed upon articles of capitulation, guaranteeing our lives and personal property. We agreed to give up all government property in our possession and to remain prisoners of war until honorably exchanged or sent to the United States, upon parole never to return to Texas. These articles were signed by both parties, and the surrender was completed.

Dr. J.H. Barnard, Dr. Jack Shackelford, and other surgeons were spared from the massacre to minister to wounded Mexican soldiers. Barnard's *Journal* told the same story:

> After a cool discussion of the chance, it was considered that if the enemy would agree to a formal capitulation, there would be some chance of their adhering to it and thus saving our wounded men. Dr. Shackelford resolutely declared that he would not agree to any alternative course that involved an abandonment of his wounded men. It was finally agreed that we would surrender if an honorable capitulation would be granted, but not otherwise, preferring to fight it out to the last man, in our ditches, rather than put ourselves in the power of such faith-

less wretches, without at least some assurance that our lives would be respected.

At first Fannin was for holding out longer, saying, "We whipped them off yesterday, and we can do so again today," Barnard recalled. However, "a capitulation with Gen Urréa was agreed upon, the terms of which were: that we should lay down our arms and surrender ourselves as prisoners of war. That we should be treated as such, according to the usage of civilized nations. That our wounded men should be taken back to Goliad and properly attended to, and that all private property should be respected. . . .We were also told we should be sent to New Orleans under parole."

Others agreed. After all, Mexican Major Juan José Holsinger greeted them as they surrendered, "Well, gentlemen, in eight days, home and liberty."

Urréa told Fannin there was no known instance where a prisoner of war who had trusted the clemency of the Mexican government had lost his life. He would recommend clemency. Fannin, B.C. Wallace, and J.M. Chadwick signed the articles.

Urréa's copy of the capitulation articles —Fannin's was apparently destroyed—included the statement that the Texians "proposed to them to surrrender . . . at descretion, to which (the Mexicans) agreed." However, the Texians' terms went on to say that the wounded and Fannin "should be treated with all consideration possible, since we propose to surrender all our arms" and that the detachment "shall be treated as prisoners of war and shall be subject to the disposition of the supreme government."

But Urréa's copy contained this notation: "Since the white flag was raised by the enemy, I made it known to their officer that I could not grant any other terms than an unconditional surrender . . . ."

In his book *Refugio,* Hobart Huson wrote: "There is no evidence whatever that Urréa's notation was contained on Fannin's copy of the treaty, nor that Fannin or any other Texian knew that Urréa had added the foregoing post-script to his own retained copy of the agreement. The document was ambiguous, but Urrea's unilateral interpretation and explanation left no room for doubt as to the construction to be given it by Santa Anna, when same came to his hands for decision."

Before that Palm Sunday morning a week later, there was a lot of activity, couriers in and out of the fort with messages to and from Santa Anna at Bexar. Therefore, many of the Texians felt something was wrong when they were lined up and marched out of La Bahía in three different directions. Urréa was at Victoria, chasing remnants of the defeated Texian armies. He, too, sent messages to camp, but stayed away, apparently knowing what his commander would do.

Santa Anna ordered the prisoners executed. A few were spared, and at least twenty-eight escaped. Several of those who survived owed their lives to Madam Alavez, known to the prisoners as the wife of Mexican Capt. Telesforo Alavez. He was a native of Toluca who rose through the ranks and later became a colonel. "Panchita" is frequently mentioned in Texas histories, but less is told of her partner in mercy, Father John Thomas Molloy.

Their story began in San Patricio four days after the Alamo was overrun on March 6, 1836. Part of it was told by Reuben Brown, who was captured as a member of Dr. James Grant's party ambushed at Agua Dulce Creek on March 2. The prisoners were carried into San Patricio, where they joined others captured by Urréa in the village and on a nearby ranch on February 27.

Santa Anna sent word that all the prisoners should be executed. Father Molloy, who had presided over the burial of both Mexican and Texian dead at San Patricio, told Urréa it would be an un-Christian act to murder the men and threatened to hold no more Masses if the orders were carried out. While the priest argued, Madam Alavez joined the argument and prevailed upon her husband to intercede.

Brown later wrote that after he was confined several days at San Patricio, "Urréa . . . said that I would have to be executed according to Santa Anna's orders. . . . I was taken out to be shot, but was spared through the intervention of a priest [Molloy], and a Mexican lady named Alvarez."

The 1859 *Texas Almanac* printed Brown's account. Mrs. Alavez's name was frequently misspelled and today is usually spelled Alvarez. She had accompanied her husband to Copano, where some eighty Tennessee volunteers under Maj. William P. Miller arrived on March 23. Celebrating the end of a voyage in which they had been cooped up for days, they jumped into the bay for a frolic. As they waded ashore, a contingent of Mexican cavalry met them. Since they were not carrying their weapons, technically they were not violating the Mexican decree that any foreigners found bearing arms would be treated as pirates and summarily executed.

Urréa's subordinate, Lt. Col. José Nicolás de la Portilla,

used this reasoning to avoid killing them, but they were rounded up and their arms tightly bound with rawhide thongs. The hides dried and tightened, cutting off circulation and causing great pain. Madam Alavez insisted that their bonds be loosened and that they be given water. Miller later wrote a letter thanking her for her kindness.

Urréa alternately resisted and obeyed Santa Anna's bloody decree. He ordered the execution of thirty-one of Capt. Amon B. King's men after they were captured near Refugio on March 15. After his army captured the remnants of Lt. Col. William Ward's command near Victoria on March 25, most were sent back to Goliad and executed with Fannin's men.

In his diary Urréa denied responsibility for the March 27 massacre. He said that de la Portilla received the orders and carried them out and that "it only came to my knowledge after the execution had taken place." Urréa ordered prisoners taken at San Patricio and at Copano sent to Matamoros, where some of them escaped. The others were eventually released.

At Goliad, when it became obvious Fannin's men were to be shot, Madam Alavez and Father Molloy hid several of them on a parapet of the fort. She had one fifteen-year-old boy pulled from the ranks and released to her care. The youth saved by Panchita's tears, Benjamin F. Hughes, became a prominent citizen of the state, living to the age of eighty.

Barnard's *Journal* tells of her actions: " . . . when on the morning of the massacre, she learned that the prisoners were to be shot, she so effectually pleaded with Col. Garey [Col. Francisco Garay], [whose humane feelings revolted at the barbarous order] that, with great personal responsibility to himself and at great hazard thus going counter to the orders of the then all-powerful Santa Anna, he resolved to save all that he could; and a few of us, in consequence, were left to tell of that bloody day."

Tragically for Dr. Shackelford, his eldest son, two nephews, and other young men he had recruited near his home in Alabama were executed. Barnard wrote that when Señora Alavez saw Shackelford a few days after the massacre and heard that his son was among the dead, "she burst into tears and exclaimed: 'Why did I not know that you had a son here? I would have saved him at all hazards.' "

Molloy, too, failed to save the life of a nephew, John Fadden, at Goliad. The priest was heartsick. His health failed, and he died in Victoria shortly after the revolution.

Captain Alavez commanded the Mexican forces at Victoria until May 14, when the retreating Mexican army withdrew from Texas. Later Panchita supplied comforts for the Texian prisoners held at Matamoros. Reports from that period say she returned to the Mexican capital with her husband, only to learn he had another wife. He abandoned her there. She returned to Matamoros and seemed to disappear from history.

But the papers of judge and noted historian Harbert Davenport in the Texas State Archives give a different story–an account by Mrs. Elena Zamora O'Shea, written in 1936. Mrs. O'Shea had taught school on the Santa Gertrudis Division of the famous King Ranch in 1902-03. Mrs. O'Shea wrote:

> Among the Mexicans there were Alfonso, an old servant to Mrs. King, and Matías Alvarez. . . . After school hours every Friday, these two old men would come to the schoolhouse and listen to me as I read to them from Spanish newspapers, or translated stories from the books studied by the children. We had been reading Mrs. Pennybacker's *History of Texas*. They followed the stories anxiously. When I read the story of the massacre of Goliad, Don Matías was alert, taking in every word. When I had finished, he asked me, "Is that all that they say about Goliad?"
>
> I told him it was.
>
> "They do not say that anyone helped those who were hurt or that any of them were saved?" he asked. . . .

She questioned him and he told the story. His father, Telesforo Alavez, had married a bride chosen for him by his parents. After years he separated from her, but could not get church approval for an annulment. Francisca, his sweetheart, went with him when the army sent him to the frontier. After the war the couple settled at Matamoros. Two children, Matías and Guadalupe, were born to them. Capt. Richard King, founder of the King Ranch, knew Colonel Alavez and knew of the mercy Señora Alavez had shown at Goliad.

According to the account, Colonel Alavez died. His children crossed the river to work on the Yturria Ranch, then the Cortina Ranch. Guadalupe died young, but Matías worked truck farms and sold vegetables at Fort Brown. He married and began to raise a family–Pablo, Luís, Dolores, Gerardo, Guadalupe, Jacinto, María and Telesforo. In 1884 Captain King offered Don Matías a job, and the family moved to the King Ranch.

Mrs. O'Shea wrote that "the boys worked at different occupations. The girls sewed for the family. María became the companion maid of Miss Clara Driscoll.

"During the two years I taught there, I had among my pupils Gerardo Alvarez Jr. in whom both Mrs. King and Mrs. Robert Kleberg took special interest. The boy finished high school and was sent to a school of pharmacy and is now [1936] a druggist at Kingsville.

"Other members of the Alvarez family live at Kingsville or on King ranches."

Father Joseph G. O'Donohoe in the same papers quotes Mrs. O'Shea as saying Matías brought his old mother with his family. Mrs. O'Shea knew Doña Panchita as a very old woman, bedridden and way up in her nineties. "She died on the King Ranch and is buried there in an unmarked grave .... Old Captain King and Mrs. King knew and respected her identity."

But that is not the last word in the story of the Angel of Goliad. After reading this account of the Alavez family in the Corpus Christi, Texas, *Caller-Times* in 1986, Gerard Alvarez III of Corpus Christi added another chapter.

"I was born in Kingsville in 1938," he wrote, "I am proud to say, the great-grandson of Matías Alvarez and fifth generation descendant of Dona Francisca 'Panchita' Alavez ...."

He told that Matías' son Gerardo became foreman of the Santa Gertrudis Division of the ranch. Gerardo died in February 1914, and the writer's father, Gerardo, Jr., was born a few months later. That Gerardo, the youth mentioned by the teacher, never completed pharmacy school. He umpired baseball professionally for twenty-five years and later worked for Civil Service in Corpus Christi. He died in 1985. Around 1933-35 he was the first Mexican-American to play high school football in Kingsville.

After Gerardo Alvarez, Sr., died, Lauro Cavazos served as Santa Gertrudis foreman. A sister of the senior Gerardo, Rita Alvarez, married a man named Quintanilla. "This union," Gerard Alvarez III wrote, "produced a daughter named Tomasa Alvarez Quintanilla, who married Lauro Cavazos."

The children of that marriage include Gen. Richard O. Cavazos; Bobby Cavazos, a country singer, Kleberg County, Texas, commissioner, and one-time foreman of the Laureles Division of the King Ranch; and Dr. Lauro Cavazos, former president of Texas Tech University and, as secretary of education, the first Hispanic to serve in the U.S. Cabinet.

"There is still a lot of Alvarez in Kingsville," Gerard III wrote.

". . . . Many are teachers and some are just plain good folks without a title. But all are still very proud of our grandparents . . . . As you can see, the Alvarez clan is alive and well in Kingsville, in Corpus Christi and all over South Texas."

As for the Goliad Massacre, it was one of Santa Anna's worst mistakes. He had executed American invaders at Tampico in 1835, and Americans did not react. He believed the death of anyone bearing arms would deter American participation in the revolt.

Had Santa Anna dumped the Goliad prisoners on the docks at New Orleans, hungry, defeated and dispirited, Col. Ethan Allan Hitchcock wrote ten years later, he likely would have discouraged American support. Texians at the Alamo died fighting. They knew what the terms of battle were. But Americans were stunned by the executions of men who had surrendered as prisoners of war. Across the United States volunteers and money headed for Texas.

Even more than the Alamo, the Goliad Massacre cost Mexico the state of Texas.

[5]

Incredible Victory

Yellow Stone

She burst around the bend with black smoke pouring from her twin stacks. Floating embers hung like stars in the smoke. Stokers crammed the firebox with wood. The captain pushed the pressure to the danger mark.

The steamboat *Yellow Stone,* flagship of the Texas Revolution, was confronting Santa Anna's army poised on the banks of the Brazos River near Fort Bend. Some of the troops had crossed over, and canoes were being loaded when the hissing, smoking apparition appeared.

Many of the Mexicans, mostly Indian conscripts, ran into the woods to hide. They had never seen a 130-foot fire-breathing monster before. Below decks and flattened on the upper decks behind bales of cotton were hundreds of Texas civilians fleeing the revolution in the desperate race to the border, a flight which became known as the Runaway Scrape.

The startled Mexicans could only gape. Finally the bravest of them began shooting, thinking bullets would halt the paddles. Two cavalrymen, apparently *vaqueros,* unlimbered their lassos and threw their loops at the smokestacks, trying to bring the dragon to bay. The paddles slashed the water, and the boat disappeared around the bend. Horsemen gave chase, but soon gave up. Santa

Vaqueros *unlimbered their lassos and threw their loops at the smokestacks, trying to bring the dragon to bay.*

Anna's soldiers were anxious to finish the rabble Texas army and return home. They continued their march as fast as they could in the muck caused by continuous spring rains. They would catch up with wiley old Sam Houston a week later at a place called San Jacinto and be beaten in one of the crucial battles of history

In December 1835 the *Yellow Stone* had brought forty-seven members of the Mobile Greys volunteers from New Orleans to Galveston. Capt. J.E. Ross took it up the Brazos to San Felipe de Austin in February 1836. He was taking on a load of cotton at Groce's Landing when Sam Houston and the Texas Army impressed the vessel to transport troops across the river. Houston kept it for fourteen days. Ross later billed the Republic of Texas $4,900 for the service. It is not recorded if part of the expense was for being shot at as an unofficial ship of the Texas fleet.

The *Yellow Stone* had been built for John Jacob Astor for use in the fur trade on the upper Missouri and Yellowstone rivers. It was constructed in Louisville, Kentucky, for $7,000 and delivered on April 1, 1831. After arriving at Fort Tecumseh June 19 and returning the first cargo to St. Louis on July 5, the *Yellow Stone* received worldwide publicity for its feat. In the winter months it plied the Lower Mississippi and went as far as the mouth of the Yellowstone River. The boat's length and deep draft caused difficulties in navigating the Missouri, and it changed hands several times before its Texas adventure.

After the trip down the Brazos with the refugees, the vessel brought back a cargo of supplies and muskets. It picked up the Texas government at Galveston and transported it to the battleground at San Jacinto. On May 9, after the Texian victory, the *Yellow Stone* carried Houston, his staff, and Santa Anna and eighty Mexican prisoners back to Galveston, then to Velasco, where the treaty was made. It performed a number of government functions in the following months and carried the body of Stephen F. Austin from Columbia to Peach Point for burial. (Austin's body later was moved to the State Cemetery in Austin.)

The *Yellow Stone* plied the Brazos for several years. How it met its fate is unknown, but the ship's bell is on display at the Alamo Museum. Texas would later have a navy, but the *Yellow Stone* had helped win a revolution.

Animals at War

Not all the revolutionary heroes were human. In the confusion of the final assault on the Alamo, a cat chose to use up his nine lives all at once as he decided his hiding place was no longer secure. He made a mad dash for freedom, and three or four Mexican muskets roared. The kitty dropped dead. Someone asked why they shot the cat. The soldiers shrugged, "That was not a Mexican cat. That was a *gringo* cat." Tabby was an uncounted victim of the Texas Revolution.

Herman Ehrenberg, the young German who had escaped from the massacre at Goliad, wrote of another unreported casualty on the side of the Texians. (He said they were no longer Germans, Scots, Irishmen, Americans or Tejanos–they were TEXANS.) As the volley of muskets cut most of the men down, he dashed for the San Antonio River, bowling over a Mexican officer waving a sword. Black smoke from the gunfire momentarily screened him from view. Bloodied by the wound of his lieutenant, he dived into the water and began swimming for the opposite shore with bullets from his pursuers splashing around him. Then, he wrote:

". . . .Another victim was to fall through the Mexican barbarity, namely, our faithful dog that had accompanied the company from the beginning to the end and that now sprang into the waters after me to share my pleasures and sufferings with me in my flight through the unknown prairie. He had already reached the center of the stream when the Mexicans made a target of him, and although they seldom hit, the faithful friend, wounded, disappeared under the waves."

Then there were the oxen Sam Houston had borrowed from Mrs. Pamela Mann. As the road forked and the Texian army turned toward Harrisburg in its retreat, Mrs. Mann wanted her oxen, which had been drawing the Twin Sisters cannon through mud bogs. Houston explained he couldn't move the cannon without the oxen.

"I don't care a damn for your cannon," she said and jumped down from her wagon, cutting the harness from the cannon. A big pistol on her hip defied opposition. The cannon went to San Jacinto by manpower.

At that time the Alamo and Goliad had fallen and the crazed population was rushing pell-mell for the Louisiana border and safety in the great Runaway Scrape. And it was the duty of Stephen Franklin Sparks to relieve these people of their horses in the name of the Republic of Texas and Ol' Sam Houston. This was no easy chore, for each rider had a rifle, pistol, and Bowie knife on his person and a very nervous trigger finger.

This story comes from a copy of Sparks' recollections, written in a letter to a friend in 1895. In 1908, at age ninety, the old fellow died in Rockport. Only one veteran of the Battle of San Jacinto survived him, Alphonso Steele, who died in 1911.

Sparks was eighteen in 1835. He left school and joined H.T. Edwards' Volunteers in Nacogdoches. He went with Col. Ben Milam to capture Bexar and was back in school when the Alamo fell. He and his teacher volunteered to try to stop Colonel Ugartechea on the Brazos. Nearly everybody had left when Texas President David Burnet ordered Sparks and three others to press horses into service for the Texas army. It wasn't confiscation, for they were to give receipts.

Two young men "who should have been in the army" rode in on fine horses. Told their horses were pressed and offered a receipt, one swore he would "press" the man who had his horse. That was Sparks. The man rushed him with a Bowie knife, Sparks recounted. But he, too, had an "Arkansas toothpick." The other man missed "so I punched it in him about an inch. I told him I would run him through if he moved .... He cried and said if his brother would get the horse, he would not mind it. That ended the strife."

Sparks went to the Texas Cabinet and asked where he would find protection if he had to kill someone while pressing horses. The Cabinet promised him protection, and the crew proceeded to press 300 horses in two weeks. Each one was a crisis.

"Our next trouble came when we pressed the president's horse," he said. "General Rusk said we had done our duty, but that we had the president's horse and asked us to release him as that was the only means Mrs. Burnet had of fleeing from the invading Mexicans. . . . We told him we would release his horse if he would send out and get a bottle of whisky." They quickly got the whiskey.

Houston's orders were to kill only beef for meat—no chickens or hogs. The volunteers found a house abandoned by a family. There were chickens in the yard, cornmeal, bacon, and pots and ovens. Sparks, promising to take the blame, killed and cooked chickens and made cornbread.

"Sparks, I will have to punish you," Houston said after he and his officers arrived.

Thomas Rusk persuaded the general to eat. As Houston continued to grouse, Rusk told him: "Gen. Houston, it is a maxim in law that he who partakes of stolen property, knowing it to be such, is guilty with the thief."

Houston snorted, but gave Sparks a second chance.

In the Battle of San Jacinto, the Volunteers performed as well as the Regulars. Sparks' unit charged the breastwork. A man in the front ranks, Elias Hamilton, fired the first shot in the battle. Sparks fired the second. Strangely enough, he was wounded by a dead man. He jumped across a small stream and landed on the bayonet of a dead Mexican dragoon. The blade, stuck in the mud, cut his leg badly.

Another among the Texian wounded was General Houston, whose ankle was shattered by a Mexican musket ball. Two horses were shot from under Houston that day. One of them was his favorite–a magnificent white stallion named Sarazan. He was brought a second horse. The stirrups were too short for Houston, so he let his legs dangle, providing an attractive target for a Mexican sharpshooter. This horse, too, was hit and sank to the ground. An aide brought the wounded general a third horse.

Yet another horse had still a greater impact on the outcome of the revolution. A beautiful black stallion named Old Whip, it was taken from William Vince, who had a farm near Vince's Bridge. Vince left, probably in the Runaway Scrape. His housekeeper, an English widow named Mrs. James Brown, stayed behind, along with her young son Jimmy. Jimmy rode Old Whip out to investigate the advancing Mexicans and soon found the horse conscripted into the invading army.

For Santa Anna, April 21 started well. He had received reinforcements to outnumber the ragged army waiting over the hill near Buffalo Bayou. Led by bickering officers, the Texians were more mob than army. It was a miracle Houston held them together until the battle. Two companies of Regulars provided the only discipline they had.

The Mexican army was disciplined. Not so their leader. He was resting or otherwise occupied in his tent. General Castrillón and his aide were sipping champagne. The men played cards or slept, their rifles stacked. They were a little contemptuous of those they called *"Soldados God Dammes"* from the profane language the Texians spoke.

Santa Anna had been up early estimating the Texian position and checking his breastwork. His cavalry was arrayed for a possible attack. At 9:00 A.M. his brother-in-law, General Cós, arrived with 500 men after an all-night forced march.

As the day wore on, Santa Anna felt there would be no battle.

He could wait for still more reinforcements. He allowed Cós' exhausted men to eat and sleep. Cavalrymen unsaddled and fed their horses. By midafternoon, the entire camp was at rest while their general dallied.

The alarm sounded only when a line of mud-covered, bearded, ragged men seemed to rise out of the ground as they rushed up from a swale in the meadow. A Mexican bugler sounded the alarm, and a few soldiers managed to fire their muskets. General Castrillón's men quickly unlimbered a cannon and fired. The aim was high.

Shots from two Texian field pieces swept through makeshift barricades and soldiers. The wave of Texians rushed forward, stopped, and fired. Every shot felled a Mexican soldier. The charging soldiers were screaming, intoxicated with anger. A big man on a horse was well out in front of the mass, booming orders. Sam Houston was bellowing for his men to fire. It was just as well they waited, or they'd have blown him away.

The battle became a slaughter. Texians liberated Santa Anna's silver service, his silver chamber pot, and $12,000 in hard money. They counted the money and recounted it until only $7,000 remained. They were ordered to stop counting before it was all gone.

When the Mexican camp was overrun, a servant brought a huge black stallion to Santa Anna for his escape from the enraged Texians, who were butchering his troops. It was Old Whip. If Santa Anna had gone south, he could have joined Generals Vicente Filisola and José Urréa with their several thousand fresh troops. Had such a force attacked the exhausted, victory-drunken Texian army on the bayou, the name San Jacinto would have joined La Bahía and the Alamo in disasters of the revolution. All Stephen F. Austin's efforts would have been in vain.

But Santa Anna let the big horse have his head. This proved to be a mistake, for Old Whip made a beeline for his barn near Vince's Bayou. The bayou was a wide, deep body of water at flood time, and Santa Anna was deathly afraid of water. Texian scout Erastus "Deaf" Smith had burned the bridge over the flooded stream, and escape was cut off. The stolen horse put Santa Anna in a trap. Unable to get away, he hid in the grass.

The next day color bearer Jim Sylvestre, hunting deer, captured the Mexican general. For his services to the Republic, Sylvestre, later an official in Jackson County and the City of Galveston, received 640 acres of land in North Texas –present-day downtown Dallas. But he traded it all for a scrawny mule, which he rode to New Orleans to set type for the *Picayune* newspaper. That mule didn't know its ultimate value.

When Santa Anna was brought in, Sparks was near the tree where the wounded Houston lay. "Zavala was there and Santa Anna was introduced to Houston. He asked if General Houston rode in front of his men on a white horse with drawn sword," Sparks reported.

"Houston answered that he rode such a horse and was in front with other officers. Santa Anna asked if it was customary for commanders of the forces of the American army to ride in such exposed positions. Houston said American generals say, 'Come on,' not 'go on' and that a general is no more than the private. They are all generals."

San Jacinto wasn't much of a fight. It lasted about eighteen minutes. The Texians had 750 men, although later more than 900 claimed to have been there. They lost nine killed and thirty wounded. Nearly all Santa Anna's 1,200 men were killed or captured.

But the little battle of April 21, 1836, ranks as one of the most important in history. It led to the annexation of Texas, the Mexican War, and the addition of New Mexico, Arizona, Nevada, California, and parts of Colorado, Wyoming, Kansas and Oklahoma to the Union.

All because Santa Anna didn't get away after he bet on the wrong horse. He might have done better with a mule.

Alphonso Steele

A private's view of a battle is never the big picture. Only a small piece of the tapestry is in view, and he's so close there is nothing pretty there at all. It's loud and dirty. It smells and sometimes it hurts.

Others were proud and amazed to find they were still alive when it was over. But Pvt. Alphonso Steele wasn't too sure he had survived the Battle of San Jacinto. He had a bullet hole in his chest, and blood was gushing out his mouth and nose. He was nineteen years old, and it appeared that he might not live out the day. Yet he would survive. In fact, he would live to the age of ninety-four. And when he died at his home in Mexia in 1911, the last of Old Sam Houston's Legion was gone. Steele outlived all the rest of the army.

His recollection of the battle, written years later, is not in the glorious stentorian style Old Sam used on the campaign trail. It is written in the more restrained manner of an eyewitness who knew only what he saw. His was the Second Regiment of Texas Volunteers, commanded by Col. Sidney Sherman.

They felt better after capturing meal and flour and feasting on bread the night of April 20. The next morning they watched General Cós arrive with reinforcements at Santa Anna's camp on Buffalo Bayou. After noon the Texians were getting restless. Finally their orders came, as reported by Steele:

> The Mexicans had thrown up breastworks out of their baggage about one hundred yards south of a point of timber.... Santa Anna's right wing was placed in a thick grove of timber....
>
> When we got within sixty or seventy yards we were ordered to fire. Then all discipline . . .was at an end. . . . As soon as we fired, every man went to reloading. And he who got his gun reloaded moved on, not waiting for orders. I got my gun loaded and rushed on into the timber and fired again. When the second volley was poured into them . . .they broke and ran. As soon as I got my gun loaded again I ran on a little in front of our men and threw up my gun to shoot when I was shot down. Dave Rusk was standing by me when I was shot. He told some men to stay with me. But I told him, "No. Take them on."
>
> One of our own men in passing asked me if he could take my pistol, but by this time I was bleeding at the nose and mouth so I couldn't speak . . . .

Another soldier went for a gourd of water. Steele tried to walk but collapsed after a few paces.

> This fellow . . . went to hand me the water, a couple of Mexicans came running toward us . . . they had hid in the grass until our men had passed . . . they stopped and threw up their hands and began to jabber. . . . I told the fellow with me to shoot one of the Mexicans. He wouldn't. He said they wanted to surrender. . . . I told him I didn't want any more prisoners. . . . I shot one of them down. The other one ran off. . . . [The Texian] . . .put me among a lot of dead Mexicans. I was so blind I could hardly see anything and I sat down on a dead Mexican.
>
> While I was sitting there some of our Regulars, who had stayed at the Mexican breastworks and were sticking their bayonets through the wounded Mexicans, came along and one of them had his bayonet drawn to stick through me, when Pvt. Tom Green of the Regulars . . . stopped him. . . .That night I was carried across the bayou to De Zavala's residence which he had given up as a hospital . . . .

In the hospital he had a row with Dr. James A.E. Phelps,

who "had been staying with a Mexican officer and neglecting Tom [another wounded soldier] and myself for several days." He accused the doctor of starving him:

> My diet was crackers and sweetened vinegar. They fed me on that until I got so weak I couldn't get up. I came to the conclusion they would starve me to death if I didn't get something to eat. There was a fine garden there and plenty of vegetables in it. Thomas Johnson waited on me. . . . Dr. Phelps told me I couldn't eat a bite of cabbage. When Johnson came in with my crackers and vinegar, I said, "The Doctor says it will not hurt me to eat a few of those cabbages." Just when I finished eating them, the doctor came in. "You'll be dead by night," he said.
>
> The next day they were cooking beans. When the doctor came in I said, "Doctor, those cabbages didn't hurt me. May I have some beans today?" He said "I don't care what you eat." From then on I had a little of anything they had to eat, and I was soon able to get up.

He became angry because the doctor spent more time with a Mexican in the other room than with him. He pulled a Derringer, told the doctor not to come near him again, and made his exit from the hospital.

Alphonso Steele apparently never knew that the doctor in the next room, under personal orders of Gen. Sam Houston, was taking care of Gen. Antonio López de Santa Anna. Had he known, he might have changed the course of history with his Derringer.

A Young Idealist

Although all sorts of ulterior motives are attached to the reasons young Americans came to fight in the Texas Revolution, time after time their writings reveal a much more idealistic point of view. A letter Giles A. Giddings wrote to his parents on April 10, 1836, illustrates this idealism. He had come to Texas to survey land for a proposed colony. He wrote:

> Since I last wrote you I have been engaged in arranging an expedition against the Indians who have committed many depredations against the frontier. On my return to the settlements, I learned that our country was again invaded by a merciless horde of Mexicans, who were waging a war of extermination against the inhabitants.
>
> A call was made for all friends of humanity to rise in arms and resist the foe. Men were panic-stricken and fled, leaving their all behind them. I could not reconcile it to my feelings to leave Texas without an effort to save it. Accordingly, I bent my

course for the army and arrived last evening at this place.

I shall enter camp this morning as a volunteer. The army, commanded by Gen Houston, is lying on the west side of the Brazos, twenty miles from San Fillippe. The enemy is in that place waiting for an attack. It is reported Houston will attack them in the morning. What will be the result, or the fate of Texas, is hid in the bowels of futurity.

Yet, I think we are engaged in the cause of justice, and hope the God of battles will protect us. The enemy's course has been the most bloody that has ever been recorded on the page of history. Our garrison at San Antonio was taken and massacred, so another detachment of seven hundred, commanded by Col. Fanning, and posted at La Bahia, after surrendering prisoners of war were led out and shot down like bears.

Only one escaped to tell their melancholy fate. In their course, they show no quarter to age, sex, or condition, all are massacred without mercy. If such conduct is not sufficient to arouse the patriotic feelings of the sons of liberty, I know not what will.

I was born in a land of freedom and taught to lisp the name of liberty with my infant tongue, and rather than be driven out of the country or submit to be a slave, I will leave my bones to bleach on the plains of Texas.

If we succeed in subduing the enemy and establishing a free and independent government, we shall have the finest country the sun ever shone upon, and if we fail, we shall have the satisfaction of dying fighting for the rights of man. . . .

Be not alarmed about my safety. I am no better, and my life no dearer than those who gained the liberty you enjoy. If I fall, you will have the satisfaction that your son died fighting for the rights of man.

Our strength in the field is about fifteen hundred. The enemy is reported four thousand strong; a fearful odds, you will say; but what can mercenary hirelings do against the sons of liberty?

Before this reaches you, the fate of Texas will be known.... The same Being who has hitherto protected my life can with equal ease ward off the balls of the enemy. My company is waiting, and I must draw to a close and bid you farewell, perhaps forever. . . .

. . . the thoughts of friends and home are fresh in my memory, and their remembrance yet lives in my affections and will light a secret joy to my heart till it shall cease to beat. . . .

Perhaps young Giddings had a premonition. He was mortally wounded at San Jacinto. The letter was the last his mother and father would ever receive from their son, who believed in the cause of freedom enough to die for it.

How It Happened

Had those Mexican armies within two days' march of San Jacinto attacked, the victory there would have been short lived—blotted from memory by another defeat as crushing as those at the Alamo and Goliad. Militarily, the Texians really should not have won to start with. But Santa Anna carelessly gave them that and, as a prisoner, the diplomatic victory, too.

A Mexican officer, José Enrique de la Peña, who analyzed the war in a journal while it was going on, was acidly critical of the leadership and of His Excellency Santa Anna in particular. His diary, published by Texas A&M University Press in 1975, is a fairly objective account, considering that de la Peña was a participant.

He felt the Battle of the Alamo would never have been fought had Gen. Joaquín Ramirez y Sesma's troops entered the town and sealed off the fort. Only ten Texians were in the Alamo when the vanguard of the Mexican army arrived, and "the enemy was still engaged in the pleasures of a dance given the night before. He could have prevented the enemy from taking refuge there, thus avoiding the painful catastrophe we witnessed."

He was critical of Santa Anna's frontal attack, which needlessly wasted Mexican lives. He saw the execution of Davy Crockett after the battle and said the act and the executions at Goliad boded ill for the future. He was outraged at the treatment of Mexican soldiers, who were starved, ill-clad, and exposed to the weather while guarding Texas corn and cattle appropriated by their commanders.

He was not surprised when Santa Anna was defeated at San Jacinto. "While General Santa Anna did nothing but sacrifice our soldiers at the Alamo, while he ordered useless executions, inviting the enmity of the army as well as that of his military family, dishonoring it and consummating his errors by allowing himself to be surprised at four in the afternoon, General Urréa was marching rapidly from victory to victory, provisioning the soldiers abundantly, even in the non-essential items and acquiring glory more by his generous and humane actions, which attracted the admiration and respect of the enemy, than by the brilliancy of his victories," de la Peña wrote.

By waiting a few days, Santa Anna would have had more than 2,000 troops, de la Peña said, but he learned that fleeing families carried valuables and he moved "with the avarice that has characterized all his actions."

If he was angry at Santa Anna, de la Peña was furious when the other generals ordered a retreat to save their leader's life, rather than attack and preserve Mexican honor and territory. More than 4,000 men were available to attack the small band of Texians who were intoxicated by the victory. A sudden thrust, he believed, would have freed most of the prisoners and possibly Santa Anna himself.

Generals José Urréa,Vicente Filisola, Antonio Gaona, Eugenio Tolsa, Adrian Woll, Ramirez y Sesma and Lt. Col. Pedro Ampudia obeyed orders to withdraw as agreed to by their captured commander. De la Peña said that of the seven, "only three were Mexican by birth, who naturally should have . . . interest in the good name and prosperity of their homeland . . . ."

Actually, only two–Urréa and Ramirez y Sesma–were Mexican. Ampudia, Tolsa, and Gaona were Cuban, Filisola was Italian, and Woll was French. It was Filisola who made the decision to retreat. It was he who was to receive the blame when the army reached Mexico after many hardships on the march home.

Santa Anna underestimated the enemy. Another reason for his failure was his ignorance of East Texas springtime weather and East Texas geography. Flooded streams impeded the progress of his supporting columns. Supplies were damaged, men sickened, and material lost. Santa Anna thought the floods came from snow melting in mountains. The Mexican commander didn't realize that the snow-crested mountains closest to southeastern Texas rise in what is now New Mexico, approximately 800 miles away.

When the order to retreat was given, mud became a greater enemy than the Texians. De la Peña recorded the miseries of the withdrawal, which was almost as disastrous as Napoleon's retreat from Russia. Instead of snow, it was the mud and floods. The Mexicans had to jettison some of their cannon and abandon many wagons. Foodstocks spoiled or were lost. The troops suffered from hunger and illness. The untreated wounded suffered mightily; many died, while officers commandeered mules to carry their loot.

Exhausted from moving mired wagons and artillery pieces in the soggy soil, de la Peña was despondent at the condition of a once proud army and the calloused attitude of the officers toward the misery and hardships of the men.

In the midst of all this, he received a letter from Mexico that caused him "greater pain than everything I have so far suffered. . .

fate takes pleasure in bringing together its deadly blows . . . ." His sweetheart had thrown him over for another and, he said, had "enlisted under the flag of my persecutors (in the Mexican army) to add affliction to the afflicted."

In December 1837 de la Peña joined Urréa in a plan supporting the Constitution of 1824. According to Carmen Perry, translator of his diaries, the effort caused him "an interminable series of humiliations, imprisonment, disillusionment and ultimately a premature death. He died in 1842, poor, ill and forgotten."

The losses of the retreat from Texas proved so staggering that Mexico had to abandon plans to raise a new army for another invasion. The economic cost to a poor nation was too great. Texas was literally saved by its bad weather. De la Peña's journal, however, answers some of the riddles of how, with relative ease, Sam Houston achieved a victory that appeared impossible.

"The Sabine Chute"

The first hint of a hot Texas summer was in the air. The afternoon heat had warmed the chill from the night's norther and created a heavy humid atmosphere as it began to dry the rainsoaked coastal turf. Ordinarily the sounds of birds and buzzing insects could be heard on the plain of San Jacinto. Now it was the soft, spongy tread of some 700 men and the strangely silent hoofbeat of fifty cavalry horses. One of the most irregular troops in history moved forward in an unsynchronized cadence of dirty, disheveled men. The line stretched for more than a thousand yards.

The silence was eerie. There were no orders, no bugles or drumbeats, only the cushioned tread of the men and an occasional clank of canteen or powder horn. Ahead of them, astride a huge, white stallion, rode a redfaced man wearing a fur hat. Years later his grandson, Temple Houston Morrow, would describe Sam Houston's uniform: a shirt that had once been white, a vest, a shabby black coat, mud-spattered yellowish brown trousers, and worn-out boots. An old U.S. dragoon sabre hung incongruously from a brightly colored silk sash around his waist. Houston brandished the sabre and urged the men on.

Behind him, the artillery company, muttering and grunting, struggled to pull two iron six-pounder field pieces. The guns were called the "Twin Sisters" in honor of two girls on the ship that had brought the weapons from New Orleans. The foundry of Greenwood and Webb in Cincinnati, Ohio, had cast the cannon, and the Ohio donors had also sent solid and grapeshot.

With George Washington Hockley, Houston's chief aide, in the lead, enlisted men and officers alike pulled and pushed as the grass gave way and the wheels grooved into the mud under the 1,600-pound burden of gun and carriage. About twenty men pulled each cannon with rawhide ropes.

Now there was commotion in the enemy ranks. A bugle sounded, as did a big nine-pound cannon. Because of the elevation, its shot passed harmlessly overhead. Spurts of orange flared from the Mexican position. Sam Houston bellowed for the men to hold their fire. The cannons continued forward at a faster clip. The breastwork was 200 yards away.

Eight gunners quickly aimed the cannon, already primed and ready. The Twin Sisters roared, and two wide gaps appeared in the barricade. Two Mexican artillerymen attempting to repair their damaged gun fell wounded. After firing an ineffectual shot, their gun was reloaded, but no cannoneers were left to fire it. Dozens of Mexican troops roused from rest were hit as they scurried about in confusion. The Texians reloaded the Twin Sisters and again fired grapeshot with deadly effect, as Mexican soldiers fled through the woods. Six hundred fifty or more muskets and rifles dropped scores of Santa Anna's troops. Then the Texians closed, attacking with bayonet and swinging rifle butts and tomahawks. In eighteen minutes the Battle of San Jacinto was over, though the slaughter continued for two hours.

The Texians had also used the six-pounders with telling effect the previous day. After a projectile from a Mexican cannon hit and seriously wounded Lt. Col. James C. Neill, chief artillery officer, the Twin Sisters replied. The newly appointed Mexican artillery officer, Col. Pedro Delgado of Santa Anna's staff, said, "Our cannon, established on a small elevation, opened its fire. The enemy responded with a discharge of grape, which wounded severely Captain Urrezza and killed his horse. Their first shot shattered the caisson on the limber; another scattered about our ordnance boxes; another, again, killed two fine mules, and they kept annoying us during the long hours it took me to remove, with only two mules, forty odd boxes of ammunition."

With absolutely no practice–since there was no powder for such a luxury–the Texian cannon were right on target. That militiamen with little experience in soldiering could be so accurate was not a matter of luck. These soldiers were disciplined and well trained. A number of them had spent hours studying different types of projectiles, pulling field pieces into position, figuring elevations, powder charges and windage, and actually firing the weapons. Operations like these required close teamwork, achieved only through rigorous training. Evidence strongly indicates that these troops, at least the key ones, had such training–in the United States Army, from which some of them had only recently deserted and others, their service completed, had brought their talents to Texas.

As Santa Anna vengefully advanced, the route of terror of those fleeing across the Sabine River to the United States was wryly called the "Sabine chute." That appellation could also have applied for the stream of volunteers and soldiers coming from the other direction.

In 1836 the six-pound cannon was standard in the U.S. Army. In early January, Pvts. Michael Campbell, George Cumberland, J.N. Gainer, and Ira Millerman were transferred from Henry Teal's Company of Texas Regulars to help man the cannon. Michael Campbell, George Cumberland, J.N. Gainer, and Ira Milliman were deserters from Companies B, E, F, and H of the U.S. 3rd Infantry Regiment, which included an artillery train and was garrisoned at Fort Jessup, Louisiana, some thirty to forty miles across the Sabine River, due east of Nacogdoches. Four other men, Ellis Benson, Joseph A. Clayton, Joseph Merwin, and Seneca Legg, were transferred to the artillery from Capt. Amasa Turner's company of Regulars. They are not shown as U.S. deserters. Benson was discharged from Company G, U.S. 3rd Infantry, in February 1834. The others were evidently expert gunners, too, with prior artillery training.

Recruiting Regulars had proved a difficult task for the fledgling Texas government, even as it offered a twenty-five dollar bounty and 800 acres of land as an enlistment inducement. As late as March 10, a committee at Washington-on-the-Brazos reported "of the regular army, there appears to be sixty privates." Of those, twenty-six had already died in the smoking ruins of the Alamo.

Attracting Regulars would have been easier if the officers could have provided housing, clothing, and arms for the troops. J.W. Bunton, chairman of the committee, reported that Capt. Henry Teal had managed to recruit some forty Regulars. These men quite likely did not need a clothing allotment, for many of them wore the uniforms of the U.S. Army. They did not need muskets, powder, or bayonets, either. They came fully equipped, either with permission to do so or without.

In *The Evolution of a State*, Noah Smithwick said, "There were said to have been a number of United States soldiers, from General [E.P] Gaines' command [at Fort Jessup and Camp Sabine] in the battle of San Jacinto. Deserters, they were called; but, after the battle, they all 'deserted' back to the United States army, and no court martial ensued."

Frank X. Tolbert, in *The Day of San Jacinto,* said, "Among Houston's men were two companies of regular infantry. In the Texan army, regulars got more land for their services than reservists (eight hundred acres as against six hundred forty in some cases), but didn't have the right to elect their own company officers as the reservists did. A number of the regulars wore parts of United States Army uniforms disguised with buckskin accessories. They were garrison troops from Louisiana who'd been allowed to 'desert' for a short, fighting vacation with the Texas rebels. The two regular companies were the most disciplined men in Houston's army of stubborn individualists."

Joseph Milton Nance in *After San Jacinto* noted that a U.S. officer came to Texas in the summer of 1836 to encourage 200 deserters still wearing U.S. Army uniforms to return to their units across the border. They refused.

In reviewing Sam Houston Dixon and Louis Wiltz Kemp's *The Heroes of San Jacinto* in 1932, pre-eminent historian Eugene C. Barker said that book "sheds light on an antiquarian historical problem of some importance. It used to be asserted, and probably was believed by some historians, that two hundred soldiers from the United States army fought at San Jacinto. If one knew when each of the San Jacinto veterans entered Texas, when enlisted, and how long he served, and how long he remained in Texas after the battle, one would be in a position to deny or verify this ancient assertion with a fair degree of certainty. The book does not give all the information necessary for a determination of the question, but that which is given tends apparently to disprove the assertion."

Although Professor Barker believed otherwise, evidence seems to substantiate the antiquarian claim. A comparison of information on Texian revolutionary veterans with information on the 1834-36 rosters and returns for the 3rd and 6th U.S. Infantry Regiments shows at least 153 instances in which men on both lists had the same or strikingly similar names. True, there were probably not 200 U.S. soldiers at San Jacinto. That figure, likely a con-

U.S. Army deserters manned the Twin Sisters with deadly effect.

servative one, was reported during the summer after the battle, for then the number of desertions increased dramatically. From May to September 1836, ninety-seven soldiers deserted from the 6th Regiment alone.

Most of the deserters who took part in the revolution came from the 3rd Regiment while it was stationed at Fort Jessup. Others from the 3rd and 6th joined them after moving to newly created Camp Sabine, right on the border to the west of Fort Jessup on the Nacogdoches–San Augustine Trail; and a few came from the 4th Infantry Regiment at Baton Rouge, Louisiana. For one thing, they didn't want to miss a good fight. They also wanted to help the outnumbered Texians and the terrified refugees fleeing for the border. Besides, the promise of free land for their services offered a better prospect for the future than their meager U.S. Army pay.

At San Jacinto many fully equipped soldiers fought in Lt. Col. Henry Millard's Regulars. They occupied the center position in the attack and offered the only semblance of stability when the Volunteers, screaming for revenge for the Alamo and Goliad massacres, became uncontrollable in their blood lust. Veteran soldiers also fought among both militia and Volunteer units of Houston's army.

U.S. soldiers still used old-style muskets, while many of the militia had more expensive and accurate rifles. One young Texian Regular, William C. Swearingen, wrote to his brother in Kentucky that riflemen opened fire at 100 yards and the "musketry" advanced farther before they fired. Swearingen was likely a former U.S. soldier, for he was a Regular equipped with musket and bayonet.

"We were ordered to charge with our bayonets," he said. "The enemy gave way except about sixty men around the cannon. They were protected by a breastwork of corn sacks, salt, barrels of meat and boxes of cannister shot. They fell by the bayonet and swam in one mangle heap from that time until they reached the bieau [bayou]."

Houston's battle report made a point of saying there were no bayonets and that the soldiers used the butts of their rifles in the assault. Ever the politician, Houston would have downplayed bayonets in the hands of U.S. troops. However, professional soldiers undoubtedly played a leading role in overcoming the critical part of the Mexican defense.

Dr. Terrence Barragy, military history professor at Texas A&I University in Kingsville, said the bayonets and the Regulars' fast, accurate fire, along with the artillery handled by experienced soldiers, may have contributed to the early panic in the drowsing Mexican army.

Just how many deserters were with the Texas Army will never be known. Rosters and returns, which show the monthly changes in regimental operations, including recruits, sick reports, discharges, and desertions, indicate that at least ninety-seven U.S. Army veterans were under arms in Texas on or before April 21, 1836, the date of the San Jacinto battle. Possibly four of them died at Goliad and three at the Alamo.

Undoubtedly U.S. soldiers were present in Texas during the revolution. Bvt. 2nd Lt. Hugh McLeod, newly graduated from West Point, was assigned to Company B of the 3rd Regiment. On the way to Fort Jessup, he stopped at Macon, Georgia, on November 12, 1835, as the Georgia Battalion was preparing to leave for Texas and promised to "resign his commision and embark as a volunteer."

He assumed his U.S. duties as a temporary company commander until March 7, 1836, when he asked for a ten-day leave of absence. He was granted leave at that time, but was later listed as absent without leave through July, when his resignation was accepted.

During the Runaway Scrape McLeod, with thirty men, garrisoned the fort at Nacogdoches. Mrs. Thomas J. Rusk, whose husband was with Houston's army, joined the flight with her young sons, but she didn't panic. She advised others to be calm, for "as long as the brave M'Leod or one of his men is living, we have nothing to fear."

It is not clear if the men McLeod commanded at Nacogdoches were volunteers or the thirty-man company he commanded in the U.S. Army.

Names similar or identical to those of some fifty deserters and thirty-two men who had been honorably discharged, some of them two or three years previously, are on Texian rosters before April 21, 1836. An additional fifteen names appear on both U.S. and Texian rosters at the time of the San Jacinto battle, indicating that soldiers could have remained on their U.S. company rolls while they were actually in Texas fighting a war.

By count, San Jacinto rosters, including those ordered to remain at Harrisburg to guard the sick and the baggage of Houston's army, list twenty-eight men who can be identified from the returns as likely U.S. deserters. There are seventeen names on Texian rolls and the discharged lists and ten that appear on Texian records and also remain on the U.S. rolls, making a total of fifty-five men possibly trained by the U.S. Army and fighting at San Jacinto.

Almost certainly there were more, for names on the reports include Smith, Jones, Brown, Johnson, and other common ones impossible to identify. Furthermore, no accounts list the men in units sent to escort panic-stricken civilians to the U.S. border or to defend Galveston or other Texian positions. And a check of rosters and returns from other U.S. frontier units might show similar results.

The official San Jacinto roster prepared for Sam Houston listed no first names for the eight artillerymen. Others in the company were fully identified. The two companies of Regulars in the Texas Army likewise were listed without first names–a strange oversight in a regular military unit, which considers drawing up rosters and calling roll a ritual.

The former U.S. soldiers further complicated matters by using initials and varying the spelling of their names from time to time. Company clerks compounded the problems by spelling some names phonetically. And adding to the difficulty of identifying troops of the 3rd Regiment, the Company D rosters for 1836 are

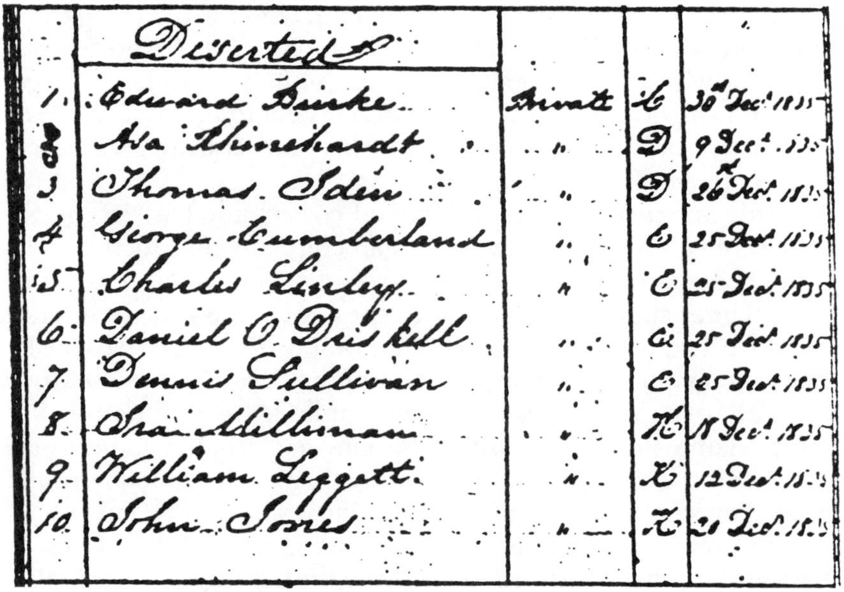

	Deserted			
1	Edward Burke	Private	C	30th Decr 1835
2	Asa Rhinehardt	"	D	9 Decr 1835
3	Thomas Iden	"	D	26 Decr 1835
4	George Cumberland	"	C	25 Decr 1835
5	Charles Linley	"	C	25 Decr 1835
6	Daniel O Driskell	"	C	25 Decr 1835
7	Dennis Sullivan	"	C	25 Decr 1835
8	Ira Milliman	"	K	18 Decr 1835
9	William Leggett	"	K	12 Decr 1835
10	John Jones	"	K	21 Decr 1835

Names of several men listed as deserters on these 3rd U.S. Infantry Regiment returns for December 1835 showed up on San Jacinto rosters.

missing.

The Texian victory stimulated a desire for freedom and land among the U.S. troops; and when General Gaines ordered an armed force into Nacogdoches in late July 1836, members of the 3rd and 6th Regiments from Fort Jessup and the 4th Regiment at Fort Towson north of the Red River took advantage of new opportunities to desert.

At the end of August, Gaines became alarmed at the scope of the defection to the foreign nation of Texas. On August 3, 1836, he wrote to Houston: "I am determined to send an officer to the Texian Government and to the Army, to reclaim the Deserts from the Corps of my Command. It is in the best interest of both Governments that their high military offenders shall be restored to their Corps and they must be so restored peaceably if possible, and forcibly if necessary. I will pardon all who return voluntarily in the present month. Those who do not avail themselves of this promise shall as far as my force and means will allow me to arrest and punish them, shall be punished to the full measure of the law."

A week later one of his lieutenants, Joseph Bonnell, wrote

that General Houston had communications to the Texas Army and "had ordered that all deserters from our army shall be given up."

Apparently, Houston used the message to get rid of a few troublemakers. Six were discharged, each "being claimed by U.S. to pay for one musket." Four others were discharged, two "by being claimed by U.S." and two others "for a demand made by the U.S. Government being deserter from that Govt." However, there seemed to be no large-scale return by the deserters to the U.S. Army.

One, John Casey, a native of Ireland who had served under Capt. Thomas H. Breece's Company of New Orleans Greys at the Storming of Bexar, was "expelled." No reason was given. Another, the artilleryman Michael Campbell, appears to have been even more unfortunate. Shortly after San Jacinto a Michael Campbell was in military confinement. Two years later Michael Campbell was hanged for murder in Victoria after an extremely fast and informal trial.

Many, however, remained in Texas as substantial citizens. One such was Daniel O'Driscoll. Driscoll family records indicate that the family patriarch enlisted in the Texas Army as a recruit from the Irish colonies. However, Hobart Huson's *Refugio* lists O'Driscoll as "among those who moved to the town of Refugio in the days of the Republic." His name does not appear on any of the land grants issued by José Jesús Vidaurri in the Power and Hewitson Colony, and he is not listed among town lot holders in Refugio before the revolution.

According to records in the National Archives, Daniel O. Driskell was born in Ireland and joined Company E of the 3rd U.S. Infantry March 16, 1835, at Frederickstown, Virginia. A laborer, he was five feet, seven and three-quarter inches tall, with blue eyes, brown hair, and a ruddy complexion.

Third Infantry returns list "Daniel O. Driskill" as deserting from Company E on December 25, 1835. On January 5, 1836, "Daniel O. Driscoll" enlisted in the Texas Army. He was a sergeant in Colonel Millard's Company A of Regulars at San Jacinto and was promoted to lieutenant by the end of the year. For his service in the Texas Army during and after the revolution, Daniel O'Driscoll and his heirs received a total of 3,080 acres in bounties and donations, including a headright grant of one-third of a league from Victoria County.

Discharged September 8, 1838, he married a Victoria widow,

Catherine Duggan. In 1839, Huson said, O'Driscoll moved to Refugio, where he established a tavern. He and his wife had two sons, Robert and Jeremiah, who dropped the O from their name and established the vast Driscoll ranching empire with their father's revolutionary land patents.

Robert's children, Robert, Jr., and Clara, became prominent South Texans in ranching and banking. Clara used family money to save the Alamo from destruction. After her death in 1945 the fortune endowed the Driscoll Foundation Children's Hospital to provide medical care for children from all over South Texas.

Some of the veterans never applied for land due them. Most sold their bounties, donations, and grants to land speculators for a pittance. Regardless of what happened to them later, however, there can be little doubt that United States soldiers had a definite impact on the outcome of the Texas Revolution.

A Question of Conspiracy

When it comes to understanding historical events, Americans like to attribute them to conspiracy rather than to conventionally accepted explanations. The struggle to wrest Texas from Mexico is a case in point, perhaps with a great deal of justification. Presence of U.S. soldiers at the Battle of San Jacinto gives rise to suspicions as to what Andrew Jackson and Sam Houston might have been up to.

Certainly, Jackson was capable of plotting a grand scheme. In 1818 Major General Jackson had taken it upon himself to cross the border of Florida and run the Spaniards out, while on a mission with the stated purpose of "chastising Indians." He accomplished this objective with a force previously commanded by Brig. Gen. Edmund P. Gaines. The 1819 Adams-Onís Treaty, signed after that incursion, gave Florida to the United States. It also relinquished any U.S. claim to Texas and set the Sabine River as the boundary between U.S. and Spanish territory.

Mexico won its independence from Spain in 1821. By 1835 Jackson was the U.S. president, Gaines was in charge of the Army's Western Department fighting the Seminoles in Florida, and trouble was brewing in the Texas–Coahuila province of Mexico. Jackson, who had endorsed the Adams-Onís Treaty when it was signed, now denied that the Sabine was part of the agreement and claimed instead that Spain had been willing to consider Texas part of the Florida agreement.

Did he have a plan to obtain California—by fighting a war

over Texas—in 1836, a plan that was thwarted by the unexpected and stunning victory at San Jacinto? There are few documents to back such a thesis, for Old Hickory preferred to have potentially embarrassing information transmitted orally. However, Dr. Anson Jones, the last president of the Republic of Texas, advanced just such a theory. He attributed his information to Sam Houston's cousin, John H. Houston, a close confidant of Andrew Jackson.

According to Jones, Sam Houston didn't plan to fight at San Jacinto. He wanted Santa Anna to follow him across the Neches River. U.S. troops under General Gaines were waiting on the banks of the Sabine River. While the Mexicans considered the Sabine the boundary with the United States, Jackson considered the Neches the border. Had such a plan succeeded, the Mexican War would have started in 1836 and there would never have been a Republic of Texas.

In an 1849 memo, Jones claimed that Jackson wanted to obtain California and a war with Mexico would have accomplished that goal. Jones wrote, "The retreat of Gen. Houston to the country between the Sabine and the Neches, the pursuit of Santa Anna and his crossing the latter stream, would have been considered an invasion of the territory of the United States, by their President, and by the [Zachary] Taylor of that day, Gen. E.P. Gaines—a conflict would have ensued between some of his troops and some of those of Santa Anna—blood would have been spilled upon [disputed] American ground—and 'war commenced by the act of Mexico!' Then Mr. Jackson would have accomplished what [President James K.] Polk subsequently did, General Gaines would have been the 'second Cortez' instead of Gen. [Winfield] Scott, and the treaty of Guadalupe Hidalgo would have been signed in 1838, instead of 1848."

Jones wrote that Houston told him during the retreat from Gonzales after the fall of the Alamo and the massacre at Goliad that he intended to retreat to the Neches and hoped for "a bloodless victory."

And evidence does point to U.S. involvement.

There is no doubt that Jones was correct in the statement that Andrew Jackson wanted California. After Joel Poinsett failed in his attempt to buy Texas for $1 million, Jackson raised the bid to $5 million; and in 1830 he sent Anthony Butler on the mission to Mexico City. As a diplomat Butler proved even less successful than Poinsett. When the Mexicans refused to accept his offer, he antagonized them by trying bribery. In 1834, while Stephen F.

Austin was being held prisoner in Mexico, Butler wrote anonymous letters trying to incite the Texians to revolt, in hopes that a revolution would encourage Mexico to sell the province.

On August 5, 1835, U.S. Secretary of State John Forsyth sent Butler a message on Jackson's behalf expressing a U.S. desire to expand the negotiations for Texas with an eye to acquiring the port of San Francisco for use by whaling vessels in the Pacific Ocean. Butler was instructed to try to obtain this boundary: "Beginning at the Gulf of Mexico, proceed along the eastern bank of the Rio Bravo del Norte to the 37th parallel of latitude, and thence along that parallel to the Pacific. . . ." The instructions went on to say that the Rio Bravo border was not essential, but that the border should stop "at the 37th parallel, or at any other line that would include the bay of St. Francisco and proceeding along such line which would include the bay of St Francisco."

Jackson definitely wanted the northern half of California.

Butler and his demands were so obnoxious that Mexico demanded his recall. Before he left, however, he sent Jackson a letter dated December 19, 1835, in which he described the following incident:

Santa Anna was in a meeting with the French and British ministers and "some eight or ten other Gentlemen." The Mexican leader began to speak of the revolt that had recently broken out in Texas and to declare that it was "his full knowledge" that it was instigated and supported by the United States. Butler said he was told that Santa Anna said he understood "that Gen. Jackson sets up a claim to pass the Sabine, and that in running the division line, hopes to acquire the Country as far as the Naches."

Butler wrote that Santa Anna then turned to a gentleman present and said, "'Sir, I mean to run that line at the Mouth of my Cannon, and after the line is Established, if the Nation will only give me the Means, only afford me the necessary Supply of Money I will march to the Capital, I will lay Washington City in Ashes, as it has already been once done.'" And at that point, Butler wrote, Santa Anna turned again and bowed to the British Minister, in a pointed reference to the damage the U.S. capital had suffered in 1814.

After he left Mexico, Butler practiced law in Washington County, Texas. He was a representative to the Texas Congress and fought in the Mexican War. Although he died heroically, trying to save fellow passengers on a burning Mississippi River steamer in 1849, he is better remembered for the notation Jackson wrote on the cover of one of his letters:

"Anthony Butler
What a Scamp"

In January 1836, shortly after recalling Butler from Mexico City, President Jackson, through Secretary of War Lewis Cass, ordered his old comrade Gaines to "repair to a proper position" somewhere on the Louisiana-Mexico border and assume command of the troops on the southwestern frontier. Gaines, who no doubt remembered Jackson's example of reading between the lines, was chosen because "public considerations demand the exercise of great discretion and experience."

In orders to Gaines, the president cautioned that the United States would remain neutral in the war between the Texians and the Mexican army. He said: "It is possible that the course of operations may induce one or other of the contending parties to approach the boundary line, with a view to cross it in arms. Should you find that the case, you will give notice to the persons having the direction, that they will not be permitted to cross into the territory of the United States: and if they attempt to do so by force, you will resist them with the means at your disposal."

Gaines assumed that his duties were important because of "recent accounts of the sanguinary manner in which the Mexican forces seem disposed to carry on the war against our Texian(s)." He said he would use force "in our own defense" and would speak in a language any belligerent would understand–the language of force to check any contending party that forgot to respect the neutral rights of the United States.

Gaines left no doubt where his sympathies lay. He offered a much stronger threat than Jackson might have wished to see in writing when he added:

"Should I find any disposition on the part of the Mexicans or their red allies to menace our frontier, I cannot but deem it to be my duty not only to hold the troops under my command in readiness for action in defence of our slender frontier, but to anticipate their lawless movements by crossing our supposed or imaginary national boundary, and meeting the savage marauders wherever to be found in their approach towards our frontier."

General Gaines was ready to start the Mexican War.

He called for mounted volunteers "with other forces, sufficient to make my numerical strength equal to the estimate strength of the contending parties, which is now estimated at eight to twelve thousand men."

Officers of the legionary brigade at New Orleans, many of whom had fought under Andrew Jackson in the famous battle there, replied that they would be delighted to come to the frontier and carry out the wishes "of the President."

Although advance word of military movements is usually highly classified, Gaines' orders were no secret to at least some of the Texians. John Thomson Mason, a close friend of Andrew Jackson and a former agent for an eastern land syndicate, was commandant of the Nacogdoches District of the Committee of Vigilance and Safety. On April 1 he wrote to Gaines at Natchitoches, Louisiana, where the general arrived that day, requesting that a detachment of troops be sent into Texas for, "after the devastation shall have been made, it is in vain to talk of protection."

This was a rather bold request, but he undoubtedly went much further. He said the messenger, William B.P. Gaines, (no relation) is "deputed to converse with you on the various subjects of deep interest to the people here, involved in the questions presented; and I beg leave to make him known to you as a gentleman claiming every confidence, and on whose discretion and intelligence the utmost reliance may be placed."

This request was made three weeks before the Battle of San Jacinto. As for Gaines' response, on April 16 Mason wrote to an unidentified person that General Gaines had marched from Fort Jessup with 600 men "to offer protection to women and children on either border of the river. He will not enter Texas till circumstances justify it."

On April 8 Gaines informed the secretary of war that Indians from the United States had crossed the boundary and that the army of Mexico, commanded by the president of Mexico, General Santa Anna in person, "is rapidly approaching in this direction through the centre of Texas; that his plan is to put to death all he finds in arms, and all who do not yield to his dictation; that as soon as he comes to the section of the country occupied by the Indians in question, on the waters of the Trinidad, or Trinity River, they will unite with him in his war of extermination; and that no boundary line, save such as that they find properly guarded with an efficient force, will be sufficient to arrest the sanguinary career of these savages, I cannot but deem it my duty to prepare for action."

To this end, he asked the governors of Louisiana, Mississippi, and Tennessee to each send a brigade and Alabama a battalion of volunteers. Jackson would later claim that Gaines made the requests without his authorization.

The threat of Indian incursions offered the general an excuse to attack, because a treaty between the United States and Mexico agreed that they would prevent by force "all incursions on the part of Indian nations living within their respective boundaries." However, while Mexican authorities sent a provocateur named Manuel Flores up from Matamoros to incite the Indians, the Indians didn't wish to get involved. Besides, Houston had used his great influence to keep them mollified.

On April 14 Gaines moved eight companies of the 6th Infantry and five companies of the 3rd, involving some 1,300 troops, to Camp Sabine. They arrived April 17 and immediately began building rafts. Gaines canceled his call for 5,000 volunteers shortly after the Battle of San Jacinto made U.S. intervention in the revolution unnecessary.

Evidence indicates that influential figures in the United States were knowledgeable about Gaines' movements. On April 23, before word of the Texian victory reached the East, Samuel Swarthout, another Jackson confidant, wrote a strong letter of support to Texian Col. John Morgan, a business associate. In it he said, "The old Chief [Jackson] and two thirds of Both Houses of Congress support the Independence of Texas. Do not be surprized if, in less than 60 days, you hear of the Government's having favorably–recognized the Government of Texas–It will be done–Already do I suspect that Genl. Gaines is in possession of Nacogdoches."

There is also a hint of conspiracy in communications from Sam P. Carson, secretary of state of the *ad interim* Texas government, one week prior to San Jacinto. On April 14 he wrote to President David G. Burnet and the Cabinet from Natchitoches:

"On my arrival here last night I met with Genl Gains; and have had with him a full and satisfactory conversation. His position at present is a delicate one and requires at his hands the most cautious movements. The object of the concentration of forces at Jessup is to protect the frontier and the Neuteral Ground also to keep the Indians in check and repress savage agressions. . .in fulfillment of treaty stipulations between the Govt of the U States and Mexico."

He said Gaines had received a report of a large force of Indians and "Mounted Mexicans" within sixty miles of Nacogdoches.

"Genl Gaines immediately on rect. of the Express issued an order to prepare thirteen companies to March this evening to the

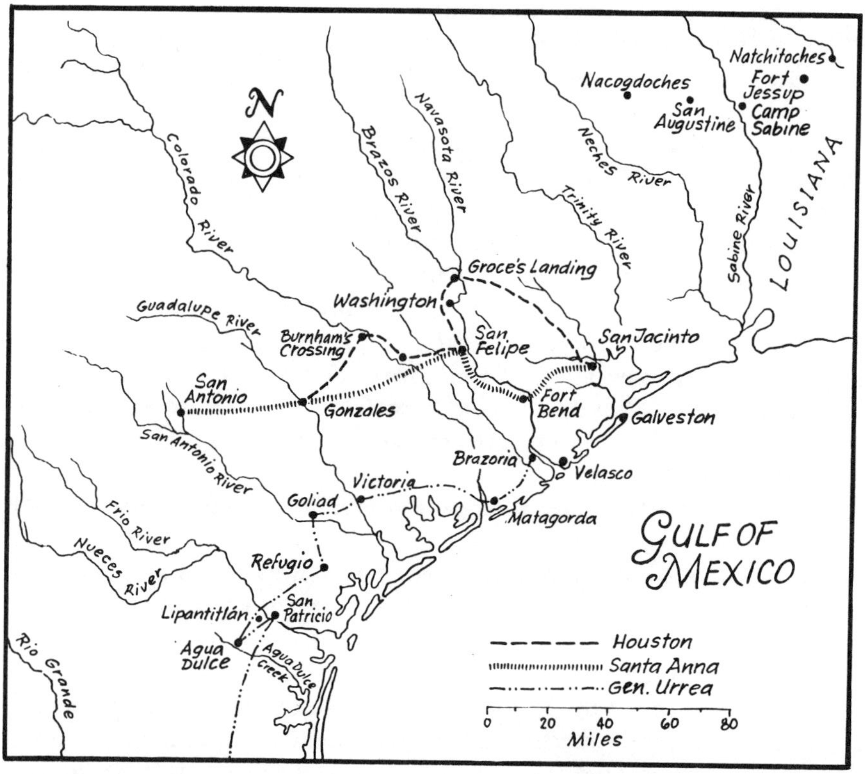

Sabean with two field peaces with 75 rounds for each and 35 rounds for the Infantry–also 12 days provisions etc."

Gaines had given him a copy of requisitions for volunteers. "He [Gaines)] will have in a few days (say 20 to 30) from 7 to 8000 men with him. . . . I cannot state positively what Genl Gains may do but one thing I think I may say that should be satisfied with the fact, that the Mexicans have incited any Indians who are under the control of the U States to commit depredations on either side of the line he will doubtless view it as a violation. . .and be assured that he will maintain the honor of his country and punish the agressor be him whome he may." If proof were found Indians were with the Mexicans, "he will cross [the Sabine] and move upon the agressors. You will remark that I can give you nothing from Genl Gains himself as to his movements."

Carson, who was on his way to Washington as an official envoy to obtain aid from the United States, added, "The departure on the part of the enemy from the useages of Civilised Warfare will doubtless have its effect with Genl Gains. . . ."

At the same time he penned a short note to Sam Houston, saying, "My view is, that you should fall back, if necessary, to the Sabine, I am warranted in saying that volunteer troops will come on in numbers from the United States. . . . You must fall back, and hold out, and let nothing goad or provoke you to a battle, unless you can, without doubt, whip them, or unless you are compelled to fight."

So Sam Houston's option was a viable one. Some Texas leaders, including Col. Sidney Sherman and the *ad interim* president, Burnet, were convinced at the time that Houston's strategy was to follow Carson's advice, to "take the Sabine chute" and retreat until U.S. forces came to his aid. Some believed the only reason he chose to fight was that his men would have mutinied if he had continued his retreat.

Indeed, the word was so widespread that the Mexican commanders drew their campaign plans on the premise that Houston was retreating to Galveston or to the Trinity. Texas colonists told Mexican Gen. José Urréa that Houston had 700 to 800 men and was on his way to defend Galveston until people and property there could be removed.

This helps explain why Santa Anna's dragoons, so devastating in earlier engagements, were feeding and watering their unsaddled horses when the Texian attack came. Had they been on the alert, the battle could have ended differently.

After the war, Urréa wrote of Houston: "Circumstances forced him to make a stand; fortune favored him at San Jacinto; and he who in the course of unfavorable circumstances could have obtained no glory as a soldier and might have perhaps disappeared from the scene, presented himself now as the conquerer and the hero."

It may be that an overconfident Santa Anna could not believe that the Texian rabble would have the nerve to attack his army across an open field. In two earlier encounters, behind a riverbank and trees at Concepción and Lipantitlán, the Texians had been almost invincible. But Agua Dulce and Coleto Creek had been a different story. Both leaders knew that the Texians were no match for the Mexicans in open country; for after they emptied their muzzleloaders, they were at the mercy of the mounted lancers. In a letter to Philip Dimmitt, Houston had written, "We must not depend on Forts" and added "the roads, and ravines suit us best."

The Mexicans agreed. After an inconclusive skirmish at Fort

Lipantitlán in 1842, Col. Antonio Canales said, "the woods [were] the only place where these vainglorious ones could stand up to us. The Texans are like tricky ladino [wild, shrewd and sly] cattle; in the forests they are brave and light, but on the open plains, they cripple up and become frightened."

And Santa Anna's own impetuosity invited an attack by the Texians, planned or otherwise. First he thought he could obliterate Houston's small band. Then he became obsessed with the idea of capturing the rebel government at Harrisburg. With the added inducement of catching archenemy Lorenzo de Zavala – vice-president of the proclaimed Republic of Texas–he charged ahead with only a small portion of his army. Thus he presented Sam Houston with an opportunity the Texian couldn't ignore.

Up to this point, his detractors believed, Houston's resolve seemed to waver, though later his retreat became a Fabian policy planned by him but explained to no one. He did give one hint when he wrote to Nacogdoches merchant Henry Raguet two weeks before San Jacinto, "Don't get scared at Nacogdoches–Remember Old Hickory claims Nachez [*sic*] as 'Neutral Territory. . . .' "

Despite claims by his enemies, however, Houston's dispatches as he retreated to the east indicated that he fully intended to attack. On March 31 he announced to the people: "My spies have just returned and report the enemy in a few miles of San Felipe, eight hundred to one thousand strong. We will whip them soon."

On April 7 he wrote: "The advance of the enemy is at San Felipe. The moment for which we have waited with anxiety and interest, is fast approaching. The victims of the Alamo, and the names of those who were murdered at Goliad, call for cool, deliberate vengeance. Strict discipline, order, and subordination, will insure us the victory. The army will be in readiness for action at a moment's warning. . . ."

And again on April 13: "The enemy have crossed the Brazos, but they are treading the soil on which they are to be conquered. . . ."

Probably the finest testimony as to Houston's resolve occurred at noon on April 21 when he called a council of war among his officers and asked their opinion. Should he attack the Mexican position or hold fast in a defensive posture?

Cols. Edward Burleson, Sidney Sherman, and Henry Millard and Lt. Col. Alexander Somervell voted to await a Mexican action. Lt. Col. Joseph Bennett and Maj. Lysander Wells voted to attack. Houston said nothing. He had already decided to charge the enemy barricades.

Houston's confidence had received a considerable boost on the eighteenth, when Deaf Smith and Capt. Henry Wax Karnes swam their horses across Buffalo Bayou and captured three Mexican couriers. Dispatches they carried contained intelligence that Santa Anna had outdistanced the other columns that had been scheduled to rendezvous with him. The odds suddenly shifted from 5 to 1 to almost dead even.

Even after winning the battle, Houston feared his ragtag army, disorganized in victory, would be an easy victim for those other Mexican columns still intact and totaling some 4,500 troops. As the Indians on the frontier were restive and the Texian army almost in revolt, Stephen F. Austin had the same sense of alarm. He wrote to Houston, "It is very desirable that Gen. Gaines should establish his headquarters at Nacogdoches. Use your influence to get him to do so, and if he could visit this place [Columbia, the seat of government] & give the people here assurances of the good faith of Gen. Santa Anna in the offers and treaties he has made you & with this Govt that would be helpful. . . ."

Before forwarding the letter to Gaines, Houston noted in the margin that he had made no treaty. At the foot of the sheet, he added: "General I refer this letter to you and can only add that such a step. . .will SAVE TEXAS. Your friend, Sam Houston."

In July, with the approval of President Jackson, the U.S. Army moved into Nacogdoches–a move that angered many Mexicans. General Urréa considered it tantamount to a declaration of war.

José María Tornel y Mendivil, Mexican secretary of war during the Texas Revolution, wrote in 1837: "The coincidence of the march of General Gaines to the frontier with the uprising of Texas after the occupation of the territory by a Mexican army naturally gives rise to the suspicion that the object of his mission, as well as that of the increase of the army of the United States, was to help the rebels in case of necessity, and to occupy, in the midst of the consequent disorder, the territory still contested, reenforcing by the presence of troops the demands which were again being presented. . . .

"Throughout the course of the incidents related, the policy of General Jackson is easily discernible in his evident desire to acquire Texas."

In the years following San Jacinto, Houston used his wartime popularity to dominate the Texas political scene, making numerous enemies, many of them former friends. Mirabeau Lamar,

Sherman, Robert Potter, and others tried unsuccessfully to paint him as a bumbling coward. President Burnet and Houston had many bitter exchanges in which Burnet called Houston a drunk Indian. Houston in turn referred to Burnet as "Wetumpka," Indian for hog thief.

After leading efforts to annex Texas to the United States, Houston's very close friend, Dr. Anson Jones, felt that his efforts were unappreciated and that Houston had claimed credit for his accomplishments. Jones was ignored when he sought nomination to the U.S. Senate and grew more and more morose, eventually committing suicide. During the period before his death, he grew to despise Houston and wrote disparagingly of him in his notebooks. He was so angry over Houston's Senate vote to exclude slavery from Oregon that he changed his son's name from Sam Houston Jones to Samuel Edward Jones, saying, "No descendant of Cromwell would bear the name of that traitor."

So was Jones' Jackson-Houston conspiracy the concoction of an isolated, depressed, obsessed person? Or was there a plan derailed by one of the most decisive victories in history? Neither President Jackson nor President Houston ever revealed the answer.

On at least one occasion, however, Houston indicated that he meant to get as close to the United States as possible in case the Mexican army was victorious. In a speech in 1845, he said that after the Alamo fell and "Deaf Smith, having returned from a scout, reported the enemy advancing, I then determined to retreat and get as near Andrew Jackson and the old flag as I could."

Was Old Sam merely jesting, or was he stating a fact? Perhaps it was both. It was vintage Houston. He kept his own counsel.

[6]

PALADINS

The Mighty Pen

A cliché is a truism that has been overworked.

"The pen is mightier than the sword" is a cliché that had real meaning when Texas was fighting for its independence, for it was the pens and printing press of the Borden brothers that held the Texian army together and made the Battle of San Jacinto possible.

Gail Borden, Jr., his brother, Tom, and Joseph Baker published *The Telegraph and Texas Register* at San Felipe. The newspaper reported the activities of the Texas government. It alerted Texians of the approach of Santa Anna's army, which, the paper said, was promising "to leave nothing of us but the recollection that we once existed."

It printed William B. Travis' famous appeal, which began, "I am besieged by a thousand or more Mexicans" and ended "Victory or Death."

A rival newspaper printed by Franklin C. Gray, the *Texas Republican,* printed the same story but ceased publication on March 2, 1836. The Bordens reported Travis' final March 3 appeal for help. The newspaper also carried the full Texas Declaration of Independence and the new Texas Constitution. On March 16 it announced the fall of the Alamo. The Bordens talked to Alamo survivors, Mrs. Almeron Dickinson and Travis' servant, Joe. They printed the first newspaper account of the disaster and listed

Santa Anna's soldiers threw the Bordens' press into Buffalo Bayou.

many of those known to have been killed.

The *ad interim* government picked up and fled to Harrisburg. This caused a general panic among the population and began the wholesale dash for the United States border that became known as the Runaway Scrape. Soldiers dropped out to help their families, and Sam Houston's army melted from around 1,200 to less than 800.

The Bordens refused to retreat. They printed hundreds of copies of the newspaper, preserving letters and documents that otherwise would have been lost to history. Only when Houston decided to retreat from San Felipe did the Bordens consider moving their operations. As the Texas Army continued to retreat, Capt. Moseley Baker, who had refused to follow Houston's order, stayed in town and helped move the press across the Brazos River. The Bordens were a rear guard in the revolution. Baker's scouts reported the approach of the Mexican army, and Baker set fire to the town, burning up much of the newspaper's supplies. Then they learned the "army" was a herd of cattle.

The Bordens considered getting out of journalism. They were in debt, their printers had not been paid, and their plant was in smoking ruins. But they obtained a team and wagon and pushed on through the mud with their heavy press to Harrisburg. There they reported the massacre of Fannin's men.

"We promise the public of our beloved country that our press will never cease its operations 'til our silence shall announce to them that there is no more in Texas a resting place for a free press nor for the government of their choice," Gail Borden wrote.

During the press run the Mexican army appeared. The Bordens grabbed the few papers printed and fled in a boat. Santa Anna burned Harrisburg and threw their press into Buffalo Bayou. After San Jacinto the Bordens got another press and reported the happenings of the new Republic of Texas.

Thomas Jefferson thought it better to have newspapers without government than government without newspapers. The Bordens proved his point. Though Gail Borden, Jr., was to win fame later as the inventor of condensed milk, his pen held the revolution together until swords could prevail. He and his partners deserve to be counted as Texian heroes.

Lorenzo de Zavala

Most visitors don't see the small family burial plot in San Jacinto Battlefield Park. There lies Lorenzo de Zavala, Texas and Mexican patriot. At his home across the bayou surgeons treated both Texians and Mexicans wounded in the battle.

De Zavala's love affair with democracy and individual freedom made it dangerous for him in his native Mexico, which later put a price on his head when he was a signer of the Texas Declaration of Independence and *ad interim* vice-president of the Republic of Texas.

A native of Yucatan, de Zavala was an active liberal, a fact that landed him in prison in 1814. There for three years he studied medicine and English. Then Yucatan elected him to the Spanish Cortés in Madrid. With Mexican independence, he was elected to the National Congress and named president of the Chamber of Deputies. He was first to sign the Mexican Constitution of 1824, but fled the country when militarists seized power. He visited the United States and formed a partnership with David G. Burnet of New Jersey and Joseph Vehlein, a German merchant of Mexico City, in the Galveston Bay and Texas Land Co.

De Zavala described American cities, government, people, and habits. He was impressed with religious freedom and the way Americans openly and peacefully debated issues. He was not impressed with slavery and treatment of blacks or the way Americans spit tobacco. The ideals he felt strongly about included free

Mexican newspapers, public education, equality of men, and the casting off of feudalism, superstition, caste privilege, and "shadows that inundate the world for twelve centuries." He believed immigrants from England, Germany, Ireland, and the United States would establish colonies under democratic institutions southward to northern Mexico, where they could be "molded to a combined regimen of the American system and the Spanish customs and traditions."

The trip to the United States had convinced de Zavala that Mexico should emulate the American experiment. In 1831 he wrote of his travels in *Journey to the United States of North America* (translated by Wallace Woolsey), trying to convince his countrymen to demand freedom and reject the peonage of Europe. Five years before the Texas Revolution, he wrote that colonists would not subject themselves to a military and ecclesiastical government, saying, "They will not want it [government] to be a deceit, an illusion, but a reality. When a military leader tries to intervene in civil transactions, they will resist, and they will triumph."

In 1827 and again in 1832 he was governor of the state of Mexico. Santa Anna appointed him minister to France. There he realized Santa Anna was a dictator who would not follow the liberal constitution. Bloody excesses of the Centralists pushed him to the revolutionary movement. He resigned, arrived in Texas in 1835, and cast his lot against the Centralist government. As Harrisburg representative to the Constitutional Convention, he signed the Texas Declaration of Independence and was elected vice-president on March 17, 1836. His wife created one of the flags Texians carried into battle.

Already in bad health, de Zavala contracted pneumonia when a boat capsized in Buffalo Bayou in November; he died days later. He was given a hero's burial and eulogized by Sam Houston and other Texas notables. Today the town and county of Zavala honor his name, and just east of the Texas Capitol in Austin stands the Lorenzo de Zavala Texas State Archives Building.

De Zavala wanted freedom and democracy for Mexico as fervently as he wanted independence for Texas. His idealism should serve to bring the two closer together.

Another Houston Love

Sam Houston winced with pain as he lay against a great oak tree on the battlefield of San Jacinto. A doctor probed to remove splinters of bone from his shattered leg.

The air was filled with the smell of spent gunpowder, burned cloth, bloody and battered human flesh, and carcasses that had been men. And an unshaven, bloodstained band of frontiersmen, their mud-spattered clothing in tatters, stood about, holding their rifles, many with the stocks broken. They wondered about the future of their leader and his next move. Moans came from the wounded among the hundreds of frightened prisoners. The enemy leader, Gen. Antonio López de Santa Anna, had not been found. There were reports to be received and a letter to the president of the new Republic of Texas to be written. But affairs of state could wait.

To subdue the waves of pain, the ashen commander-in-chief concentrated with great intensity, weaving magnolia leaves into a small garland crown. Then he reached into his coat, pulled out a card, and wrote this note:

"To Miss Anna Raguet, Nacogdoches, Texas: These are laurels I send you from the battlefield of San Jacinto. Thine. Houston."

Who was the woman who could bring this great warrior to interrupt such a dramatic moment in history for a romantic gesture?

She was a nineteen-year-old beauty who had been in his mind for some time. Pretty young girls generally caught the eye of Sam Houston, then forty-three, but this one had a special attraction as a damsel who had sent her knight off to battle.

Anna Raguet was the daughter of Ohio merchant Henry Raguet, who had moved to Nacogdoches in 1832 to open a business on Sam Houston's recommendation. Houston practiced law near the Raguet mercantile store. Anna, educated in the best schools in Philadelphia, was fluent in several languages. She gave Houston lessons in Spanish, an essential knowledge in Mexican Texas. He spent many hours in the Raguet home, visiting and talking to Anna, her father, or both.

Stephen F. Austin and other early settlers became fluent *en español,* conversing and writing in the language. Just how much Spanish Houston learned is not known. Likely not much, for he was fully smitten by his young mentor. He dropped in a few words occasionally, but not often.

He corresponded with her father, then more and more with Anna herself. To her he confided the problems of commanding troops in Texas, the shortcomings of the Texas government, the state of foreign affairs, and other subjects normally discussed in

To subdue the waves of pain, the ashen commander-in-chief concentrated with great intensity, weaving magnolia leaves into a small garland crown.

those days only by men.

After Houston was named commander-in-chief in 1836, a sharp division arose between Governor Henry Smith and the General Council; and four different men–Houston, James Fannin, and F.W. Johnson and James Grant–were named to command the troops. At Refugio, Houston dissuaded most of the men of Johnson and Grant from invading Matamoros. He then left for East Texas to treat with his Indian friends, to whom the Mexicans were offering inducements to attack the colonies.

On his way to visit his friend Chief Bowles of the Cherokees, he stopped off at the Raguet home in Nacogdoches. As he sat with his back to an open door and talked to Anna and her father, a swarthy man suddenly appeared behind him, dagger upraised.

Before the attacker could strike, Anna jumped up and grabbed his hand, saving Houston's life. What happened to the would-be assassin is not recorded. Houston, already enamored of his sparkling teen-aged teacher, was now fully hooked.

As he left to sit as a delegate to the March Convention, to rejoin the army as commander-in chief, and face the full might of a battle-hardened Mexican army, he asked her for a talisman to carry into battle. She gave him a silken sash she had knitted to serve as a belt for his sword.

Houston was a throwback to the Age of Chivalry. He was the knight, and she was his sweet maiden. Hence, when the knight was victorious, though wounded in deadly combat, his first thoughts through the waves of pain were of his ladylove. So he fashioned a garland of magnolia leaves and sent it to her as a token of the victory at San Jacinto.

Sam Houston could handle any situation—almost. He stood his ground against tyrants, fought bravely, and bore great punishment from his wounds in several battles. He stood toe-to-toe, never giving an inch in contests of will with some of the strongest men in the United States, outmaneuvered some of the most devious diplomats of his day, and refused to be stampeded by an impetuous Texas Congress. He held sway over a rowdy, rebellious army of ambitious adventurers and out-thought their leaders, who sometimes plotted to lynch him. While he could be refined and charming, he could also be crude, cunning, and egotistical; but he was always dedicated to his sense of personal honor. He proved his courage in battle and in standing alone against the multitudes in support of unpopular causes. He was strong physically, mentally, and emotionally, winning duels, battles, and great debates—all against men.

Jousting with women, Houston was neither confident nor skillful. Except with Indian maidens, his efforts were usually unsuccessful. Early in life, when he ran away from home to live with the Cherokees, he enjoyed the carefree life and liberal sexual standards of the tribe. He said he was "wild and impetuous" during this period. He danced, participated in tribal celebrations, frolicked and walked in the woods, reading the *Iliad* to Indian girls. And when they did not understand, he spoke the universal language of the heart. With his wild nature, he was comfortable with them. He seemed to have trouble finding full acceptance only among the women of his own people.

Perhaps from the almost religious esteem he held for his

mother, he viewed all womankind in the same light, as though they were on a pedestal. He greatly admired beautiful young women. He never sought any other variety. As early as 1824, when he was a member of Congress, he planned to take a wife and start a family. He wrote to a friend advising him the best way to rebound from an unsuccessful love affair was by "taking a new chase. As for my single self, I do not know yet the sweets of matrimony, but in March or April next I will; unless something should take place not to be expected or wished for. . . . My errand here is to attend to the business of my constituants, and not to spend honey moons. Every thing in due season."

But by the following April he wrote his cousin John H. Houston, "I am this far on my way west, in the full enjoyment of the sweets of single blessedness. . . . The political ferment at home is very great. My summer must needs be very active, and of these facts I felt bound in honor to let Miss M- - - know all the facts, and she concluded to defer matters until fall."

Matters were so pressing that he never returned to his lady. And there were other romances that did not work out. In 1826 he said, "I am making myself less frequent in the Lady World than I have been. I must keep up my Dignity, or rather I must attend more to politics and less to love."

Early in 1828 the Tennessee congressman called on Mary Custis, the daughter of George Washington Parke Custis and great-granddaughter of Martha Washington. In *The Raven*, Marquis James wrote, "Representative Houston was chairman of the Congressional Board of Visitors of the United States Military Academy, the annual inspections on the Highlands of the Hudson where a shy third classman was writing letters to the same Mary Custis. The young lady was so indifferent to the claims of fame as to prefer this quiet youth who did not drink or smoke, and eventually to marry 2nd Lt. Robert E. Lee, Corps of Engineers."

Then, after he was elected governor of Tennessee, thirty-five, and still a bachelor: "I have as usual had 'a small blow up,' " Houston wrote to Dr. John Marable. "What the devil is the matter with the gals I cant say, but there has been hell to pay and no pitch hot. May God bless you, it may be that I will splice myself a rib."

It was a matter of weeks when he did just that on January 22, 1829, marrying a trim, blue-eyed, eighteen-year-old with long yellow hair–Eliza Allen of Gallatin, daughter of John Allen. Of her, James wrote, "No other woman by such womanly means or by any means, has so strangely changed the face of American history."

This fateful marriage has received much historical attention. Within three months it had ended. The separation resulted in Houston's resignation as governor and disgrace in Tennessee society. It very likely cost him the nomination to succeed Andrew Jackson as president of the United States.

On April 9 Houston wrote to the bride's father that he believed Eliza to be virtuous: "That I have & do love Eliza none can doubt–that she is the only earthly object dear to me God will witness. . . . She was cold to me, & I thought did not love me. She owns that such was one cause of my unhappiness. You can judge how unhappy I was to think I was united to a woman that did not love me."

He blamed busybodies who pried into the affair, saying they were "robbers of others' good name–assassins of characters of the innocent."

His only words about the cause of the breakup appeared in a statement, in which he said that it was a private affair and the public had no right to interfere in it. "And remember that, whatever may be said by the lady or her friends, it is no part of the conduct of a gallant or a generous man to take up arms against a woman. If my character cannot stand the shock, let me lose it. The storm will sweep by and time will be my vindicator."

Houston begged Eliza to forgive him and take him back. She declined. He took a steamboat for the West to find solace among his friends the Indians, his pride wounded and his ambitions in shambles. Political enemies, fearful of his return, continued to spread rumors about his personal life. They told stories of his drinking problem, which was prodigious, and called him a "Squaw Man."

Even after Houston left the Indian Territory for Texas, he often returned to visit his red brothers. When he prospered, he had a horse and could travel forty miles a day. When he was broke, he walked, traveling only ten miles a day. A year later, so the story went, his route could be traced by the half-breed babies born either ten or forty miles apart.

Houston did know and understand the Indians. He was inducted as a citizen into the Cherokee Nation. He knew their customs and spoke their language and later, when he was chief executive of the Republic of Texas, treaties were always honored. After the separation from Eliza, he took an Indian wife, Diana Rogers. Magazines and newspapers said the former governor of Tennessee had "sunk to the lowest depths of humanity with a filthy Indian Squaw."

Diana Rogers, however, was a tall, willowy beauty of almost regal bearing. Her father, Capt. John Rogers, was one of the most prominent men in the Cherokee Nation; and her mother was the sister of two Cherokee chiefs. She was less than one-quarter Cherokee, probably closer to one-sixteenth, and fifteen-sixteenths Scotch and English, according to the authors of *Sam Houston with the Cherokees*.

Diana was only ten years old when Houston knew the family in Tennessee. She was married to David Gentry before the tribe was removed to Arkansas Territory. He was a white man, a blacksmith of considerable wealth, who was killed in a battle with the Osage. Tiana, as her people called her, was educated. The Rogers family, whose progeny includes a humorist named Will, owned plantations and a considerable number of slaves. They moved west before the forced removal of Cherokees from Georgia.

Houston and Tiana renewed their acquaintance at a dance and were married by Cherokee law. Since Tiana had been married previously, there was not much of a ceremony. The wedding was held in John Rogers' home on Spavinsaw Creek in 1830. They moved to a rambling log cabin near Cantonment Gibson in Arkansas Indian Territory, near present-day Muskogee, Oklahoma. At that time Fort Gibson, the westernmost outpost, was known as "the graveyard of the U.S. Army." Houston opened a trading post and at once began defending the Indians from unscrupulous agents.

Tiana apparently ran the store, and Houston maintained a political center, carried on correspondence, entertained visitors, and drank to excess. He made two trips to Washington on behalf of his red brothers. As he returned through Nashville, it was said, Eliza asked for a reconciliation and Houston, possibly thinking of Tiana, declined. But by 1831 the lure of Texas was calling.

His parting with Tiana has been greatly fictionalized–that she died in his arms, that she grieved herself to death and was buried beside a clear stream, or that she threw herself off a cliff. According to Cherokee law, the marriage ended when the husband left the Cherokee Nation.

In Washington, D.C., in December 1831, Houston composed a poem, apparently with Tiana in mind. The final verse reads:

Farewell! I wish it were not so.
That we must part and part forever,
But let the wandering exile go,
My heart from thee no change can sever.

He gave Tiana all his property at Wigwam Neosho, as he called their home. She did not die of a broken heart, but married Sam D. McGrady. It is not known what happened to him, but Tiana died of pneumonia in 1838 and was buried at a place called Wilson's Rock. Her remains were later interred in the National Cemetery at Fort Gibson, Oklahoma. Her tombstone carries her name as "Talahina," because a newspaper reporter misinterpreted her Indian name, which is similar to the Choctaw word "Talihini," meaning "railroad."

In 1856, when a friend mentioned placing flowers on Tiana's grave, tears came to Houston's eyes. He loved her, he said, and always remembered those days. But Texas called, and Houston came, applying for a land grant as a "married man," a condition that produced more acreage.

His relationship with Anna Raguet shows something of his problems of courtship. Half his age, Anna seemed to see Houston as a commanding public figure but held him off as a suitor and teased him while remaining at a distance. As he awkwardly courted the younger woman, Houston confided the almost unsurmountable problems facing the emerging republic. He sent her gifts, among them a snuff box and a horse.

Anna greatly admired Houston, his feats, and his position. She accepted the attention, but not from a romantic viewpoint. She always owed him several letters. However, she was filled with patriotism for Texas; and Houston was a part of this emotion.

Anna wrote poems. In December 1835, she wrote:

Shall these rich vales, these splendid sires
E'er brook oppression's reign?
No! If the despot's iron hand
Must here a sceptre wave,
Raz'd be those glories from the land,
And be the land our grave.

Small wonder she would admire a warrior. A portion of another poem from her notebook reads:

To arms! To arms! Let each firm hand
Its battle sabre wield.
The oppressor comes–but stand;
To Tyrants never yield.

And bloody be his welcome here,
Who would our soil enslave.
This myriad host we cannot fear:
Who would? 'Tis not the brave.

And Houston returned the compliment in poetry.

Should I return from well-fought fields
I'll bring again thy warrior's shield
And at thy feet I'll proudly yield
The laurels won for thee.

What woman could resist that sort of testimonial, particularly when he sent her the laurels he won at San Jacinto?

Anna wrote in her diary, "On the 2nd of March the Texans declared their Independence–the anniversary of the birth day of Genl Houston. A remarkable coincidence.

"On the 21st of April, 1836, was gained by Genl Sam Houston and his brave followers the glorious victory of San Jacinto. This gallant Commander in 'war excelling as well as peace' dashed bravely in advance of his little band fronting the Mexican army. Santa Ana taken prisoner Apr. 23rd."

Four months after San Jacinto, she wrote her father from Philadelphia:

"I hope our gallant General has recovered. Tell him I think he has slighted me. He might have deigned to write to me, but I suppose he has so many more interesting correspondents that I am entirely forgotten. I should like to tell him all the compliments I hear paid him. I am loudest in his praise. I hope he will retrieve himself in my estimation by writing. It would not do to tell him a lady asked me the other day if he was not a ferocious, savage-looking fellow. She was quite surprised when I described him as a handsome man, accomplished and fascinating in his manners."

She followed by asking about "our dear friend Dr. Irion."

Answering a letter addressed to "My Charming friend" in which she described the architecture of Philadelphia, Houston wrote "I admire taste as well as fine feeling in a Lady." He hoped that young lawyers moving to Texas would not rob Texas "of her richest Ruby, and fairest flower. . . ." He concluded by saying, "You made me a Hero. I will place my laurels at your disposition, if you will not trample on them. The Civic wreath I must take care of when the next Laurels are won . . . ."

By this time Houston was president of the new republic. He called on Anna to collect and preserve his papers, which were being scattered among various departments. Some were lost in a burglary of his office. Since there was no seal, Houston detached a cuff link from his sleeve and used it as a personal seal on state papers. It pictured a collared dog's head, encircled by an olive wreath over a script capital H. Above the dog's head was a cock with the motto: "TRY ME!"

He then asked Anna to help design a national seal of the Republic. Her seal was a five-point star at the center of a circular disk with the words "THE REPUBLIC OF TEXAS" around the outer edges. In 1839, under the next administration, a laurel of oak and olive leaves was added. That seal is similar to the present official seal of the State of Texas.

In February 1837 he told Anna that a Mexican army menaced invasion. "I do not wish that it should require so many battles to make a 'True Knight' of Miss Anna. These broken bones are a painful price to endure for greatness."

Just as Houston fell for Anna Raguet, so did many other younger suitors. For a time there were various reports that Anna was to be married. Houston agonized each time. She did not like the new town of Houston and would not visit it. He teased that he might look out for a "spare rib."

Houston continued to long for a wife. He wrote to his good friend Dr. Robert Irion, "My only wish is to see the country happy, at peace, and retire to the Red Lands, get a fair, sweet 'wee wifie,' as Burnes says, and pass the balance of my sinful life in ease and comfort (if I can) . . . ."

He noted that many fine ladies were expected at the new town of Houston on the first anniversary of San Jacinto, but "We will not have the fair Miss Anna there, for she has a great aversion to 'Houston,' and I dare not invite her, or I would wait upon her and ask her to a 'Levee' of the President. How sad the scenes must be at my Leevees. No Mrs. H—— there, and many who will attend can claim fair dames as theirs!!! You know the old adage, 'every dog', etc. etc. My day may come!"

A month later he called Anna "the Belle of New Orleans"

after her visit there. She had referred to "your Miss Barker." She had met another young woman who also had received a Houston memento from the Battle of San Jacinto. He apparently had to scramble for an answer. "When I saw her, she presented to me a beautiful image so much resembling Miss Raguet that really I thought the world was compelled to admire and wished to see her," he wrote.

"Miss B. had received a trifle from the spoils of San Jacinto when she was kind enough to dispense with Prudery and visit a soldier, prostrate and suffering under the influence of his destiny. If I admired Miss Barker, it was because I admired others to whom she bore a striking resemblance. Is she not beautiful? Tell me!"

He added that if Miss Anna were getting married, he would play the part of God Father, to tell posterity. She continued to tease him about his Miss Barker.

A pamphlet circulating at that time accused Houston of cowardice and opium use at San Jacinto. In June she wrote to say that the effort to defame Houston "will have a contrary effect . . . .the efforts of all these aspiring demagogues cannot rob from the brow of the hero of San Jacinto laurels so justly earned–His fame is fixed."

By this time Houston's romantic efforts were becoming serious. In a letter to her he said he had received a beautiful ring with instructions "that I should present it to the most lovely, intelligent, and excellent single lady in Texas. Who will get it? I have not made public the conditions on which it is to be disposed of. If I should find any difficulty, I will just have it advertised in the Telegraph and receive sealed proposals."

Her letters, he said, were "like angel visits."

In February 1838 he wrote that Jefferson Wright, known as the artist of the Republic, had completed his portrait "for your father's parlor, until I have as good a masion [*sic*]. It is said to be best likeness ever taken of me."

On May 15, 1838, he wrote that "I will in a few days write again and present to you some matters of consideration which I deem due to myself, as a man whose only glory is to wear the mantle of unsoiled honor and untarnished truth . . . ." He also noted that he wasn't getting tight and that "I never drinks nothing."

Apparently he planned to send her a memorial of divorce he had submitted to the General Assembly of the State of Tennessee and a judgment by a Texas judge declaring his divorce from Eliza Allen was legal. Someone had told Anna his divorce was a fraud.

On June 4, after she had questioned its validity, he wrote: ". . . had I addressed you or sought to win your love when I was aware that the same must have taken place at the expense of your happiness, and pride, and peace, and honor, in life I must have acknowledged myself a 'lily liver'd wretch.' I was honest. I was devoted!"

In 1833 Mexican law did not allow divorce. In 1837 the process would ordinarily have been conducted through the Congress, but Houston had managed it by presidential decree. A judge declared the divorce legal, but a question remained in Anna's mind. From that point on, the romance was over.

Though Houston continued to hold out hope, the long shadow of his tragic marriage to Eliza Allen had doomed his hopes of life with Anna Raguet. He wrote Dr. Irion from Nashville in July 1839: "My love scrapes here are pretty well over . . . .Fine girls here are very abundant, but they don't take my eye."

He added, "You have basked this summer in sunshine of Miss Anna's countenance . . . . She is a great woman. I admire her for herself . . . .What is she at? Who will marry her? If she were out of the way, I would be better off in my feelings."

He and Anna remained friends and continued to correspond. He sent presents and recommended several young bachelors to her. Nearly all his letters mentioned his good friend Irion. Sometimes the doctor himself delivered them to Anna. And on March 30, 1840, Dr. Robert A. Irion and Miss Anna Raguet were married in Nacogdoches. The couple named their first son Sam Houston Irion.

Houston was not crushed by the end of his romance with Anna, for in January 1840 he had told Irion he planned to be married. "She is a 'clever Gal' and I hope to show her to my friends as such, in March at furthest."

Houston had been in Alabama on a horse-buying trip in the summer of 1839 when he met Margaret Moffette Lea, daughter of Temple and Nancy Lea. Marquis James said that Margaret was in the crowd on the docks in New Orleans in 1836 when the battered hero of San Jacinto was brought ashore more dead than alive. She, too, was drawn to this man who had so altered the course of history. And three years later, when Houston looked at the tall beauty with the fair skin, violet eyes, brown hair with golden ringlets dangling over her forehead, he forgot the earlier romances altogether.

Houston waited for Margaret in Texas, but her mother came and said the wedding, if there was to be one, would be in Alabama. As the orchestra prepared to play, the Lea menfolk said the wedding could not continue unless the bridegroom told why he had separated from Eliza Allen. It was a subject he had never disclosed, he told them politely, and they could "call off the fiddlers." They relented and the May 9, 1840, ceremony took place. The newlyweds moved into the house he had prepared for Anna Raguet at Cedar Point, on Galveston Bay.

Asked why, in light of Houston's excesses, she risked unhappiness by linking her destiny with his, Margaret replied that "not only had he won my heart, but I conceived the idea that I could be the means of reforming him. And I mean to devote myself to the work."

She did, and quite successfully. After he married Margaret Lea, Houston was baptized in the Baptist Church, saying the fishes downstream would surely be polluted by the washing of his sins. He gave temperance lectures. When they were apart, he wrote Margaret a brief summation of the Sunday sermons. He wrote often, always professing his love for her.

The couple had eight children: Sam Houston, Nancy Elizabeth, Margaret Lea, Mary William, Antoinette Power, Andrew Jackson, William Rogers, and Andrew Temple. Margaret apparently forgave him for his former transgressions, for the name of one of their children was the same as that of Tiana Rogers' brother, William.

Upon hearing of Houston's marriage, Gen. Barnard Bee predicted the worst. "I see with great pain the marriage of Genl. Houston to Miss Lea! I had hoped it would never have been consummated. In all my intercourse with life I have never met with an individual more totally disqualified for domestic happiness."

Bee was wrong, for Houston's marriage marked the beginning of the happiest part of his life. He was the model husband–devoted, caring, solicitous and a model of sobriety. As he had said all along, all he ever wanted was a "Wee Wifie."

A Different Santa Anna

Texans have had few kind words for Antonio López de Santa Anna Pérez de Lebron, but the "Napoleon of the West" squared a debt with Dr. James A.E. Phelps in a display of a human side seldom reported.

General Santa Anna was alternately a hero and villain in his own country. He was cited for bravery in battle. He defeated a Spanish invasion, overthrew the government in the name of liberalism, and lost a leg in a battle attempting to repel the French in the 1838 Pastry War.

On the other side, he repudiated democracy and installed himself as dictator. He was ruthless to opposition; and many Mexican villages felt the same harsh wrath he unleashed upon the Alamo, San Patricio, and Goliad. His generalship was disastrous to Mexico. He ordered his armies to retreat after his capture at San Jacinto. He cost his country a lot of real estate by losing the Battle of Buena Vista to Gen. Zachary Taylor and the Battle of Cerro Gordo to Gen. Winfield Scott. He briefly returned to power and promptly sold the United States another chunk of Arizona in the Gadsden Purchase before his overthrow. He rose to power five times before his death in 1876.

He was a vain, pompous man with a reputation for more amorous conquests than military ones. To Texans, he was a man completely without honor. But this story indicates that their assessment was not altogether true:

It began with Santa Anna's capture the day following San Jacinto, when Texians found him hiding in the woods near the battlefield in the clothing of a peasant soldier. He was exposed when his captured troops hailed him as "*El Presidente.*" He was taken before Sam Houston, who declared him a prisoner of war despite cries from the soldiers to execute their hated enemy.

But Houston soon left for New Orleans for treatment of his shattered leg. The rabble Texas Army wanted to lynch the Mexican general, but he was taken aboard various Texas Navy vessels for safekeeping while the Texas Congress negotiated a treaty with him. The Texians sent him ashore, where he had justifiable fear for his life, especially after Mexico rejected the treaty.

He and several of his officers were told they were going to Goliad to be executed on the grounds where James Fannin's men had been shot. Instead he was moved to Columbia and placed in the plantation home of Dr. James A.E. Phelps, Orozimbo, where there were few hecklers. James "Snuffy" Creighton, former Corpus Christi teacher and author of a book on the history of Brazoria County, recounted the story of a woman visitor who brought the general a bottle of poisoned wine. Dr. Phelps pumped out his stomach and saved his life.

Santa Anna was back in power in 1842, when a company of

Texians invaded Mexico in an attempt to avenge Mexican raids on South Texas. However, of the 276 who set out, many would not survive. Some died in the battle for the town of Mier. Seventeen were executed after drawing black beans at Salado. Others died in captivity.

One of those captured was Orlando Phelps, son of the doctor who had treated Santa Anna. He was ill, Creighton noted, and in prison when Santa Anna learned of him and ordered him sent to Mexico City for treatment by Santa Anna's personal physician. When young Phelps recovered, he was sent back to New Orleans with the Mexican leader's best regards and $500 in gold.

The Phelps family never shared the dark Texas view of General Santa Anna.

John Files Tom

No, she told her stepson, he couldn't go to war. He had no warm clothing.

Young John Files Tom was upset and disappointed over this because his father was shouldering his rifle and preparing to march away with Stephen F. Austin to attack the Mexicans at San Antonio. As the oldest son, John felt he should be in the war, too, though he was only sixteen. His father, William, said it was all right with him, but he would have to get his stepmother's permission to go.

That's when a neighbor girl came to the rescue. She donated her wool knit stockings to the cause. And that's how part of John Tom's uniform in the Texas Army came to be girls' stockings.

He and his father arrived in Gonzales October 10, 1835, a week after the opening skirmish of the revolution. They followed Austin, James Bowie and James W. Fannin, Jr., along with ninety other men, to San Antonio.

Young Tom was a member of an artillery team under Lt. Col. James C. Neill during the Siege of Bexar. After Cós capitulated, Tom and his father joined the rest of the Texas Army in Fortress Alamo. But there they found few supplies and little food.

After William Barret Travis arrived, the Toms left with Neill. They had intended to see that their family was safe, but they soon joined Sam Houston's army at Gonzales as it began its retreat toward the border. The elder Tom was assigned to protect settlers in the retreat as news of the massacres at San Patricio, Agua Dulce, San Antonio, Goliad, Refugio, and Victoria reached the colonists.

Johnny Tom was still with Houston April 21, 1836, when the Texians surprised the sleeping Mexican camp and destroyed Santa Anna's army in eighteen minutes of savage revenge at San Jacinto. But Tom saw little of it. On the first charge, a musket ball smashed his leg below the left knee, and he fell into the high grass of a hog wallow. He packed soft mud around the crushed bones to slow the bleeding. The battle moved on, and he fainted from loss of blood.

After the battle a report of casualties was drawn up for Houston. Others in his troop had seen Tom fall and reported him dead. He is listed as killed on Houston's official report.

Two friends, John Milton Swisher, also sixteen, and Louis Clemens, returned to where he had fallen and carried him to Lorenzo de Zavala's home nearby for treatment. He recovered, but he would walk with a limp for the rest of his life.

John Files Tom lived to be an Indian fighter, sheriff of Guadalupe County from 1856 to 1860, and captain of a Texas Ranger company for frontier defense during the War Between the States. He was elected to the Texas legislature in 1874. He and other legislators defied Governor Edmund J. Davis and the Reconstruction government by taking control of the state Capitol when the defeated governor refused to leave. A battle was averted only when President U.S. Grant advised Davis to withdraw from office.

Likely nobody ever teased Tom about wearing female stockings.

Their Blood Ran Red, Too

The first Texian blood shed in the Texas Revolution was red. The man who shed it was black. That man was Sam McCullough, Jr.

The Handbook of Texas quotes W.P. Zuber as saying that McCullough was born in Abbeyville, South Carolina, in 1810, a free Negro and the son of Sam McCullough, Sr. Zuber said the McCulloughs came to Texas in May 1835. Others have reported that McCullough was the former slave of George Morse Collinsworth, who granted him his freedom. However, it is more likely that Zuber was correct and that the senior McCullough was white, for he came from Montgomery County, Alabama, with his son and three daughters. He received a headright certificate for one-third of a league of land in Jackson County.

When Collinsworth recruited his troop of men at Matagorda

in October 1835, Sam McCullough, Jr., was one of them. He was also one of the sixty-six who signed the Victoria compact of loyalty to the Mexican Constitution of 1824. Apparently he had learned to read and write, a privilege not often available to blacks, as such instruction to slaves was illegal in the South.

When Collinsworth's Texians captured fortress La Bahía on October 9-10, their only casualty was McCullough, who sustained a wound in the shoulder. He recovered and was able to participate in the Storming of Bexar in December 1835, but the wound would trouble him the rest of his life.

Although Congress had passed a law prohibiting Negro freedmen from residing in the Republic, he and his family were exempted from its provisions and the Republic of Texas granted him one league of land for his service. McCullough fought in the Plum Creek Fight against the Comanches in 1840. He went on a spy mission to San Antonio after Mexican Gen. Adrian Woll captured that city in 1842. One of his sons, William, served in the Confederate Army, and McCullough himself was active in the Texas Veterans Association until his death in 1893.

The role of McCullough and other African-Americans in early Texas has been largely ignored, but a number of black men took part in revolutionary battles. One of them, Hendrick Arnold, was a key figure in the capture of Bexar in December 1835 and was a close friend of the famous scout Erastus "Deaf" Smith. At Bexar, Smith was scout for the group led by Ben Milam, while Arnold was scout for a contingent led by F.W. Johnson. When it was time for the move, Arnold was not there; the troops had such confidence in his scouting ability, they would not attack until his return.

Smith was married to Guadalupe Ruíz Durán, a native of Bexar and a descendant of Canary Islanders who had come to San Antonio in the 1700s. To protect her, he tried to remain neutral as the threat of revolution grew. However, when he sought to enter San Antonio in December 1835, Mexican sentries shot off his *sombrero* and chased him toward the rebel camp. Soon after that he joined the rebel forces.

Arnold was married to Smith's stepdaughter and served with Smith's spy company at the Battle of San Jacinto. Some said that Smith, who spoke Spanish and looked like a Mexican, wandered about the Mexican camps while Arnold played the part of a runaway slave. Arnold received a grant of 640 acres of land for his service at Bexar.

Mention is made of another African-American at San Jacinto. The little band that struck up the bawdy tune "Will You Come to the Bower" as the battle opened included a huge black man known to history only as Dick, playing the drums.

Greenberry Logan was born a slave in Kentucky in 1799 and came to Texas from Missouri as a freedman in 1831. He received one-fourth of a league of land on Chocolate Bayou in Brazoria County, where he operated a blacksmith's shop. He took part in the Battle of Velasco in 1832. In 1834 he purchased a slave named Caroline, set her free, and married her. For a time they operated a boardinghouse in Columbia.

Logan joined the Texas Army and fought in the Battle of Concepción on October 28, 1835; he then participated in the Siege of Bexar and was wounded in the arm in the assault and capture of San Antonio, crippling him for life. Thirty-seven prominent Texians, including Henry Austin, cousin of Stephen F. Austin, signed Logan's petition requesting the right to stay in Texas as a freedman. He received a league of land as a disabled veteran of the Texas Revolution. He had land in Brown and Callahan counties and had filed for another grant in Zavala County in 1881, the last recorded mention of him.

Then there was a clerk in Francis DeSauque's San Antonio store in March 1836. Only in recent years has he had the identity of a name–John. He had no last name. It is not known whether he was a freedman or a slave. Yet he fought to the death as a rifleman alongside the other heroes in the Alamo and lies buried with his comrades in an anonymous grave. He fought and died for a freedom he may never have had.

A fellow defender was Joe, Col. William Barret Travis' slave, who also defended the Alamo with his rifle. When the Mexicans attacked, Joe accompanied Travis to the wall where the Texian leader fired his shotgun into the mass of attackers and fell backwards, a bullet wound in his head.

William Fairfax Gray said a Mexican general leaped upon Travis, who ran him through with his sword, and they both died. Joe ran to the chapel and fired more shots before Mexican troops entered and allowed him to surrender. He was released and accompanied Susanna Dickinson to Sam Houston with a warning. He is said to be buried in Austin.

A third black in the Alamo was named Charlie. This account appears in *A Mexican Sergeant's Recollections of the Alamo & San Jacinto* by Francisco Becerra:

With every thrust, Charlie parried with the frightened officer. After several passes, the soldiers broke into laughter.

A black woman named Betty, who had been a cook for James Bowie, said she was in the kitchen after the attack when a group of Mexican soldiers came in. Charlie tried to hide but was pulled out. The officer in charge of the detachment was a small man; and when the soldiers lunged at Charlie with bayonets, he grabbed the officer and held him as a shield.

With every thrust, Charlie parried with the frightened officer. After several passes, the soldiers broke into laughter. The officer didn't find his situation amusing, but he promised Charlie his life would be saved if he put him down. Charlie complied and became one of the few survivors of the Alamo, probably escaping his bondage in Mexico.

Another black man deserves mention as a hero from the days of the Republic. As a slave he had a single name–Griffin. It isn't a name that rings familiar from the history books, yet he fought as valiantly and died as heroically as any of the storied Texian leaders.

The revolution had been over for six years, but the fighting was not finished. In September 1842, Gen. Adrian Woll led 1,000 Mexican troops into San Antonio. The courts and city government were in session. Judges, officials, and clerks were captured, along with the city's merchants, militiamen, and other leading citizens.

One of these was Samuel Augustus Maverick. He had been held there earlier, when General Cós occupied the city in 1835, but he escaped and subsequently scouted for the Texians retaking the village. He was elected an Alamo delegate to Washington-on-the-Brazos and was one of the signers of the Declaration of Independence. For that reason he was not in the Alamo to die with his comrades.

As threats of Mexican invasion grew in 1842, he sent his family to live with friends near La Grange. When San Antonio was taken, Maverick's slave, Griffin, hurried to tell Mary Maverick of her husband's capture. She suggested that he return to San Antonio and pass himself off as a runaway. He would be free to move about and might be able to free his master. She promised him his freedom if he would do so.

In her memoirs Mary Maverick said he jumped at the chance and told her, "[A]s for freedom, I do not want any more than I have. Master has always treated me more like brother than a slave."

Taking a gun, a mule, and money, he was on his way in a short time. He overtook and joined Capt. Nicholas Mosby Dawson and fifty-three men from Fayette County. They were rushing to aid Mathew Caldwell, whose 252 men were standing off General Woll from behind an embankment at Salado Creek, six miles east of San Antonio, now near the edge of Fort Sam Houston.

Within the sound of that battle, Mexican infantry, cavalry, and artillery surrounded Dawson's men in an exposed mesquite grove on open prairie. At first the Texians, with their long rifles, repulsed the attacks; however, Woll pulled his men back out of rifle range and his artillery raked the Texas force with grape. Then his cavalry and infantry charged. The assault swept forward, and the fighting was hand-to-hand, knife-to-sword, lance-to-rifle butt.

Dawson stood up, waved a blanket, and attempted to surrender his men. He was shot down. He rose again. The firing continued. He ordered the men to fight to the end. Thirty-six Texians were killed, fifteen wounded were taken prisoner, and two escaped. Thirty Mexicans were killed and more than sixty wounded.

There were many heroes, but Griffin, big and strong, stood out. He emptied his rifle and started swinging it, clubbing the enemy right and left until the stock shattered. Finally he was swarmed under by a wave of troops and was killed.

Mrs. Maverick wrote:

> Our poor Griffin was with Dawson and was slain. He would go into the battle with them, and, though offered quarter several times, refused because he was thinking of his master, now a prisoner and too, of his young masters, William and Andres, now possibly slain [with Caldwell]; the desire for vengeance seized his brave and trusty soul, and he wanted to kill every Mexican he could.
>
> He was a man of powerful frame, and he possessed the courage of the African lion. And this faithful and devoted African performed prodigies that day. . . . When his ammunition became useless, because of the proximity of the enemy, he fought with the butt end of his gun, and when the gun was broken, he wrenched a limb from a mesquite tree and did battle with that until death closed his career. He received more than one mortal wound before he ceased fighting.
>
> Mexican Col. Carasco himself afterwards told Mr. Maverick that he had witnessed feats performed by "that valiant black man," and he pronounced Griffin the bravest man he had ever seen.

Samuel Maverick wrote his wife: "The slaughter of Capt. Dawson's company from your neighborhood I truly deplore and my poor Griffin, God knows I feel his death as the hardest piece of fortune we have suffered in Texas. Poor faithful, brave boy! I owe thee a monument and a bitter tear of regret for the fall. I mourn thee as a true and faithful friend and a brother – worthy dear brother in arms!"

Maverick, who was taken to prison in Mexico along with fifty-two others, was elected to the Texas Congress during his imprisonment. He was released in 1843. Though he often spoke of a monument, he never built it. He was known as a man who was close with a dollar.

The African-American who may have had the greatest influence on Texas history was a young mulatto woman, Emily, who belonged to Col. James Morgan. Morgan, to circumvent the Mexican law, had nominally "freed" his slaves, signing them instead to a ninety-nine-year term as indentured servants.

He was away with his command on Galveston Island, so the story goes, when the Mexican army appeared near Harrisburg. Morgan's servants, including Emily, were loading a flatboat. Santa Anna saw her and admired the tall, long-haired, "very comely Latin looking" woman of about twenty. The president ordered her assigned as a servant in his marquee, or presidential tent. An inveterate womanizer, Santa Anna had staged a fake wedding in San Antonio to convince the mother of one young girl that his intentions were honorable. He saw no need of such formalities with Emily, who had no choice in the matter.

William Bollaert was an English ethnologist who talked with James Morgan during a visit to Texas in 1838. In *The Day of San Jacinto,* Frank X. Tolbert quoted Bollaert as saying Emily was in Santa Anna's presidential quarters at 4:30 P.M., when the alarm of the Texian attack was given. According to Bollaert, it was probably due to Emily's influence that the Texians won the battle.

"She detained Santanna so long," he said, "that order could not be restored readily again."

Some historians believe the story of Emily Morgan and her part in the revolution is an interesting piece of fiction, a ribald tale that Texans like to tell because it shows Santa Anna "caught with his pants down." After all, they point out, no Mexican reports of Emily exist. Col. José Enrique de la Peña, Ramón Martinez Caro, and others who criticized the Mexican leader would surely have added an afternoon tryst to the list of his shortcomings if one had taken place. Nevertheless, the story, like Travis' line, has become a part of Texas lore.

In recent years the indisputable contributions of Sam McCullough, Hendrick Arnold, Greenberry Logan, and other African-Americans have gained some recognition. Unfortunately, many deeds of other black Texians are probably lost to history. But the story of Emily Morgan, though it may not be widely recognized, will live on, for it is Emily Morgan who is immortalized in story and song as "The Yellow Rose of Texas."

And Griffin does have his memorial. It is on Monument Hill, overlooking the Colorado River high above La Grange, where he and the other victims of the massacre lie in a common grave. The memorial honors two groups, Dawson's men and the prisoners executed after drawing the black beans on the Mier expedition.

Griffin—a Texas hero—earned equality the hard way.

¡Recuerden!

Gen. Antonio López de Santa Anna's troops were startled as a Texas Army seemingly rose out of the ground a couple hundred yards away. The tall *gringos* had approached in silence without being seen. Now they were coming at a trot after leaving the cover of a swale. A drum was beating, fifes were playing, and the earth was shaken by cannon shot. The faces of the grimy figures, who wore brown and black buckskin or homespun rags, could be seen as they sighted down their rifles to fire. Faces were contorted with rage, and they were screaming an unintelligible *grito.*

In his final instructions Gen. Sam Houston had cautioned his men not to forget the Alamo and "Labadie," as the Texians called La Bahía. Col. Sidney Sherman is generally credited with spreading the cry "Remember the Alamo! Remember Goliad!" up and down the lines. It spread like wildfire and terrified the Mexican troops behind the barricade of saddles, foodstuffs, and brush.

The furious giants, now crashing the barricades and swinging rifle butts and Bowie knives, were seeking a terrible revenge for the deaths of their friends and relatives at the Alamo and at Goliad. Suddenly, over the din of battle, amid the terrible screams, came a booming roar: *"¡Recuerden el Álamo! ¡Recuerden La Bahía!"* The deep bass voice was that of Antonio Menchaca, sergeant in Capt. Juan Seguín's troop of Tejanos.

For too many years Anglo-Saxon historians ignored the contributions of Seguín's Tejanos and other native-born Texians. The clash at Gonzales, where the opening shots of the revolution were fired, became the Lexington of Texas, but historians did not record that the Tejanos at Victoria did the same thing. They stood firm in their "Round House" fortress and refused to surrender their cannon to Capt. Manuel Sabriego, who had been ordered there by the commandante at Goliad. Strangely, this act of defiance has never received recognition, possibly because the affair at Gonzales was the one that opened hostilities.

After the Battle of Gonzales, Austin was elected commander-in-chief of the Federal Army of Texas. Juan Seguín, a twenty-nine-year-old *Bejareno,* was commissioned a captain in that army and raised a company of mounted Tejanos, including his brothers-in-law, Manuel and Salvador Flores. A contingent of Tejanos under Placido Benavides, the *alcalde* of Victoria, joined George Collinsworth's volunteers in capturing La Bahía, the Presidio of Goliad, on October 9-10, 1835. Seguín and Benavides raised two companies, totaling some 150 men, with Benavides deferring to the *Bejareno* as commander. Their men were couriers, scouts, spies and foragers during the Siege of Bexar and fought with distinction during the Storming of Bexar and the Battle of San Jacinto.

Immediately after the Storming of Bexar, William B. Dewees, a participant in the battle, said, "Our army owe many thanks to the brave inhabitants of San Antonio, who, although native Mexicans, still ranked themselves on the side of liberty, and fought bravely with the Texan forces. Were all the Mexicans such ardent lovers of liberty as the citizens of San Antonio, we should not now be left to fight our battles alone."

Many of the Nordics, especially those who had been in the state for some time, got along well with their Tejano neighbors. Jim Bowie, Philip Dimmitt, and Erastus "Deaf" Smith, for example, were married to Mexican women and had close ties to the Tejano communities.

Some, however, did not like or trust the native-born Texians. For some reason Col. Francis W. Johnson, who assumed command of the Federalist army after Ben Milam was killed in the assault on San Antonio, did not mention the Tejanos in his report of the campaign. Tejanos at Agua Dulce and San Patricio, where ten fought and four died, were likewise slighted.

Even so, Tejanos probably would have played a much larger role in the revolution if it had not been for the attitude of Governor Henry Smith. After the General Council, the provisional governing body, passed an ordinance on December 10, 1835, allowing "all white men and Mexicans opposed to a Central Government" to vote, Smith claimed that Tejano attitudes could not be accurately tested. "I consider that they who are not for us, must be against us," he said. He did not trust the inhabitants of Bexar, who he believed had not shown friendship to the Texas cause. He singled out the San Antonians as untrustworthy even after they had fought alongside their Nordic comrades.

"In many instances they have been known to fight against us," he said. "I therefore consider that they should neither be entitled to our respect or favor and as such, not entitled to a seat in our councils." Still later he said it was "bad policy to fit out, or trust Mexicans in any matter connected with our government; as I am well satisfied that we will in the end find them inimical and treacherous."

He believed Tejanos would fight against Centralist tyranny or for the liberal Constitution of 1824. But he did not believe they would fight for Texas independence. When Smith's sentiments became known after the Storming of Bexar and when many of the later arrivals were unable to recognize the difference between Tejanos and other Mexicans, some native Texans withdrew to neutrality. Others became Centralists and took to the field as Texas Tories. They were invaluable as scouts, spies and militia cavalrymen for Gen. José Urréa's invading army as it swept up the coast, crushing San Patricio, Refugio, and La Bahía.

Still, many continued to fight for the Federalist cause. The war became a joint effort of Nordics and Tejanos to win a revolution against overwhelming odds. Eight Tejanos died in the Alamo. Four of Placido Benavides' men died at Agua Dulce and San Patricio. An unknown number of Tejanos died with James Fannin at Goliad. And Juan Seguín's company fought with great courage at San Jacinto. Another company of his men helped escort civilians over flooded rivers in the Runaway Scrape as terrified civilians hurried to get out of the path of Santa Anna's army. But it was the logistical support the Tejanos gave–horses and cattle and other foodstuffs–that was crucial to the success of the revolution.

"Had the Tejanos joined forces with the Centralists," Refugio historian Hobart Huson wrote, "it is entirely likely that General Houston would have been unable to muster the strength [he had] at San Jacinto."

Menchaca, Seguín's second sergeant whose voice boomed over that battle, was described as a man six feet two inches tall, with a massive build, fair complexion, and blue eyes. He was also a *Bejareno*, a member of a family that had suffered greatly during the Mexican revolution against Spain. In 1830 he became friends with James Bowie.

In his memoirs Menchaca told of returning to San Antonio on December 20, 1835, after the Storming of Bexar. He was greeted by a tearful Bowie, who was still mourning the death of his wife. That evening, Menchaca said, Bowie introduced him to Travis and "Col. Niel" at the Alamo. Menchaca told of the arrival of Davy Crockett and fourteen young men from Tennessee on January 13, 1836. Crockett, Bowie, Travis, "Niell," and all the other officers put guards around the city because they feared the return of the Mexican army, he said.

Menchaca wrote his memoirs many years after the events, and the old soldier's memory was probably clouded by time. Archie McDonald wrote that Travis had left San Antonio by December 10. Bill Groneman, in *Alamo Defenders*, said Crockett arrived February 9.

"On the 10 February, 1836," Menchaca wrote, "A. [he spoke of himself in the third person by his initials or "he"] was invited to a ball given by officers in honor of Crockett, and was asked to invite all the principal ladies in the city to it . . . . While at the ball, at about 1 o'clock, A.M. of the 11th, a courier, sent by Placido Benavides, arrived, from Camargo. . . ."

The courier asked for Seguín. When told Seguín was not there, he asked for Menchaca and gave Menchaca the message that Santa Anna was marching on the city with 13,000 troops. As Menchaca was reading the letter, Bowie came to see it and then called to Travis to read it; but, Menchaca wrote, "Travis said that at that moment he could not stay to read letters, for he was dancing with the most beautiful lady in San Antonio."

After Bowie insisted, "Travis came and . . . then said, it will take thirteen thousand men from the Presidio de Rio Grande to this place thirteen or fourteen days to get here; this is the 4th day. Let us dance to-night and tomorrow we will make provisions for our defense."

The ball continued until 7:00 A.M.

After hearing Benavides' warning, Menchaca said, he followed advice from Bowie and Seguín and left San Antonio to take his wife to safety. At Gonzales he joined fourteen other Tejanos from San Antonio. In the meantime Seguín, who had been sent from the Alamo to seek help from James Fannin at Goliad, received word from Fannin that he was unable to respond. Seguín then went to Gonzales to meet with Sam Houston. There he organized a company of twenty-four men. Menchaca, who had accompanied Bowie on a tour of the United States, signed on as interpreter.

On the morning of April 21, Houston's retreating army was camped near the San Jacinto River. Word came that "Deaf" Smith, following Houston's orders, had burned the bridge over Vince's Bayou. In his memoirs Seguín wrote that he and Gen. Thomas Rusk shared dinner in Seguín's tent. After dinner, Rusk asked Seguín if the Mexicans "were not in the custom of taking a siesta at that hour. I answered in the affirmative adding, moreover, that in such cases they kept their main and advanced guards under arms with a line of sentinels. General Rusk observed that he thought so too, however the moment seemed to him favorable to attack the enemy. He added: 'Do you feel like fighting?' I answered that I was always ready and willing to fight, upon which the general rose, saying: 'Well, let us go.' "

When the battle started, the Mexicans were so surprised they left eleven rows of stacked arms untouched. "The fight lasted two hours and a quarter, when those who were not killed, taken prisoners or wounded, fled in great disorder," Menchaca wrote. The next day Santa Anna was brought in. "Many were in favor of putting him to death. But as he was a Mason and most of the officers were Masons, he was protected." Menchaca and Seguín also belonged to the order.

"The next day a steamboat from Galveston arrived with three hundred men, four guns and provisions. Houston ordered that the provisions be divided into two equal parts, one for his troops and the other for prisoners and wounded," Menchaca reported. The Mexican army was in retreat as Santa Anna had ordered. Colonel Ampudia was allowed to remove the Mexican sick and wounded, and "two men with two horses loaded with roasted meat and gourds of water for the wounded and sick were sent with Filizola [Mexican Gen. Vicente Filisola]."

Menchaca, wounded later in the Woll invasion of San Antonio, became a civic leader in that city and prominent in the affairs of the San Jacinto Veterans Association.

Placido Benavides, who sent the message warning the revolutionaries about the advancing Mexican army, is sometimes known as "the Paul Revere of the Texas Revolution." A native of Reynosa, he and his brothers were colonists in Martín de León's colony that became Guadaloupe Victoria, later shortened to Victoria. He issued land titles, then married Augustina, daughter of the empresario, and eventually took charge of the colony after his father-in-law died.

His land was on Placedo Creek, which may be an English corruption of Placido. Earlier he had built a fortress-like Victoria home, which was a bastion for the community when the Comanches attacked. He was elected *alcalde* of Guadaloupe Victoria in 1834 and won a captaincy in the Texas cavalry for bravery leading his troop in the Storming of Bexar.

On March 2, 1836, Benavides was helping Dr. James Grant round up wild horses near Agua Dulce when Mexican cavalry surrounded the party and killed Grant and twelve others. Benavides escaped, riding hard all the way to Goliad, warning colonists along the way of Gen. José Urréa's approach. He gave Col. James Fannin the last message from Grant and Col. Francis Johnson and then spread the alarm up the coast, allowing hundreds of refugees to escape.

After San Jacinto, Benavides and his family moved away. The family went back to ranch in Victoria County, but Placido Benavides never returned to the land whose independence he helped win. He died in Louisiana in 1837. His nephew Placido settled in Duval County at a railroad stop that came to be known as Benavides Station—later the town of Benavides.

Another noteworthy Tejano family was the Losoya family, also of Bexar. Losoyas were heroes in the Alamo and at San Jacinto. Bernice Strong, librarian at the Daughters of the Republic of Texas Library at the Alamo, felt deeply about them, for the Losoyas' home was within the Alamo compound, on present-day Alamo Plaza. Toríbio Losoya had the unusual distinction of dying for Texas liberty in his own front yard, yet despite the fact that he is listed on the Alamo roll of heroes, he was ignored in *The Handbook of Texas* and in Lon Tinkle's *Thirteen Days to Glory.* And writer James E. Ivey, in a publication of the *Alamo Lore and Myth Organization,* says Walter Lord erred and removed Toríbio Losoya from the rolls in *A Time to Stand.*

Lord confused Toríbio with his uncle, José Domingo Losoya, who is listed among those receiving benefits as a veteran of the Battle of San Jacinto, and drew the conclusion there was no Losoya in the Alamo. But there was.

José Toríbio Losoya was the son of Domingo's older brother, Bentura, and his wife, Concepción Charli. The family moved from Los Adaes settlement in far East Texas when it was ordered evacuated in 1773. When the Bexar missions were secularized, some forty Adaesanos were given land in a drawing. The Losoyas drew a grant that included two houses formerly occupied by Indian Christian neophytes in the southwest corner of the Alamo compound. One of the houses, a part of the Alamo structure proper, was the base for the eighteen-pound cannon. This well could have been the emplacement from which William Barret Travis fired his famous answer to Santa Anna's surrender ultimatum.

Toríbio's family, ardent Federalists, left their home when General Cós took command of the Alamo in the fall of 1835. Toríbio returned as one of Seguín's contingent that participated in the Siege and capture of Bexar in December. And he was among Seguín's volunteers who occupied the Alamo in February 1836 and prepared to meet the full fury of the enraged dictator's army.

This was Toríbio's last trip home. He would never leave. But his mother returned to live across Alamo Plaza for a number of years after the Alamo fell. Toríbio's wife, María Francesca, was the granddaughter of Andres Benites Curier, prominent Indian agent during the years of Spanish rule. Apparently she and their young son, Juan, were among the Alamo survivors.

Toríbio's body was found in the chapel, where Mexican soldiers overwhelmed barricades and killed all within. This brave Tejano's body was dragged out, thrown on the heap, and burned with those of the other Texians.

It is ironic that this native Texian was all but denied a heritage that gave him the purest of Texan credentials. His death as an Alamo hero was verified after the battle by San Antonio Alcalde Francisco Antonio Ruiz and Augustín Barrera. Largely through efforts of Strong and others, in 1986 a statue was erected in his honor on Losoya Street above the River Walk at Paseo del Alamo opposite the Hyatt Regency Hotel in downtown San Antonio.

Toríbio's uncle, José Domingo Losoya, was born a Spanish subject in San Antonio in 1783. Most likely he was a soldier from an early age, for San Antonio was often threatened by Comanche raids, and able-bodied males were accustomed to defending their homes. Domingo was swept up in the Mexican Revolution against Spain and probably was involved in the battles and skirmishes that culminated in the disastrous Battle of Medina in August 1813, when Gen. Joaquín de Arredondo crushed the army of Mexican patriots and American filibusters.

Losoya, like many other San Antonio residents, fled to Louisiana. Listed as Domingo Losana, he was a member of Capt. Jean Louis Buard's Company in the 2nd Division, Louisiana Militia Consolidated. Louisiana Governor William Claiborne noted that many members of the company were survivors of the Medina and Trinity massacres. Other members included Francisco Alvardo, James Bowie, "Reason" Bowie, John D. Bradburn, Richard D. Bradburn, Jose Leal, Rueben Ross, and Samuel Ross. The unit left for New Orleans on the day of Andrew Jackson's famous victory, and therefore arrived too late to fight the British at Chalmette.

Historian Ivey says Losoya returned to San Antonio after Mexico won its independence from Spain. During his long exile he had become familiar with Americans and their language.

In 1834 he received a land grant on the Medina River just west of the point where it joins the San Antonio River, not far from the site of the Battle of Medina. Ivey suspected that he might have used what became known as Losoya's Crossing in his escape and chose that spot for his land grant for sentimental reasons. It was there that the townsite of Losoya was established. Earlier Losoya had owned a lot just south of Alamo Plaza, where he and his young wife, Guadalupe Ramón, lived.

When Santa Anna reversed his liberal stance and backed a dictatorial central government, Federalists in the area began to organize. Domingo joined Juan Seguín's original volunteer company and was accepted into the Texas Army by Gen. Stephen F. Austin on October 22, 1835. Domingo served under James Fannin and James Bowie at the Battle of Concepción and under Bowie in the Grass Fight, an encounter in which some fifty members of the Mexican army were killed during the Siege of Bexar. He participated in the assault on Bexar under Sgt. Manuel Flores, attacking Main Plaza and capturing the Garza House. At that time Domingo Losoya was fifty-three years old and was described as a "good man and an efficient soldier and a true patriot." He joined Sam Houston at Gonzales early in 1836 and served as forage master, collecting food and supplies for the army. It was a critical service, for the army was dreadfully short of everything.

Losoya served at San Jacinto in Seguín's company in the Second Regiment of Texas Volunteers under Col. Sidney Sherman. He received a land patent for his service and died at his ranch at Losoya in 1869. There he is buried, along with his younger friend Enrique Esparza, who was eight years old when he and his brothers and sisters survived the Battle of the Alamo. José Domingo Losoya is another of the overlooked patriots who should receive recognition.

It is unfortunate that the sacrifices and accomplishments of the Hispanic Texians have been slighted. Although recent research has brought them increased recognition, it is sometimes grudging, negative, erroneous, or incomplete. Rudy Acuña, a Chicano historian at California State University, Northridge, compared them to the Vichy French of World War II, a view that seems incomprehensible to anyone acquainted with the Federalist-Centralist conflict. Others have focused their attention on injustices heaped upon them after the revolution.

One widely circulated error concerns Sgt. Manuel Flores, Seguín's brother-in-law who fought alongside José Domingo Losoya at Bexar. Unfortunately, many histories have reported that he turned against Texas and died at the hand of Texas Rangers. As *The Handbook of Texas* points out, they have confused him with another Manuel Flores, the Mexican agent sent to Texas in 1836 and 1839 to instigate Indian wars.

On April 20, 1836, the day before Sgt. Manuel Flores fought for a free Texas at San Jacinto, 1st Lt. Joseph Bonnell of the U.S. Army wrote the following to Gen. Edmund Gaines from Camp Sabine, Louisiana:

". . . . One 'Manuel Flores,' a Mexican, has passed up to the Caddo villages. . . and had been endeavoring to prevail upon the

Caddo Indians to join him, and go against and fight and plunder the white inhabitants of Texas. . . .

"This Manuel Flores passed himself off for a Mexican officer. . . was formerly a trader among the Caddoes; he held a lieutenant's commission in a [Mexican] militia company a few miles distant from Fort Jesup, Louisiana."

That Manuel Flores was killed by Rangers in 1839 in the "Cordova-Flores Incident," in which a group of Mexicans was bringing arms to be used in an Indian uprising they hoped to incite. The Texian Flores and his wife had established a ranch on the south side of the Guadalupe River near the town of Seguín in 1838. Flores fought for Texas again in the spring of 1842 in a force that pursued the army of Rafael Vásquez after Vásquez invaded San Antonio. He received a donation land grant of 640 acres in Zavala County on April 17, 1850, for his service at Bexar and San Jacinto.

Perhaps the story of Juan Seguín himself, summarized by Jesús F. de la Teja in *A Revolution Remembered, the Memoirs and Selected Correspondence of Juan N. Seguín,* best illustrates the confusion and ambivalence that cloud the history of the Tejanos. The Seguíns had been friends to the Texas colonists since the earliest days of Anglo settlement. Juan's father, Don Erasmo Seguín, had helped Moses Austin obtain permission on January 17, 1821, to settle 300 families in Texas. The Seguíns aided the colonists with money and supplies. In March of 1836, as Santa Anna's army advanced, Erasmo Seguín was driving thousands of sheep eastward as food for the fleeing refugees.

Juan Seguín began recruiting troops for the Federalist cause in 1835 and was appointed captain of the regular cavalry under William Barret Travis. He would have perished with Travis if he had not been sent through Santa Anna's lines as a messenger to go plead for help from Col. James Fannin at Goliad. At least six of Seguín's Tejanos died in the Alamo, and historian Hobart Huson believed his company at San Jacinto was several times larger than was officially listed.

A letter Seguín wrote to the Texas State Comptroller in 1874 would seem to reinforce this belief. "You should not think it strange," he wrote, "that of so large company, containing over one hundred men, only over twenty were at the battle of San Jacinto, because Genl. Sam Houston sent Lieutenant Salvador Flores from Gonzales with over forty men to escort the families that were on the farms exposed to the attacks of Indians and which

Santa Ana considered as enemies, and that many previous to our being surrounded at the Alamo had received furloughs from Bowie and Travis in order to look after their families who were exposed to the same dangers."

Seguín's men had several bloody clashes with Santa Anna's cavalry as they fought a rear-guard action covering Houston's retreat. They joined Moseley Baker's men and prevented the *Santanistas* from crossing the Brazos at San Felipe, a move that could have been disastrous for the Texians.

Houston asked the Seguín company to stay and guard the sick at Harrisburg. He may have feared Seguín's Tejanos might be shot by mistake in a pitched battle. Seguín had other ideas:

"If we'd wanted to be camp guards, we would have stayed with our old people and our women and children, who are out there now driving their sheep and cattle toward the United States border. We did not join your army, General, to ride herd on sick folks. We men from Bexar have more grievances to settle with the Santantistas than anyone, for we have suffered the most from them. We want to fight."

Houston agreed. He ordered Seguín's company into the line. Dressed in ragged clothing like the others in Houston's army and wearing white pasteboard in their hats to distinguish them from the Mexicans, the captain and his men helped carry the day.

De la Teja said, "Juan and his men earned Sam Houston's respect at San Jacinto." Years later Houston complimented them, citing Seguín's "brave company in the army of 1836, and his brave and gallant bearing in the battle of San Jacinto, with that of his men."

After San Jacinto, Seguín served as commander of San Antonio. In that capacity, he had the ashes of the Alamo victims buried. He served in the Texas Senate, fought the Comanches, and was mayor of San Antonio. Then his fortunes changed. He made political enemies among the Anglo newcomers and, like many other figures of the day, was involved in land speculation. He suffered financial reverses. He moved to Mexico in 1842 after Mexican leader Rafael Vásquez spread the rumor that Seguín had joined his force occupying San Antonio. Actually, Juan had led a group searching for the invaders.

In Mexico, he wrote in his memoirs, he was given the choice of going to prison or joining Adrian Woll's Mexican army, which captured San Antonio later that year. He joined Woll's force and later fought for Mexico in the Mexican War. Many in Texas branded him a traitor.

However, Sam Houston never wavered in support of his friend. On July 6, 1842, Houston had written to Erasmo Seguín:

> I am aware that you are unhappy in consequence of the absence of your son, Colonel J.N. Seguín, from Bexar. I deplore his absence much. . . . What his motives are for absenting himself from home at this time, I cannot imagine; but you may be assured . . . that I cannot, nor will I ever entertain a suspicion of his fidelity to the Republic of Texas; until I have the most conclusive evidence–and that, I trust I shall never have.
>
> The conduct of Captain Seguín and his brave company . . . have afforded me too much happiness to sacrifice my estimation of his worth and character to idle rumor, or unexplained circumstances.
>
> I pray, Sir, that you will not suppose for one moment, that I will denounce Colonel John N. Seguín, without a most perfect understanding of the circumstances of his absence. I rely upon his honor, his worth, and his chivalry.

By early 1848 Seguín had decided to try to return to Texas. In February, Texas Mounted Volunteer Capt. John A. Veatch reported to President Mirabeau Lamar that Seguín had asked permission to bring his family back home. "He said he will return to Texas and risk consiquences. . . ," Veatch said.

Seguín also wrote to seek Houston's help, and by the end of the year he and his family were back in San Antonio. In spite of the charges of disloyalty against him, his political career was not over. He was elected justice of the peace in largely Hispanic Bexar County in 1852 and also was the featured Tejano and a member of the platform-writing committee in the formation of the Bexar County Democratic Party. After the Civil War, the Seguín family moved back to Mexico. Juan Seguín died in Nuevo Laredo on August 27, 1890.

Despite his participation in politics in the 1850s, de la Teja says, Seguín must have felt increasingly alienated during his later years as the English-speaking, Anglo-American domination of Texas increased. Even so, he was recognized as a revolutionary hero, and his writings show no bitterness or regret. Perhaps Seguín's own words in remarks at the end of his memoirs speak for him best:

> I have related my participation in Woll's expedition and have only to say, that Neither I nor any of my posterity will ever have reason to blush for it.
>
> During my military career, I can proudly assert, that I never

deviated from the line of duty, that I never shed, nor caused to be shed, human blood unnecessarily; that I never insulted, by word or deed, a prisoner; and that, in the fulfilment of my duty, I always drew a distinction between my obligations, as a soldier on the battle-field, and, as a civilized man after it.

. . . . I have attempted a short and clear narrative of my public life, in relation to Texas. I give it publicity, without omiting or suppressing anything that I thought of the least interest, and confidently I submit to the public verdict.

It is sad that the Seguíns, the Losoyas, and all the other Tejanos, so involved in Texas history, have been so ignored in the telling of it.

The Fightingest Texian

The Texas Revolution was over, and friends and relatives waited at dockside in Alabama to celebrate the homecoming of a hero. They knew only that he had been there at the start of the trouble and had written home about the horrible bloodshed at the Battle of San Jacinto. They couldn't wait to hear him tell of his feats in battle.

The two-masted schooner crossed Mobile Bay, furled sails and drifted to the dock. The family and friends leaned forward to see their hero. He was not among the passengers lining the rail. Then they saw a disheveled figure on the deck.

Judges R.E.B. Baylor and Walker Keith Baylor scarcely recognized young John Walker Baylor as their nephew–the robust young man who had marched away so confidently just a year earlier to fight for freedom in Texas. The figure on a sailcloth pallet was a living specter–almost skeletal. His clothing hung in rags. Even though the air was hot and humid, he pulled a tattered blanket around himself for warmth. His body clattered against the wooden deck as the rigors of another bout of fever attacked him. The crew had not expected him to survive the stormy voyage from Brazoria, below San Felipe on the Brazos River. Yet he survived on to Mobile, then by small steamer up the Alabama River to Cahawba.

John Walker Baylor, who had not reached his twenty-third year, was dying–an unreported casualty of the Battle of San Jacinto. He had received a wound so minor he didn't even report it. As the summer wore on, infection set in. His clothes were worn to tatters, his money had run out, and he was getting weaker by the day. He decided to return to Alabama, where he died five months after the battle.

Perhaps his uncles thought him not lucid when he told them he had been in the Texas Revolution from beginning to end. Judge R.E.B. Baylor, prominent jurist, Indian fighter, and congressman, could have easily brushed off young Baylor's stories as delirium.

Had Walker lived, he undoubtedly would have left his mark in Texas. His death brought his brothers and uncles to Texas, and they helped shape the affairs of the Republic and the state. John Walker Baylor has never been listed among the heroes—Travis, Crockett, Bowie and the others. Yet perhaps he was the fightingest Texian of them all.

Walker Baylor wasn't cut out to be an officer and a gentleman. He was a fighter, descended from a long line of warriors. The United States Military Academy at West Point was unable to teach him much about the art of warfare. It failed miserably to teach him discipline.

Gen. Sam Houston probably understood the young cadet's problem. He himself had left mathematics and rules he considered superfluous at Porter Academy in Maryville, Tennessee. The rules there forbade students from getting drunk, playing cards or other games of hazard, using profane, irreverent or obscene language, or being "guilty of conduct tending thereunto. . . . No student shall attend a horse race, a ball, or other frolicking assembly . . . .No student shall be guilty of fighting."

These rules were in force because temptations like gambling with dice and cards, cock fighting, and drinking were common pastimes on the Tennessee frontier.

From his experiences Houston believed it was impossible to mold ready-made leaders in a military academy. He thought officers should learn their trade on the job. In his recollections, *The Evolution of a State*, Noah Smithwick said Houston "was a living exponent of the natural law alluded to by him in Congress when one United States Military Academy bill was under consideration. Said he, 'You might as well take dung-hill fowl's eggs and put them in eagles' nests and try to make eagles of them as to try to make generals out of boys who have not capacity, by giving them military training.' "

Walker Baylor probably personified Houston's candidate for military leadership, for he was a frontiersman who could not fit the West Point mold. With a long military background, he was the type to learn the killing trade on the job. He became very good at it.

Born at Woodlawn on Stones Creek, near Paris, Bourbon County, Kentucky, he was the eldest son among seven children. The family traveled from camp to post to fort—wherever the father, Dr. John Walker Baylor, was stationed as assistant surgeon with the U.S. 7th Infantry. There was fighting enough to go around for a youngster on the frontier where, if there were no Indian uprisings, there were always schoolmates, the sons of other soldiers, to fight.

In the late 1820s the doctor was assistant surgeon at Cantonment Gibson in Indian Territory near the Arkansas border in present-day Oklahoma. Sam Houston visited the Baylor family often and hosted Dr. Baylor in the home at Neosho he called "The Wigwam," where he lived with his Indian wife, Tiana Rogers. Through this relationship and a mutual friendship with Andrew Jackson, Houston probably knew the doctor's brother, R.E.B. Baylor. Houston wrote his cousin John Houston in Washington from Cantonment Gibson in 1829:

"My friend Dr. Baylor will hand you this letter. He is worthy of your friendship; and that is all that I could say of any man. He will Kiss My dear God Daughter, and will tell you all about me. . . . Write to me. My letters will reach my wigwam, and they will give me happiness."

The Baylor family had a fighting tradition. Young Baylor's grandfather, Walker Baylor, commanded Gen. George Washington's Life Guard in the Third Continental Division at the Battle of Germantown, where he was disabled for life when a spent cannonball crushed his foot. Walker Baylor's brother, Col. George Baylor, was commended by his commander-in-chief for valor at the Battles of Trenton and Princeton. He was wounded at Monmouth.

Young Walker's uncle R.E.B. Baylor fought under Gen. William Henry Harrison in the campaign against the Indian chief Tecumseh and served in Colonel Boswell's Regiment in the War of 1812. He commanded a regiment of Alabama volunteers in the Creek Indian Wars of 1836.

Because of the family history in the American Revolution and because Dr. Baylor was a friend of President Jackson, young Walker Baylor received an appointment to West Point after spending a year attending Bardstown College in Kentucky. His father applied for Walker's entrance to the Military Academy from his post at the Arkansas fort. West Point Archives show this letter, dated July 25, 1831, from leading citizens of both Kentucky and

Alabama to the U.S. House of Representatives:

"We feel a very good solicitude towards and appreciation for Walker Baylor, son of Doct. John W. Baylor as cadet from Arkansas. He is very promising, has not the means of education and he is descended from Col. Baylor who fought so gallantly in the Revolutionary War and was wounded in his country's cause."

Academy records show that Walker Baylor entered West Point July 1, 1832, on an at-large appointment. He was eighteen years and seven months old.

Almost from the beginning he was in trouble. Walker's brother George Wythe wrote in 1900: "Walker . . . unluckily got into a quarrel with Cadet Freeman and they concluded to settle it by a duel with naked bayonets. Walker, proving quicker at fence, punched more holes in Cadet Freeman than Army regulations allowed and [he] was dismissed. But as his father . . . and President Andrew Jackson were warm personal friends, the president said, 'I don't believe fighting should be a drawback for a soldier.' "

According to another Baylor family account, Jackson, upon hearing of the incident, "turned the air blue around the White House with an occasional streak of red."

Disciplinary reports from the Academy show that the president of the United States on November 27, 1832, directed "that the proceedings of the General Court Martial convened at West Point, N.Y. by virtue of M.A. Order No. 30, in the case of Cadet Baylor, be annulled. . . ."

That order does not specify the offense. It is possible this was the bayonet fight. Baylor family recollections say Cadet Freeman later entered the ministry, became a bishop in San Antonio, and was minister at St. Mark's Church for some Baylors living there.

But Walker was soon in trouble again. He was court-martialed once more, on December 18:

> Specification. In this the said Cadet Walker Baylor, of the U.S. Corps of Cadets, did thrust or strike with his fist Cadet C.H. Simons of the same Corps, this in the Cadet Barracks at West Point, N.Y., on or about the 25th of October, 1832.
>
> Specification. In this he, Cadet Baylor aforesaid, after having been duly arrested, did leave his quarters at the Cadets Barracks, this on or about the 2nd day of November, 1832.
>
> The prisoner pleaded in bar of the trial that he had been once tried for the same offense.
>
> After mature deliberation, the court sustained the plea of the prisoner.

Again he had won. Then, on January 7, 1833, Cadets Baylor, Crittendon, R.G. Stockton, Churchill, Seall, Martindale, Waggaman, and Hathaway were placed under arrest for "a violation of paragraph 9b of the regulation; by using playing cards on the 5th of January."

There was no need for another court-martial, for on February 1 Order No. 18 said "on the recommendation of the Academic Board approved by the Secretary of War, Cadets W. Baylor [and 10 others] who were found deficient at the late General Examination of cadets, are hereby discharged from the service of the United States. By order of Lt. Col. Thayer."

A family version indicates that Walker may have been less than truthful in explaining his discharge to his parents. George Wythe Baylor wrote that after the bayonet incident Jackson "restored young Baylor's appointment. But instead of returning as he should have done and going through the course prescribed, Walker returned and showed his restoration to the commandant, resigned and then left for his home in Natchez, Miss."

Walker may have concocted that story himself. It probably sounded better than admitting he had flunked out.

If it was such a ploy, it was not entirely successful. "His mother and sisters greeted him with love," George Wythe continued, " but his father felt aggrieved and was only pacified by promises of good behavior in the future."

Walker was listed as an assistant surgeon before he went to West Point, indicating he had some medical training before 1832. After he returned home in 1833, he studied medicine under his father, apparently until the time of his father's death, on January 5, 1835, at Second Creek, near Natchez. With as much medical training as most physicians of the day, he is listed as one of the doctors of the Texas Revolution.

After the father died, Walker's mother moved to Pine Bluff, Arkansas, to live with her daughter Sophie Marie, who was married to U.S. Army Capt. James L. Dawson. Walker apparently accompanied her. He probably then went to visit relatives, likely his uncle R.E.B. Baylor, in Alabama and went from there to Texas, for he was listed as an Alabama volunteer. He was twenty-one years old in 1835.

Just how and when he arrived in Texas is not clear. He may have been one of Col. John Henry Moore's 160 volunteers at Gonzales, where the opening shots of the revolution were fired on October 2 of that year. A few days later he joined Capt.

George M. Collinsworth's recruits. Collinsworth was the Missourian who had been in Texas four years and had participated in colonist attacks on Mexican authority at Brazoria and Velasco. On October 5, 1835, he recruited twenty volunteers in the Matagorda area to capture La Bahía, the *presidio*, or fortress, at Goliad. On October 9 Baylor was one of the men at Victoria who—before they started a twenty-five-mile forced march to Goliad—pledged "our lives, our property, and our sacred honour" to defend the liberal Mexican Constitution of 1824.

The recruits captured Goliad with a minimum of bloodshed. The Mexican garrison lost three killed, seven wounded and twenty-one captured. Sam McCullough was wounded in the shoulder. Baylor became a member of the garrison at Goliad, but reserved the right to leave when the fighting was going on elsewhere.

"The Texan volunteer of that period respected authority, but he was an individualist and respected it according to his own lights," Hobart Huson wrote.

"He was outspoken in expressing his personal opinions and was not modest in his disputations. By and large they craved excitement and longed to be where there was likelihood of fighting to be done. . . .

"Dr. John Walker Baylor is a good exemplar of the spirit of that stirring age. Wherever there was a prospect of a fight, he managed to get to it. He joined [Philip] Dimmitt's garrison [at Goliad] and was appointed assistant surgeon. The prospects of storming Bexar lured him thence, where he was in the thickest of the fray."

Actually the young volunteer was in the thick of things before the Storming of Bexar, for he left Goliad on October 15, carrying a letter from Dimmitt to Stephen F. Austin, who commanded the Texians on their march on Bexar. Baylor accompanied J.A. Padilla, a former Spanish official in Texas, an empresario and land commissioner in Martín de León's Colony who sided with the Texas rebels and later served on the General Council. They rode with the troop of thirty Tejanos commanded by Placido Benavides, the Guadaloupe-Victoria *alcalde*.

Dimmitt wrote in the letter, "Doct Baylor goes with them, and can give you much important information. He is a gentleman, and a soldier. Was in action in the Storm of this post, and behaved bravely."

After Baylor delivered the letter, he followed James Bowie and James Fannin and fought in the Battle of Concepción on

October 28. No rosters of that battle have been found, but Col. Joseph L. Bennett signed this affidavit that is on file at the Texas State Archives: "I hereby certify that I was acquainted with J.W. Baylor of the State of Alabama. Was with him in the Army of Texas in the Fall of 1835 at the Battle of Concepcion . . . ."

In the margins of a copy of H.S. Thrall's 1878 *History of Texas* in the Texas Collection at Baylor University, Walker's brother George wrote this comment about the battle:

"My brother, J.W. Baylor, was in the mission fight opposite the wilderness . . . it was near [the later site of] General John B. Baylor's house. Dick Andrews, brother of Redding Andrews, [died when] a copper grape shot struck a tree and glanced off and killed him."

Baylor carried another message from Austin to Dimmitt describing how the Texians had inflicted heavy casualties on the 400 Mexicans attacking at Mission Concepción. Baylor arrived back at Goliad on November 5, thus missing the Battle of Lipantitlán, which occurred on that date when men from the Goliad garrison and Refugio under Capt. Ira J. Westover captured a small Mexican outpost on the Nueces River near San Patricio. Mexican losses were heavy; one Texian was wounded.

Meanwhile, Augustín Viesca, who had been deposed by Santa Anna as governor of Texas–Coahuila, had escaped from prison and appeared at Goliad. He was incensed when Dimmitt did not recognize him as governor of Texas and obey his orders as such. Dimmitt gave him a reception but told him he would leave it to the government of Texas to determine who would be governor. Viesca, insulted, complained to Austin. Dr. James Grant, who accompanied the governor and his party, also clashed with Dimmitt and wrote to Austin. Austin ordered Dimmitt removed from command on November 18. On the twenty-first, Baylor was one of five who drafted a stirring defense of Dimmitt. Sixty-seven members of the garrison signed the letter.

Dimmitt refused to give up his command. Instead, he marched to Bexar, where Austin's force had laid siege to the town. Some of the men who served under Westover in the Lipantitlán expedition accompanied Dimmitt to San Antonio in time for the Storming of Bexar. Baylor was also with him.

Nine of Baylor's comrades in Dimmitt's Goliad garrison would die in the Alamo. Others would perish in the Goliad Massacre. Most were members of the twenty-eight-man contingent Huson says participated in the five-day house-to-house battle that was the Storming of Bexar.

Among those from Dimmitt's garrison who took part with him in the battle at Bexar were José Miguel Aldrete, Milton B. Atkinson, Baylor, Samuel Blair, Lt. John P. Borden, William Bracken, James Brown, Capt. William S. Brown, Manuel Carbajal, Joseph Benjamin Dale, Jeremiah C. Day, Jr., William G. Hill, Augustus H. Jones, William Langenheim, William D. Lightfoot, Armand Victor Loupy, Edward McCafferty, Thomas J. Mitchell, Benjamin J. Noble, James Nowlan, Charles J. O'Connor, C.A. Parker, Robert L. and William G. Reddin, John M. Thruston, David Wilson, and William E. Howth.

After the capture of San Antonio, Dimmitt's men returned to Goliad. Baylor was one of the signers of the declaration there on December 20, 1835, when the garrison got the jump on the rest of Texas and declared for independence, to the dismay of the government at San Felipe. However, the Goliad garrison voted in disgust to disband shortly after Dr. Grant came through and impressed the entire *caballada*, or the garrison's herd of horses, on his ill-fated Matamoros expedition.

Walker Baylor's records show his service at the Goliad garrison lasted from October 5, 1835, until January 11, 1836. Before the troops' departure, James Bowie stopped by; some of the old garrison troops may have gone with him to San Antonio. As Dimmitt and his followers marched back to Matagorda, they met Sam Houston with a small detachment on the way to Goliad. Houston listened with sympathy as Dimmitt detailed how Grant had taken his supplies and horses. Capt. Peyton S. Wyatt was now in command at Goliad. Before Dimmitt's followers had proceeded far, a messenger from Houston overtook them, ordering Dimmitt to recruit as many men as possible and proceed to reinforce Col. James C. Neill at the Alamo.

Baylor and others of the Goliad garrison arrived at the Alamo with either Bowie or Dimmitt. Since most of those with Dimmitt were colonists from the Matagorda area, it is likely Baylor was with Bowie. Among the Goliad garrison contingent, Samuel Blair, James Brown, Jeremiah C. Day, Jr., Charles M. Despallier, Edward McCafferty, Christopher A. Parker, Isaac Robinson, John M. Thruston, and David Wilson would die with William Barret Travis.

It is uncertain when Baylor left the Alamo, but a plaque just inside the shrine lists him as a courier. Travis sent him to plead with Fannin, by now the commander at Goliad, for help.

John Sowers Brooks, Fannin's aide-de-camp, mentioned in letters to his family that four messengers arrived from the Alamo from February 25 to March 9. Herman Ehrenberg said, "At the risk of their lives, one or two came daily through the enemy lines and brought us the pleadings of the garrison, especially the private letters of Travis, the commander, and of Bowie and [David] Crockett."

Mrs. Mary Austin Holley wrote in March 1837: "Mrs. Baylor's oldest son was a cadet of West Point. He joined the army of Texas and was with Travis at the Alamo, but he was sent out on some service and thereby escaped the massacre at the time of its fall. He was then with Fannin's corps but was one of those who escaped the massacre . . . ."

After he reached Goliad, Baylor enlisted in Capt. Jack Shackelford's Red Rovers. Dr. Shackelford had served in the Alabama legislature with R.E.B. Baylor and would have had an interest in the young doctor.

On March 13 Col. Albert C. Horton arrived at Goliad with thirty-two horsemen from Victoria. (Horton later became lieutenant governor, then acting governor of Texas when James Pinckney Henderson took leave of absence during the Mexican War.) Baylor and other men who had horses were assigned to Horton's command, to report to Fannin the strength of the Mexican army. In 1913 George Wythe Baylor reported that Horton called Walker "one of the most daring men I ever saw in battle."

On March 18 Horton's men had a spirited skirmish with the Mexican cavalry near the fort. As the battle see-sawed back and forth, troops watching the sport left oxen hitched all day without food or water, a critical mistake. The next day, on March 19, Fannin ordered the ill-fated retreat. After his army was surrounded by the superior Mexican force, a group of horsemen was cut off from the main body. They were pursued by Mexican cavalry, but escaped into the deep woods where the pursuers dared not follow.

Baylor's name is on the list drawn by historian Harbert Davenport of "Mounted Men Under Capt. Horton Not Captured on March 19-20, 1836." Others include Thomas Jefferson Adams, Norman Austin, Jacob Betts, Garrett E. Boom, George J. Bridgeman, George Whitfield Brooks, J.W. Buckner, Thomas Cantwell, Joseph Clemens, Lewis DeMoss, William DeMoss, Nicholas W. Eastland, Joseph Fenner, William C. Francis, Jefferson

George, Francis Jones, John Jones, Augustus S. Kincheloe, James W. Moore, Charles Morgan, John L. Osborn, Thomas Osborn, Michael Riley, George N. Robinson, Levi Pendleton Scott, Christopher Terrell, Thomas S. Thompson, George W. Wheelwright, and Ralph Wright.

Several of Horton's men managed to reach Houston's army and fight at San Jacinto. Among them was "Doct." Baylor. That is the way he appears on the San Jacinto battle roster, in Capt. William H. Patton's Company in the Second Texas Volunteer Regiment, commanded by Col. Sidney Sherman. The roster lists three killed and eight wounded in the battle. Young Baylor received a slight wound on his thigh.

His brother George said, "[A]s he had studdied medicine, his knowledge of medicine stood in demand at that time, but having been at West Point, he was more useful as a drillmaster for his company and put them in good fighting trim for the battle that won for Texas her liberty.

"Letters from him at that time gave an account of the battle which he said was more of a surprise and a massacre than a fight and he wrote the sight of the dead Mexicans and the smell of blood was something horrible."

The statement of Col. Joseph L. Bennett, one of several collected by Baylor on July 25, 1836, when he was attempting to collect something for his service to Texas, said that he "new him in the spring of 1836 in the army of Texas. Was in the Battle of San Jacinto on the 21st of April. After the Battle I heard him say that if he can get a furlow, he would go to Alabama for the purpose of gitting money and clothing for he said his cloathes was worn out and his money spent. The above is a true statement of facts relitive to the service of Doct. Baylor."

But he did not go yet. Very likely Baylor accompanied the army commanded by Gen. Thomas J. Rusk that followed upon the heels of the retreating Mexicans. Rusk was in charge of the Texas Army while Sam Houston recuperated from the wound he suffered at San Jacinto. The force arrived at La Bahía the last of May.

Rusk wrote: "[W]e found no difficulty in discovering the ground upon which Fannin and his gallant men were shot by order of Santa Anna. Most of their bodies were burned, while there were many bones and some entire skeletons scattered over the plain for some distance. . . .

". . . . As a token of respect, as well to the men who fell a sacrifice to the treachery and bad faith of our enemy as a duty that we owe to the relatives of the unfortunate deceased and ourselves, it is ordered that the skeletons and bones of our murdered countrymen be collected into one place in front of the fort, and buried with all the honors of war. Thomas J. Rusk, Brigadier General Commanding."

The following day the funeral was conducted under the command of Col. Sidney Sherman. Rusk gave a eulogy in which he said: "In that mass of remains and fragments of bones many a mother might see her son, many a sister her brother, and many a wife her own beloved and affectionate husband. But we have a consolation yet to offer them. Their murderers sank into death on the prairies of San Jacinto under the appalling cries: 'Remember La Bahia!'

". . . . He [Santa Anna] must sometimes reflect on the tragedy of La Bahia! While the names of those whom he murdered shall soar to the highest pinnacle of fame, his shall sink down to the deepest depths of infamy and disgrace . . . ."

Sam Dexter, Rusk's aide-de-camp, said: "I saw tears flow from the eyes of more than one brave man . . . and observed many . . . involuntarily grasp their weapons more firmly, as if they felt that the holocaust of San Jacinto had not compensated them for the brutal murder of their comrades at La Bahía."

Five of the mourners were "those of Col. Fannin's command who are with the army, and who so miraculously escaped." Those survivors looking at the charred bones of their comrades likely made disparaging remarks to Baylor.

Some of Fannin's men were bitter because Horton's cavalry troop did not return to help the army reach the protection of the woods. A few of the New Orleans Greys assigned to Horton did break through the Mexican lines to die with their comrades.

Gen. José Urréa wrote: "The enemy's cavalry, which was small in number, had escaped the moment we overtook them, thanks to their good horses. Some there were who, choosing the fate of their brave companions, dismounted and abandoned their horses. I took advantage of this to replace the worst mounts of our dragoons."

Horton put it to a vote, and James W. Moore made a heated argument that such a charge would be fruitless. The men voted overwhelmingly to stay in the cover of woods some distance from the battle site. Horton later said that Doct. Baylor was one of a few who argued passionately to help their beleaguered friends.

Of this, George Wythe Baylor wrote: "My brother, so Gov. Horton told me, made an earnest appeal to the men to cut their way through to Fannin, but at that time, every man had his say and the majority voted not to go."

Moore and the men who voted with him were wise. Had Horton ridden in to aid Fannin, his troop would have been cut to pieces by Mexican lancers and all his men would have been added to the list of dead.

At the same time Rusk was holding the memorial service at Goliad, Mexican Gen. Juan José Andrade was retreating across the San Antonio River a few miles from La Bahía. He sent a message to the Texian commander, complaining that Rusk had not complied with the stipulation of the treaty of San Jacinto that the "Texan army should not approach within less than five leagues of the retreating Mexicans."

"General Rusk informed Andrade that he had better push on in conformity to other stipulations of the same treaty, as the Texans were exasperated by the scene of demoniacal barbarism which they had just witnessed, and if the Mexican army came in sight, he could not answer for the acts of his men," Dexter reported. He said that Andrade, one of the bravest and most efficient of the Mexican general officers, headed 750 fresh troops. It looked as if another battle was inevitable, but Andrade thought it over and turned his columns toward the Rio Grande. Even so, there was more fighting at hand.

On May 29 Rusk sent Maj. Isaac Watts Burton with a company of twenty mounted rangers to search the coast from the Guadalupe River to Mission Bay to keep watch against a possible Mexican strike from the sea. The men were well mounted and armed. John Walker Baylor was one of them.

On June 3 they saw a Mexican ship off Copano and signaled distress. The ship replied first with a United States, then a Texas flag. The Texians remained silent. The ships then hoisted the red, white, and green Mexican flag, and the Texians repeated the distress signal. The captain and five sailors came ashore and were made prisoners. Sixteen Texians rowed out and captured the *Watchman* without firing a shot.

Col. Juan Davis Bradburn, a Kentuckian whose unpopularity as *alcalde* and tax collector at Anahuac had led to the first disturbance by Texians against Mexican authority, reportedly escaped in a rowboat. He had left Texas to return with the invading army. His capture could have considerably shortened his life.

The *Watchman* was filled with foodstuffs, clothing, and military supplies for the Mexican army. Rusk was upset when he heard of the capture because he was afraid it could bring harm to Texians held prisoner in Matamoros. He gave orders to release the vessel and send it back to Mexico. Major Burton couldn't understand such an order. While he was trying to figure it out, Rusk changed his mind and ordered the *Watchman* sent to Galveston.

As the rangers waited for a favorable wind, the schooners *Fanny Butler* and *Comanche* entered the anchorage. The Texians ordered the captain of the *Watchman* to decoy his fellow captains aboard. They and their vessels were captured. The cargoes, valued at $25,000, were taken to Velasco.

The seagoing safari launched the gaudy legend of Texas Ranger exploits, and it also accomplished far more. After San Jacinto, the Texas Army had continued to grow. There was little food and no pay. The troops, many newly arrived from the United States, had come to fight. They had been manageable, but without food they were uncontrollable. The captured bread, rice, and beans cooled a heated confrontation that had threatened to become a revolution against the transitional government.

Therefore the rangers did not share in the booty of captured ships as seamen of the age often did. The ships were returned to Americans who owned them. The Mexican government called the act piracy. But the new Republic of Texas had survived its first crisis–all because twenty horsemen went to sea as "Horse Marines."

Baylor returned to Velasco and languished there most of July, his battle wound festering and his clothing in tatters as he waited for some pay. On July 25, 1836, he signed a receipt for sixty-four dollars–"payment in full" for his services from October 5, 1835, until January 11, 1836. With the money, he paid his passage to New Orleans and Mobile.

From Brazoria he wrote to his father's old friend, Sam Houston: "I am sorry that circumstances have prevented me from returning to Nacogdoches as soon as I intended. My health is such that I cannot travel and I need not say what has been my anxiety to return. . . .

"I will be in Nacogdoches as soon as my health will allow me to travel. I have suffered more from the villainous aspersions that have been put in circulation agin me than from my bodily disease. I did try and pay to a man fifty dollars. But that it was bad money, I, at that time, had no idea whatsoever."

It appears that Baylor, like many other newcomers to Texas, had discovered the realities of the colonial monetary system. Noah Smithwick said colonial Texians used counterfeit coins and later fake U.S. dollars as legal tender because hard specie was so scarce. The Texians knew the money was bogus, but they used it as long as it held its par value. New arrivals did not find redeeming value in the practice.

In the letter, dated September 14, 1836, the young soldier asked the general to "sell both the horses I left there, settle all my affairs and if there is a ballance in my favour, I wish you to send it to me here—the stallion I paid a large price for—I don't know what he will bring at this time. The other horse I sent in the direction of Col. Rusk. . . . You can sell him for what you think him worth . . . ."

He asked Houston to send the money to Brazoria, where he planned to return after he regained his health. But eight weeks later he was dead.

His uncle, Robert E.B. Baylor, gave this deposition in Bastrop County, Texas, January 2, 1840:

> I learnt the following facts from the late Dr. J.W. Baylor on his deathbed. [Young Baylor died at Cahawba, then capital of Alabama, where his uncle was practicing law.] He stated that he entered the Army of the Republic of Texas from the commencement of the Revolution until his death which took place some time after the Battle of San Jacinto.
>
> There may have been short intervals during the war that he was not attached to the Army. He was at the taking of Goliad and was at Bexar during the time Genl. Cos had possession of that place. I do not think he was at the storming of Bexar with Milam.
>
> He was at the Battle of Concepcion, the Battle of San Jacinto and in several other battles with the Mexicans.

The judge did not grasp what his nephew had told him. There is no documentation to place Walker Baylor at Gonzales, but if he was in the Texas Army "from the commencement of the Revolution," he was there and therefore in the war from beginning to end.

Dr. John Walker Baylor has the unique distinction of having been at the Alamo, at Goliad, and at San Jacinto—at every battle of the revolution with the exception of Lipantitlán and possibly the skirmish at Gonzales. Yet he remains almost unknown to history.

R.E.B. Baylor claimed Walker's land headrights and bounties for Walker's brothers and sisters and said in 1840 that the full

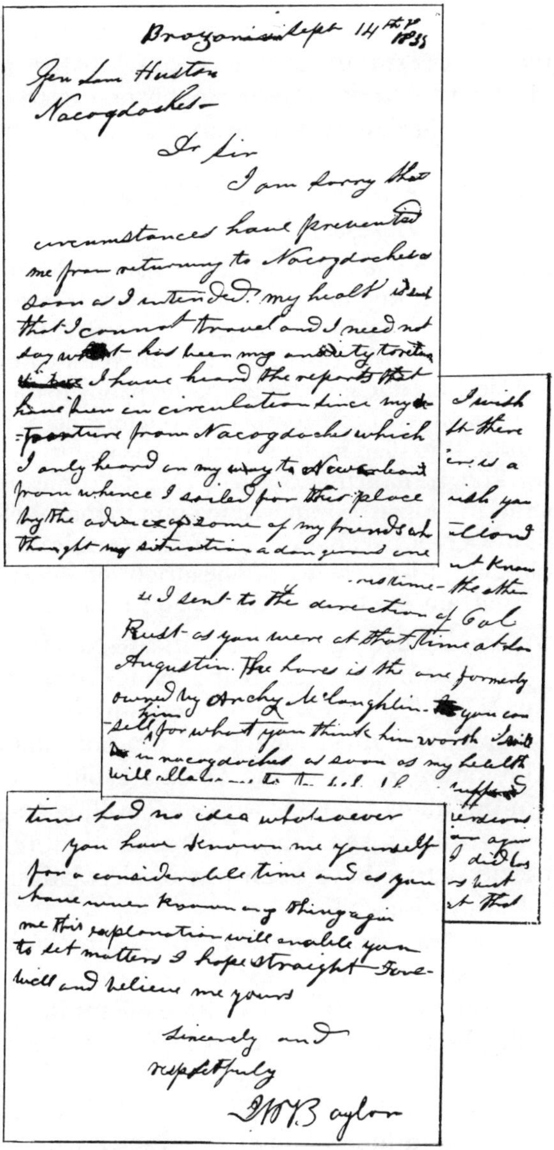
Brazoria Sept 14th 1835

Gen. Sam Huston
Nacogdoches—

Dr Sir

I am sorry that circumstances have prevented me from returning to Nacogdoches as soon as I intended. my health is such that I cannot travel and I need not say what has been my anxiety to return. I have heard the reports that have been in circulation since my departure from Nacogdoches which I only heard on my way to New Orleans from whence I sailed for this place by the advice of some of my friends who thought my situation a dangerous one

... no time – the other I sent to the direction of Col Rusk as you were at that time at San Augustin. The horse is the one formerly owned by Archy McLaughlin – you can sell him for what you think him worth. I will be in Nacogdoches as soon as my health will allow ...

time had no idea whatsoever

You have known me yourself for a considerable time and as you have never known any thing agin me this explanation will enable you to set matters I hope straight. Farewell and believe me yours

sincerely and respectfully

J. W. Baylor

The young soldier wrote to his father's old friend, Sam Houston.

facts of his nephew's record "will appear by a reference to the different Departments. The others are within the knowledge of the officers of Govt. and members of Congress.

"Doctor Baylor's constitution was entirely broken down in the service of his adopted country. How he performed his duty as a soldier, I leave to others to say. I refer for further information on this subject to President Lamar, Genl. Huston [*sic*], Col. Bennett, Mr. Jack and others. I now leave this matter to the justice and magnanimity of the Congress to grant such relief as they think proper."

On February 5, 1840, President Mirabeau B. Lamar signed the following act of Congress:

> Section 1st. Be it enacted by the Senate and House of Representatives of the Republic of Texas, in Congress assembled. That the Secretary of War, be required to issue to R.E.B. Baylor, heir of Dr. J.W. Baylor deceased, a certificate for six hundred forty acres of land as a donation for the participating in the battle of San Jacinto, and a certificate for six hundred forty acres of land allowed to those who died in the service of the country.
>
> Section 2nd. Be it further enacted. That the commissioner of the general land office be required to grant to the said R.E.B. Baylor, heir of Doctor J.W. Baylor deceased, a certificate of one third of a league of land, being the headright of Doctor J.W. Baylor deceased, any law to the contrary notwithstanding.

Dr. Baylor's heirs also received Certificate No. 2956 for 320 acres of land for Baylor's service in the army from October 5, 1835, to January 11, 1836 – in Dimmitt's command.

John Walker Baylor must have been the only man to have fought in all the major battles of the Texas Revolution. He died young as one of the many paladins who were willing to give their lives for an ideal. And before he died he "suffered more from the villainous aspersions that have been put in circulation agin me than from my bodily disease."

Perhaps it was the "bad money," perhaps some accused him of deserting the Alamo, or perhaps it was a story that he, as a member of Horton's band, had abandoned Fannin's men that troubled him. But he never regained his health to rebut the false reports.

He remained a hero only in the eyes of his younger brothers, who also became fighters. Henry Weidner Baylor was a surgeon in John C. Hays' regiment in the Mexican War. Baylor County, Texas, is named in his honor. John Robert Baylor was an Indian fighter, a Texas Ranger, and Confederate colonel. High water prevented Henry and John Robert and a cousin, also a Dr. John Walker Baylor (son of William Baylor), from joining Nicholas Dawson's Fayette County volunteers, those massacred near Salado Creek in 1842 as they marched to the assistance of Texians being attacked by Mexican Gen. Adrian Woll at San Antonio. The youngest brother, George Wythe Baylor, was a Confederate officer, Ranger, and Indian fighter.

Yet even more influential would be Walker's uncle, Robert Emmet Bledsoe Baylor, soldier, judge, preacher, Indian fighter and a major force in the Baptist movement in Texas. He traveled hundreds of miles on a court circuit, holding court by day and preaching at night. He had served as a U.S. representative from Alabama, but came to Texas to handle his nephew's affairs and stayed to become Supreme Court justice, district judge, member of the Texas Congress, member of the committee reporting on the ordinance accepting the terms of annexation, one of the authors of the Texas Constitution, and founder of the university that bears his name.

Dr. John Walker Baylor, forgotten hero, never saw the fruits of his sacrifice. His death brought R.E.B. Baylor and thereby a legacy of law, culture, and religion to the new Republic of Texas in 1839, but the young soldier lies in an unmarked grave in the old cemetery of the abandoned townsite of Cahawba, Alabama, twelve miles southwest of Selma.

Sadly, even in his own mind his reputation was not redeemed before he died. In his final plea to Sam Houston, he wrote: "You have known me yourself for a considerable time and as you have never known anything agin me, this explanation will enable you to set matters, I hope, straight. Farewell and believe me Yours Sincerely and respectfully, J.W. Baylor."

Appendix A
U.S. Army Deserters or Discharges With Names Similar to Those of Men Who Served in the Texas Revolution

Names of 3rd and 6th U.S. Army Infantry Regiment desertions and 3rd Regiment discharges show a striking similarity to names of men listed on the rosters of the Army of the Republic of Texas and in Republic of Texas land grants, donations, and bounties. Names the same as or similar to those of five other Texas veterans, all of whom fought at San Jacinto, also appear on the post returns of the U.S. 4th Infantry Regiment at Baton Rouge, Louisiana, in 1836.

****Denotes present or former U.S. troops with the same names as men in the service of Texas on or before April 21, 1836, the date of the Battle of San Jacinto.**

United States Army 3rd Regiment deserters with the same names as men who served during the Texas Revolution:

****Adkins, William,** Co. I, deserted August 1835. A **William Atkins** served in the San Augustine Volunteers from April 1, 1836.

****Barry, David,** Co. D, deserted January 4, 1836. **David Berry** received a 640-acre bounty in Williamson County for service from April 10 to October 10, 1836.

****Bear, Isaac,** Co. F, deserted June 17, 1834. An **Isaac Bear** served in Lt. Col. Henry Millard's Command at San Jacinto and received one-third of a league of land in Houston County as a headright grant.

****Beck, John,** Co. E, deserted in December 1834. **John Beck** served in Capt. W.D. Ratliff's San Augustine Volunteers from April 1, 1836. **John Beck** received 320 acres for service from April 1 to July 17, 1836.

Beckley, Thomas, Co. D, deserted December 1835. **Thomas Beckley** received a 320-acre bounty in DeWitt County for service in the San Augustine

Volunteers in 1836, dates not specified.

Bennett, John, Co. H, deserted December 1834. **John Bennett** is listed with volunteers from Jasper County under Capt. M.B. Lewis in July 1836 and served in Capt. John Ingram's Company, beginning in July 1836. He received 320 acres in Jack County for service from July 6 to October 6, 1836.

****Boling, John**, Co. F, deserted January 15, 1836. **John Boling** served in Capt. John M. Bradley's Company of San Augustine Volunteers in April 1836. Bradley's unit served at San Jacinto.

Boyd, William, Co. H, deserted November 8, 1835. **William Boyd** received a 640-acre bounty in San Patricio County for service beginning in May 1836.

Brown, William, Co. B, deserted December 12, 1832. **William Brown** enlisted in Capt. John Chenowith's Company of Zavala Volunteers in Gen. Green's Brigade April 27, 1836, and received a 1,280-acre bounty in Matagorda County.

Bush, John, Co. B, deserted December 15, 1835. **John Bush** received a 320-acre bounty in Smith County for service from July 8 to October 7, 1836.

****Byrnes, John**, Co. F, deserted August 17, 1835. **John Byrnes** was awarded a 320-acre donation in La Salle County for service from March 1 to June 1, 1836.

Cahill, John, Co. H, deserted August 1834. **John Cahill** received a 640-acre bounty in Victoria County for service from May 18 to November 18, 1836. He later served in Lt. Col. Juan N. Seguín's Co. A, Second Regiment of Cavalry, in the Regular Army of Texas.

****Campbell, Michael.** His desertion from Co. B was reported January 4, 1836. **Michael Campbell** served under Col. George Washington Hockley as an artilleryman at San Jacinto. He enlisted January 6, 1836, and served until January 1838. He received land bounties totaling more than 2,000 acres in Llano and McLennan counties.

****Carr, John,** Co. F, deserted June 17, 1834. **John Carr** received 160 acres in San Saba County, 160 in Matagorda County, and 640 acres in Throckmorton County for serving at San Jacinto.

****Casey, John**, Co. F, deserted August 17, 1835. **John Casey** was a member of Capt. Thomas H. Breece's Company of Texas Volunteers before Bexar in 1835. He was expelled from the army. However, he received a 320-acre land bounty for service from February 27 to September 5, 1836.

Clark, John, Co. C, deserted February 24, 1835. **John Clark** received 179 acres of bounty land in Tyler County for service from July 6 to October 1836 in Capt. B.J. Harper's Company.

****Cleveland, Joseph W.**, deserted an unknown U.S. unit. On April 8, 1836, **Joseph Cleveland** was promoted to "principal musician." On August 30 he was dropped from the rolls "by being claimed by the U.S."

****Cumberland, George**, Co. E, deserted December 25, 1835. **George Cumberland** enlisted in Teal's Company on January 5, 1836, and served as an artilleryman at San Jacinto. For that service he received a 640-acre donation in Cooke County. He received a 1,280-acre bounty for land in Fayette County.

Davis, John, deserted an unknown U.S. Army unit. **John Davis** enlisted in Capt. E.L.R. Wheelock's Company May 8, 1836. He was discharged "for a demand made by the U.S. Government being deserter from that Govt. on Aug. 28, 1836."

****Driskill, Daniel O.**, Co. E., deserted December 25, 1835. **Daniel O.**

Driscoll served as third sergeant on the staff of Lt. Col. Henry Millard's Co. A at San Jacinto. He enlisted January 5, 1836, and was promoted to lieutenant by the end of the year. He served until 1839. **Daniel O'Driscoll** received a headright of one-third of a league of land in Victoria County "upon proof that he was a citizen of Texas prior to March 2, 1836." He also received a bounty of 1,200 acres in Marion County and 480 acres in King County. He received a 640-acre donation in Refugio County for his service at San Jacinto.

****Dutcher, Alfred**, Co. H, deserted January 5, 1836. **Alfred Dutcher** enlisted January 13, 1836, in Lt. Col. Millard's Co. A Regulars and served at San Jacinto. He served until September 1837 and received 1,280 acres in Van Zandt County and 640 acres in Johnson County. He was granted a headright certificate for one-third of a league of land by Washington County because he was a resident of Texas prior to March 2, 1836.

****Fishbaugh, William,** Co. B, deserted November 23, 1834. **William Fishbach (Fishbaigh)** was among the Gonzales Ranging Company of Mounted Volunteers mustered into the service February 23, 1836, by Byrd Lockhart. He died in the Alamo on March 6. **William Fisbaugh's** heirs received 1,920 acres of bounty land in Terrell and 640 acres donation in Kinney County for his having fallen in the Alamo.

****Flynn, Thomas**, was reported as a deserter from Co. H February 15, 1836. **Thomas Flynn** joined Lt. Col. Millard's Co. A of Texas Regulars on January 15 and fought at San Jacinto. He was promoted to corporal June 28. He received 1,120 acres in Atascosa County.

****Gainer, J.N.**, Co. F, deserted January 7, 1836. **J.N. Gainer** enlisted in Capt. Henry Teal's Co. A, Regular Infantry, January 9, fighting at San Jacinto. He received a one-third league headright from Harris County in 1838.

****Gill, John**, Co. B, deserted February 7, 1835. **John Gill** fought at San Jacinto as a first lieutenant in Thomas H. McIntire's Company, Col. Sidney Sherman's Command. He received 640 acres in Washington and Lavaca counties and a 640-acre donation in Hunt County.

****Gough, Henry**, Co. K, deserted July 17, 1835. **Henry Gough** received a 320-acre bounty in Nacogdoches County for service from October 1835 to January 4, 1836.

****Greaves, David**, Co. F, deserted January 7, 1836. **David Grieves** was in Lt. Col. Millard's Command on January 12, 1836. He fought at San Jacinto, was appointed quartermaster sergeant May 9, 1836, and died June 15, 1837, after being promoted to lieutenant.

****Hamilton, John,** Co. B, deserted August 24, 1832. **John Hamilton** served from February 1836 to May 1837, when he died in the service. His heirs received bounties for a total of 3,200 acres in Cooke and Bexar counties.

****Husband, John,** Co. B, deserted January 4, 1835. **John Husband** was at the Siege of Bexar and at Harrisburg helping guard baggage during the Battle of San Jacinto. He later served as a Ranger. He received a 320-acre bounty in Madison County.

****Iden, Thomas,** Co. D, deserted December 12, 1835. **Thomas Iden** enlisted in Capt. W.D. Ratcliff's Company, San Augustine Volunteers, April 1, 1836.

****Jackson, Edward,** Co. D, deserted October 14, 1834. **Edward Jackson**

received a bounty of 320 acres in Clay County and 320 acres in Brown County for service beginning in May 1836. An **Edward Jackson** was also present at the Siege of Bexar.

****Jackson, John**, Co. K, deserted in December 1835. **J. Jackson** is listed in Maj. McNutt's Command guarding the baggage at Harrisburg during the Battle of San Jacinto. **John N. Jackson** fell with Fannin.

****Jones, John,** Co. K, deserted in December 1835. **John Jones** was drafted into Capt. Peter Duncan's Company at Lynchburg March 8, 1836.

****Kelley, John,** Co. F, deserted September 27, 1834. He may have been the **John Kelley** who perished in Capt. David N. Burk's Mobile Greys in Fannin's Command.

****Lee, Henry,** Co. D, deserted June 23, 1835. **Henry Lee** served in Capt. Matthew Kuykendall's Company, guarding baggage at Harrisburg during the Battle of San Jacinto.

****Linley, Charles,** Co. E, deserted in December 1835. **Charles Linley,** a thirty-one-year-old Englishman, enrolled in the Volunteer Auxiliary Corps at Nacogdoches January 14, 1836.

****McLeod, Hugh,** was last in his class at West Point. In March 1836 he took leave of absence from temporary command of Co. B, of which he was second lieutenant. By the end of March, he was declared absent without leave. He resigned his commission in July. He became a lawyer and a brigadier general in the Texas Army. He led the battle against the Cherokees in 1839, commanded the ill-fated Santa Fe Expedition in 1840, served as adjutant general of Texas in the Mexican War, and served in the legislature. He served the Confederacy as colonel of the First Regiment, Texas Infantry, and died at Dumfries, Virginia, in 1862. He is buried in Austin. **Hugh McLeod** received a bounty for 1,280 acres of land in Van Zandt County for service from March 7, 1836, to December 21, 1837.

****Miers, William** (also listed as **Miars, Myers**), deserted Co. F as a sergeant November 25, 1835. He was listed as a private on rosters until September, when he was again listed as a deserter. **William Miar** signed up with Capt. John Hart at Velasco January 30, 1836.

****Milliman, Ira,** Co. H, deserted December 18, 1835. **Ira Melleman (Millerman)** enlisted in Capt. Lynch's C Co. January 9, 1836, and transferred to the Artillery Company at San Jacinto. **Ira Milliman** received a 640-acre donation in Llano County and a bounty of 1,280 acres in Gonzales County.

Moorehead (Moorhead), John S., Co. B, was reported as a deserter in June 1834. **John T. Moorehead** signed up June 1, 1836, as 1st sergeant in Capt. James Allen's Company of "Buckeye Rangers."

****O'Driskill, Daniel (O'Driscoll). See Driskill.**

****Parce, Edward,** Co. F, deserted January 3, 1836. **Edward Pierce** enlisted January 12, 1836, and served in Lt. Col. Millard's Co. A of Regulars at San Jacinto.

****Phillips, Samuel,** Co. D, deserted June 20, 1835. **Samuel Phillips** received a headright in Houston County and a bounty of 320 acres in Leon County for service from March 1 to June 1836. He served at San Jacinto in Hayden Arnold's Company, Sidney Sherman's 2nd Regiment.

****Rhinehart, Asa,** Co. D, deserted December 12, 1835. **Asa Rhinehart** enlisted January 12, 1836, and fought under Lt. Col. Henry Millard at San Jacinto. He received a 1,280-acre bounty in Titus County. Robertson County issued him one-third of a league of land as a headright grant.

****Rockwell, Chester,** Co. H, deserted December 8, 1833. **Chester Rockwell** served in Capt. B. Bryant's Company, Col. Sherman's Command, at San Jacinto. He participated in the taking of the schooners *Watchman, Fanny Butle*r and *Comanche* in Major Burton's "Horse Marines" and received a 1,280-acre bounty in Travis and Bell counties.

****Smith, Thomas S.,** Co. A, deserted in October 1833. **Thomas Smith** received a 640-acre bounty in Travis County for service from December 1835 to June 1836 and for participating in the Battle of Refugio.

****Stevenson, Robert,** Co. B, deserted November 28, 1835. **Robert Stevenson** fought at San Jacinto in Capt. William Kimbro's Company in Col. Sidney Sherman's Command and received a donation of 640 acres in Navarro County and a headright in Sabine County .

****Sullivan, Dennis,** Co. E, deserted December 25, 1835. **Dennis Sullivan** enlisted January 5, 1836, and served in Millard's Regulars at San Jacinto. He served in the army until his death on August 1, 1836. His heirs were awarded bounties of 1,440 acres in Limestone and 480 acres in Navarro County.

****Tyndale, William,** Co. K, deserted January 14, 1836. **William Tyndale** enlisted in Capt. Andrew Briscoe's Company in Lt. Col. Millard's Regulars January 15, 1836, and fought at San Jacinto. He was promoted to sergeant in August, when he transferred to Capt. Nicolas Lynch's Company. He received a bounty for 1,280 acres in Upshur and Gregg counties for service from January 1836 to August 1838. He was given a donation of 640 acres for San Jacinto in San Saba and Eastland counties.

Deserters from the 6th Infantry Regiment:

From the time 6th Regiment troops arrived at Camp Sabine in April until September 1836, ninety-three of them deserted. The list of those ninety-three names includes the following names that also show up on Texas rolls or bounty lists.

Adams, John, deserted from an undetermined U.S. Army unit and enlisted May 8, 1836, in Col. Jesse Benton's Ranger Company as second corporal. On August 30 he was discharged, "being claimed by the U.S. to pay for one musket."

Archer, John, Co. K, deserted May 1, 1836. **John Archer** enrolled May 8 in Capt. E.L.R. Wheelock's Rangers.

Boyer, John, Co. C, deserted May 1, 1836. **John Boyer** joined Capt. Henry Teal's Company May 23. **John Boyer** received 640 acres in Llano County for service from July 1 to October 9, 1837.

Brown, John, deserted from Co. K. **John Brown** was in Capt. John N. Bradley's San Augustine Volunteers April 30, 1836. **John Brown** received a 320-acre bounty in Van Zandt County for service from May to September 1836.

Brown, William, Co. H., deserted May 1, 1836. **William Brown** enrolled in Capt. Charles L. Durocher's Company June 3, 1836.

****Campbell, James W.,** Co. F, deserted March 14, 1836. **James Campbell** received a 1,280-acre bounty in Coryell County for service from June 4, 1836, to December 14, 1837. **J. Campbell** is on the roster of Capt. Palas Love's Company

June 4, 1836. **J. Campbell** is also listed as serving under Capt. Kuykendall guarding baggage at Harrisburg during San Jacinto. (See **James Campbell** in list of men discharged from 3rd Infantry Regiment.)

****Cole, David,** Co. H, deserted May 1, 1836. **David Cole** was a corporal in Capt. W.E. Howth's company May 23, 1836. **David Cole** received a bounty for 320 acres in Trinity County for service from May 23 to September 1, 1836. However, a **David Cole** also received a 320-acre bounty in Wilson County for service from March 6 to June 6 and fought at San Jacinto under Capt. William M. Logan in Sherman's Command. It is likely that the first-mentioned **David Cole,** a corporal, is the one who on August 28, 1836, was dropped from the rolls "by demand made by the U.S. Gov't being a deserter from that Gov't."

****Goulden, William,** Co. K, reported as deserting April 12, 1836. **W. Golden** received a 320-acre bounty in Camp County. He served March 17-September 17, 1836, and in 1837-38.

Granard, Sam'l, deserted from an undetermined U.S. Army unit. He enlisted in Capt. Henry Teal's Company August 6, 1836. On August 30, 1836, he was "discharged being claimed by U.S. to pay for one musket."

Hanson, Thomas, a deserter from unspecified U.S. Army unit, enlisted in Capt. Henry Teal's Company August 6, 1836, and was discharged August 30, 1836, "being claimed by U.S. to pay for one musket." However, through a special act of the legislature in 1858, **Thomas Hanson** received a 640-acre bounty in Jackson County for service "in the years 1836 and 1837."

Holmes, Martin, Co. D, deserted March 3, 1836. **Martin Holmes** received a 1,280-acre bounty in Fayette County for service from March 1837 to March 1838.

McClusky, James, deserter from unnamed U.S. Army unit, was discharged August 30, 1836, "being claimed by U.S. to pay for one musket." At the time he was in Capt. Henry Teal's Company, in which he enlisted August 8, 1836.

****McPhea, Archibald,** deserter from unknown U.S. army unit. On April 8, 1836, he was promoted to "Principal Musician." On August 30 he was dropped from the rolls "by being claimed by the U.S."

****Miller, William,** deserted from Co. K. There are five **William Millers** in the bounty listings. One signed up with Capt. James Chessher's Jasper Volunteers on March 23 with Joseph Pennington. All four served after San Jacinto. However, **William Miller,** who fought in Lt. H.H. Swisher's Co. H, Burleson's Command, at San Jacinto, signed up with Teal's Company May 16 and was appointed corporal June 27. On August 31 he was charged to pay the U. S. Army "for one musket." Evidently he evaded arrest and sent the musket back, for on August 31 he enrolled with Capt. Jacob Snively's Co. B, 1st Regiment. **William Miller** received a 1,280-acre bounty in Brown County for service from May 8 to January 1, 1837. **William Miller** also received one-third of a league of land in Milam County as a headright.

****Monroe, William H.** Apparently he deserted from the 6th Regiment, for he joined Chessher's Jasper volunteers on March 23 , 1836, with Miller and Pennington. He enlisted in Teal's Company May 16, 1836, with William Miller. He, too, was appointed corporal on June 27. However, he was discharged "being claimed by U.S. to pay for one Musket." **William Monroe** received a bounty for 1,280 acres in Williamson County for service from April 8, 1837, to April 8, 1838.

****Pennington, Joseph,** Co. K, is listed as a deserter on April 8, 1836. **Joseph Pennington** was thirty-two years old when he enrolled in Capt. James Chessher's

Company of Jasper Volunteers, of which he was first corporal, on March 23, 1836. He was on the roster from July 3 to October 3 ,1836, for which service he received a bounty of 320 acres in Hill County.

Shell, John, Co. K, deserted in March 1836. **John Shell** served in Capt. J.M. Bradley's San Augustine Volunteers and received a 320-acre bounty in Bosque County for service from April 30 to August 1, 1836.

****Spilman, James,** deserted Co. A, 6th Regiment. **James Spillman** served under Capt. William H. Patton's Company, Col. Sherman's Command, as 4th Corporal at San Jacinto. In May 1836 **James Spillman** was court-martialed by the U.S. Army at Camp Sabine, La. **James H. Spillman** was given a 640-acre donation in Ellis County for service at San Jacinto, and **James Spillman** received a 320-acre bounty in Travis County.

Stafford, Henry, Co. K, deserted May 1, 1836. **H. Stafford** served in Capt. W.H. Secrests' cavalry company in June 1836. **Henry Stafford** appears on Capt. D. Brown's militia roster. **Henry Stafford** received a 320-acre bounty in Live Oak County for service from July 4 to October 4, 1836.

Warden, Philip H., deserted from Co. K. **Philip Warden** joined Capt. John M. Bradley's Company of San Augustine Volunteers on May 30, 1836, and Henry Reed's Company June 4. He received a 320-acre bounty in Coryell County for service from May 26 to August 26, 1836.

Weeden, Leven B., Co. A, deserted May 20, 1836. **Leven B. Weeden** received a 320-acre bounty in Caldwell County for service from February 14 to December 11, 1837. He also received a 960-acre warrant in Coryell County.

****Wilson, Joseph,** Co. F, deserted May 26, 1833. **Joseph Wilson's** heirs received 1,920 acres in Bosque County for "his having fallen with Fannin at Goliad."

Men discharged from the 3rd Infantry Regiment with the same names as men who later served in the Texas Revolution:

****Benson, Ellis,** was discharged from Co. G, February 28, 1834. **Ellis Benson** enlisted in Capt. Asa Turner's Company and transferred to Lt. Col. J.C. Neill's Artillery Company before San Jacinto. He received a 1,280-acre bounty in Freestone County for service until September 4, 1837, and a 640-acre donation in Harris County for his service at San Jacinto.

Boyle, John, was discharged from Co. B, December 21, 1836. **John Boyle** served under Capt. Joseph Soverein beginning September 5, 1836.

Brooks, William, was discharged from Co. D, August 20, 1833. **William Brooks** received a 320-acre bonus in Navarro County for service July 6-September 30, 1836.

****Brown, David H.**, was discharged from Co. E, November 6, 1833. **David Brown** (no initial) received a 640-acre donation in Panola County for service at San Jacinto. **"D" Brown** served as a private under Capt. William Kimbro, Sherman's Command, at San Jacinto.

Campbell, James, was discharged from Co. D, June 3, 1834. **James Campbell** received a 1,280-acre bounty in Bell and Coryell Counties for service from June 4 to December 14, 1836. (See **James W. Campbell** in list of 6th Regiment deserters.)

****Campbell, William,** was discharged from Co. D, July 19, 1835. **William S. Campbell** served April 1, 1836, to July 1, 1837. He served with Capt. L.H. Mabbitt's Company of Volunteers from May 9, 1836, and received 1,280 acres in Goliad County and 320 acres in Henderson County.

****Cole, William,** was discharged from Co. E, June 14, 1835. **William Cole** is listed as serving two months during 1836 under Capt. William Bicknell. He received a bounty for 320 acres in Clay County for three months of service "to May 18, 1836."

****Craig, Henry,** was discharged August 1, 1835. **Henry Craig** enlisted in Capt. Henry Teal's Company January 9, 1836. He served at San Jacinto, was promoted to 3rd sergeant in August and 2nd sergeant in October, then was in Capt. Jacob Snively's Company, in which he was promoted to lieutenant in December. He was detained as a prisoner at Matamoros and received a bounty for 1,280 acres in Johnson County.

Crawford, James, was discharged from Co. E, September 16, 1836, as a musician. **James Crawford** received a 320-acre bounty in Grayson County for service from July 20 to October 6, 1836.

****Davis, George,** was discharged in June 1834. **George Davis** enlisted in Capt. Henry Teal's Company January 14, 1836, and participated in the Battle of San Jacinto. By September he was quartermaster sergeant in Col. E. Morehouse's command. He received a bounty for 320 acres in Falls County and 1,280 acres in Frio County.

****Day, William,** was discharged from Co. B, January 4, 1833. **William Day** was awarded a 320-acre bounty in Maverick County for service from March 16 to June 6, 1836, and a bounty of 320 acres in Leon County for service from June 26 to September 26, 1836. He fought under Capt. William S. Fisher in Co. I at San Jacinto.

****Dyer, John,** was discharged from Co. K in January 1833. **John Dyer** served in Thomas Robbins Company of cavalry, "formerly William H. Smith's Company, and subsequently John Dyer's Company in the Campaign of 1836."

****Ellis, Sgt. William,** was discharged from Co. A, June 8, 1835. **Willis L. Ellis** served in Capt. Galaspy's Company, Col. Sherman's Command, at San Jacinto. **Willis L. Ellis** received a 640-acre donation in Brazos County.

****Fitch, Jabez,** discharged February 17, 1836, from Co. I, received a 320-acre bounty in Bexar County for service from December 17, 1835 to April 26, 1836. **J. Fitch** served as a lieutenant in Col. J.C. Neill's Artillery Company at San Jacinto.

Ford, William, was discharged in June 1833 from Co. H. **William Ford** received a 320-acre bounty for service from July 8 to October 8, 1836.

Francis, James, was discharged from Co. D, March 28, 1834. **James Francis** served in Capt. L.H. Mabbitt's Company of Volunteers May 9, 1836. He received a 320-acre bounty in Comanche County.

****Fraser, Alexander B.,** was discharged October 20, 1834, from Co. E. **Alex. Fraser** enrolled in Capt. Allen's "Buckeye Rangers" June 29, 1836. **Alex. Frazier** enrolled in Capt. McClure's Company of the Texas Army in June 1836. **Alexander Frazer** was 3rd corporal in Captain John McClure's Company of Permanent Volunteers. He received a 1,280-acre bounty for service from January 1836 to January 21, 1838.

Green, Edward, was discharged January 31, 1836, from Co. G. **Edward R. Green** served in Capt. Flores' Company C from November 16 until December 31, 1836, and received 640 acres in Comanche County for service from November 16, 1836, to November 13, 1837. **Ed R. Green** served June 10 to December 1836 and received a 640-acre grant in Navarro County.

****Griffin, William,** was discharged December 12, 1834, from Co. I. **William Griffin** fought at San Jacinto under Capt. William Wood in Col. Burleson's Command. He received a 1,280-acre bounty in Washington County for service from February 22 to October 23, 1836.

****Heath, Ebenezer S.**, was discharged from Co. K, July 23, 1835. Heirs of **Ebenezer S. Heath** received a 1,920-acre bounty for his service from October 1835 to March 27, 1836. A native of Massachusetts, **Ebenezer S. Heath** was a member of the New Orleans Greys under Capt. William G. Cooke before Bexar in 1835 and "Fell with Fannin" as a member of Samuel O. Pettus' Company.

****Henry, John,** was discharged as a 1st sergeant from Co. G, August 4, 1834. **John Henry** received a 640-acre bounty in Navarro County for service from April 15 to October 1837. He enrolled in Capt. W.E. Howth's Co. C of Regular Infantry January 5, 1836. In May he was promoted to 2nd corporal. He was in Capt. Alfred P. Walden's Co. A, Texas Rangers, in October. Therefore it is likely that he was not the same **John Henry** who was sentenced to death by a general court-martial on January 5, 1836. The sentence was "mitigated by the Commander in Chief to imprisonment and hard labor during the term of service and to forfeit all claims on the Government General Order No. __July 1, 1836."

****Hodge, James H.,** was discharged from Co. H, December 11, 1835. **A J Hodge** served under Capt. P.R. Splane, guarding the baggage for the army at Harrisburg during the Battle of San Jacinto.

Hunt, Thomas, was discharged from Co. H, January 4, 1834. **Thomas Hunt** served in Capt. Thomas S. McFarland's Company as a volunteer during the Revolution. He received a 320-acre bounty in Wood County.

****Johnson, John,** was discharged from Co. C, February 12, 1836. Five **John Johnsons** are listed on the Texas muster rolls. A **John Johnson** received a bounty for 320 acres in Tom Green County for service from March 2 to June 2, 1836.

****Johnson, William C.**, was discharged from Co. A, December 24, 1835. **William Johnson** enlisted January 26, 1836, in Capt. J.P. Lynch's Company, First Regiment, Texas Volunteers. A **William Johnson** is on the muster roll of Lt. Thomas' Co. C, Texas Rangers, December 1-December 31, 1836; and another **William Johnson**, a Philadelphia native, fell at the Alamo. **William Johnson** received a 1,280-acre bounty in Blanco County for service from January 17, 1836, to January 17, 1837. Six William Johnsons received bounties.

****Kelly, James,** was discharged from Co. H, August 16, 1835. **James Kelly** was ordnance sergeant for Capt. D.N. Burk's Mobile Greys from November 2, 1835, to February 29, 1836, and died with Fannin on March 27.

Kelly, William, was discharged from Co. G, January 11, 1836. **William Kelly** was a volunteer in August in Capt. Bird's Company. There are one William Kelley and four William Kellys in the bounty listings, one for "his service during the War."

****Lamb, John,** was discharged from Co. G, March 8, 1836. **John Lamb** was enrolled in the San Augustine Volunteers in Capt. Henry Reed's Co. Reed's unit was at San Jacinto.

****Lee, James,** was discharged from Co. C, February 7, 1834. **James Lee** enrolled as a volunteer for three months in the Texas Army in Washington County June 30, 1836. **James S. Lee** was listed with Capt. J.D. Elliot's Co. A, 1st Regiment Dragoons, September 19. **James Lee** was awarded a 320-acre bounty in Calhoun County for service from June 29 to August 31, 1836. **James S. Lee** was awarded 1,280 acres in Leon County for service from April 12 to June 26, 1836.

****Lewis, Sgt. William P.,** was discharged from Co. A, February 7, 1834. **William Lewis** joined Capt. James Chessher's Jasper Volunteer Company March 23, 1836. **William Lewis** enlisted July 1, 1836, in Capt. B.F. Ravill's Company, First Regiment, Texas Volunteers, and served in this unit until it was disbanded by Gen. Thomas J. Rusk in July. **William Lewis** was among those issued donation certificates for 640 acres of land for having participated in the Storming and Capture of Bexar. The name appears seven times on the bounty lists, three without additional initial.

****Littlewood, John,** was discharged from Co. D, June 6, 1834. **John Littlewood** joined the Army of Volunteers at Velasco January 30, 1836. He was promoted to 2nd corporal November 15. He served under Maj. J.N. Moreland in the Regular Infantry. **John Littlewood** was awarded 1,280 acres in Bandera County for service from February 13, 1836, to October 26, 1837. He received 320 acres in Colorado County for service from July to September.

****Malone, John,** was discharged from Co. B, October 17, 1835. **John Malone** enlisted in Capt. William Rufus C. Hays' Company, 1st Regiment, 2nd Brigade, on April 20, 1836. In October he transferred to the cavalry, then to Capt. Alfred P. Walden's Texas Rangers. He received a bounty of 320 acres in McLennan County.

****Martin, John,** was discharged from Co. F, April 5, 1834. The bounty list shows **John Martin** received 320 acres in Fort Bend County for service from September 29 to December 29, 1835; 320 acres in Bosque County for service from May 25 to September 6, 1836; another 640 acres in Frio County for service from July 15, 1836, to January 15, 1837; and 480 acres in Uvalde County for service from January 27 to November 8, 1837. Obviously at least two **John Martins** are involved here, since there is an overlap in the times of service. **John Martin** is on the rolls of Capt. W.E. Howth's Company, Regular Infantry, January 3, 1836; Capt. N. Lynch's Company, Millard's Command; and W.D. Burnet's Company, July 15, 1836. A **John Martin** enlisted in Co. D, 3rd U.S. Infantry Regiment, in 1834; but Co. D rosters for 1836 are missing.

McMahon, Martin, was discharged from Co. F, March 17, 1836. **McMahan,** no first name or initial, enlisted in Capt. John Ingram's Company July 1, 1836.

****Nelson, Edward,** was discharged from Co. I, in January 1833. **Edward Nelson** was mustered into Capt. John Chenoweth's Company January 1, 1836. **Edward Nelson's** heirs received 1,920 acres in Blanco County for his "having fallen at the Alamo."

****Phillips, Elijah,** was discharged from Co. I, July 19, 1835. **Eli Phillips** enlisted in Capt. John Smith's Co. A, 1st Regiment, Regular Infantry, Maj. Moreland's Command, on February 13, 1836, and served until October 24, 1837. This unit was at San Jacinto. He received a 1,280-acre bounty in Wilbarger County and a headright grant in Bastrop County.

****Rounds, Lyman F.**, was discharged from Co. A, June 1, 1834. **Lyman F. Rounds** enlisted January 19, 1836, and served as first sergeant in Capt. Andrew Briscoe's Company, M.B. Lamar's Command, at San Jacinto. He was promoted to second lieutenant April 28 in Capt. W.E. Howth's Regular Infantry Company but deserted August 28. He received a bounty for 1,280 acres in Williamson and Milam counties.

Scroggy, John, was discharged from Co. G, August 6, 1835. **John Scroggy** received 640 acres in Dallas County for service from May 8 to November 8, 1836. He was a 1st lieutenant beginning May 18, 1836, in Capt. A.W. Fowler's Company, 1st Regiment, 2nd Brigade.

****Simpson, John,** was discharged from Co. J, October 11, 1835. **J. Simpson** is listed under 1st Lt. H.H. Swisher in Col. Burleson's Command at San Jacinto.

Smiths who deserted and were discharged from the 3rd Regiment undoubtedly participated in the Texas Revolution, but it would be very difficult to identify them in the Texian ranks because the name is so common.

Winkler, William, was discharged from Co. D, August 24, 1834. **William Winkler** joined Capt. R.B. Irvine's Company October 9, 1836, and received a 640-acre bounty in Bosque County and 640 acres in Zavala County for service from October 9, 1836, to November 4, 1837.

****Wright, 1st Lt. George,** was discharged from Co. E. **G. Wright** served under Capt. William H. Patton in the Battle of San Jacinto. **George W. Wright** enlisted in Capt. Hart's Mounted Men, Gen. Green's Brigade, July 20, 1836, and was elected 1st lieutenant that same day. Heirs of **George Wright** received 1,920 acres in Wise County for his service from July 1 to October 15, 1836, "and having died in the service." **George W. Wright** received 320 acres for service from July 5 to October 5, 1836. **George W. Wright** also received 1,280 acres for service from January 16, 1836, to March 22, 1837.

A considerable number of names that remained on U.S. Army rosters are identical to some found on Texas Army rolls for the same time period and on Texas land records. Noah Smithwick and others reported that many U.S. troops crossed the Sabine and returned to their units when the fighting was over. This list of soldiers whose names remained on the muster rolls of the 3rd Infantry Regiment would seem to lend credibility to those reports:

Allen, Corp. Eathern, Co. K. **E. Allen** was in Captain E.L.R. Wheelock's Company May 6, 1836.

Allen, William, was listed on the roster of Co. F. **William Allen** signed on with Capt. Bird's Four-Month Volunteers August 2, 1836, and received a bounty for 640 acres in Erath County for service from April 19 to October 1837.

****Barker, William S.,** was on the roster of B Company. **William Barker** served under Capt. P.R. Spiller at Harrisburg, guarding the sick and baggage during the Battle of San Jacinto.

****Brown, Alexander,** remained on the roster of Co. I at Camp Sabine. His name never left it. He was listed as being on "Detached Service." A **Pvt. Alexander Brown** served in Capt. Gibson Kuykendall's Company at the camp at Harrisburg during the battle. **Alexander Brown** received a 320-acre bounty in Walker County for service from March 1 to May 30, 1836. He received a 640-acre donation in

Anderson County for service under Capt. Gibson Kuykendall, Maj. Robert McNutt, guarding baggage at Harrisburg during the Battle of San Jacinto.

****Brown, George,** was on the roster of Co. G and was discharged September 14, 1836. **George Brown** served in Capt. Richard Roman's Company, Burleson's Command, at San Jacinto.

Caldwell, Andrew, Co. A. **Andrew Caldwell** was in Capt. Thomas S. McFarland's Company of Texas Volunteers "in 1836."

Clark, William, Co. C. **William Clark** served in Capt. Richard Hodges' Company, starting September 19, 1836.

Collins, Anthony, remained on the roster of Co. F. **A. Collins** enrolled in T.H. Barron's Texas Rangers November 1, 1836. **Anthony Collins** was in J.D. Elliott's Company November 20, 1836.

****Crawford, John,** remained on the roster of Co. I. **John B. Crawford** received a 320-acre grant in Wise County for service from January 14 to May 29, 1836. He also received a 640-acre donation grant in Karnes County for service guarding baggage at Harrisburg during the Battle of San Jacinto, in which he served under Capt. P.R. Splane. At twenty-two, the South Carolinian had enrolled in the Volunteer Auxiliary Corps at Nacogdoches January 14, 1836.

Elliott, James, Co. B. **James Elliott** received a 1,280-acre bounty in Tarrant County for service from April 28, 1836, to January 1, 1838. He served in Capt. Henry Teal's Company.

Gibson, William, was on the roster of Co. G. **William Gibson** received a 1,280-acre bounty in Ellis County for service from May 18, 1836, to December 18, 1837. **William Gibson** served in Capt. John McClure's Company, beginning May 18.

Gorman, Patrick, Co. B. **Patrick Gorman** received a 1,280-acre bounty in Kinney County for service from September 1836 to May 1838.

****Griffith, John,** was discharged from Co. E, December 23, 1836. **John Griffith** served in W.H. Patton's Company at San Jacinto. **John Griffith** received a bounty of 1,290 acres in Goliad County for his service from February 1836 until his death in the service in July 1837.

Harrington, John, Co. D. **John Harringon** received a 1,280-acre bounty in Newton County for service from May 10, 1836, to August 14, 1837.

Heyder, John G., Co. A. **John Hyde** was on the roster of Capt. William D. Ratliff's Militia Company. He served from May 10, 1836, to an unknown date when he "left the country."

Jackson, Edwin, Co. A. **E. Jackson** served under Capt. Thomas S. McFarland, date unspecified.

Jacobs, John, was discharged from Co. D, October 8, 1836. **John Jacobs** was granted a 320-acre bounty in Bosque County for service from June 4 to September 4, 1836, under Capt. William Hamilton.

****King, William,** served in Co. A, where he was listed on "detached duty." **William King** served under Capt. Henry Karnes at San Jacinto. The heirs of **William King** received a 640-acre bounty in Jefferson County for service from March 24 to October 4, 1836.

****Lewis, Abel,** was listed on "Detached Service" from H Company in April 1836. But **A. Lewis** appeared on the roster of Capt. W.H. Patton at San Jacinto. He received a 320-acre bounty, which was later rejected.

Loyd, John, remained on the roster of Co. F. **John Loyd** received a 320-acre warrant for service from May 30 to December 30, 1836.

Lucas, John, Co. G. **John Lucas** served under Capt. Thomas McFarland "in 1836."

Lynch, Patrick, Co. G. **Patrick Lynch** joined Capt. C.A.W. Fowler's Company May 18, 1836.

Martin, Thomas, Co. F. **Thomas Martin** received a 640-acre bounty in Rains County for service from October 23, 1836, to November 24, 1837.

****Mattison, Andrew,** was in Co. H. He was not on the roster from April through June. **Mattison,** with no first name or initial, signed up April 12, 1836, with Capt. John Quitman at Nacogdoches. **Andrew Mattison** was discharged from the U.S. 3rd Infantry Regiment, December 15, 1836.

****McGee, Joseph,** Co. I. **Joseph McGee** was given a 320-acre bounty in Live Oak County for service from March 15 to July 23, 1836.

****Miller, James,** was carried on the roster of Company D through December 1835. No Co. D rosters are available for 1836. He would have been eligible for discharge December 13, 1836, but he was not on the discharge list for that month. **James Miller** fought at San Jacinto in Capt. Moseley Baker's Company, Burleson's Command. Another **James Miller** fought in Capt. A.H Wiley's Company at San Jacinto.

Norris, Thomas, Co. E. **Thomas Norris** enlisted in Capt. Benjamin Read's 1st Regiment Volunteers, June 1, 1836, and was with James L. Holmes' Kentucky Volunteers by August 1836. He received a 640-acre bounty in Coryell County.

Pool, William, Co. A. **William Pool** served in Capt. B. Enloe's Militia. Date not specified.

Riley, John, Co. G. **John Riley** received a 480-acre bounty in Hamilton County for service June 4, 1836, to November 15, 1837.

****Swarts, John,** Co. D, was discharged August 23, 1836, after serving only half of his enlistment. **John Swarts** was granted a 640-acre bounty in Lavaca County for service from March 2 to November 2, 1836. **John Swarth** was enlisted in Capt. McClure's Company June 1. **John Swarty** served in Maj. Isaac Burton's "Horse Marines" as they captured three Mexican supply ships on Copano Bay, June 3, 1836.

****Thompson, John,** remained on the roster of Co. B. **John Thompson** received a 320-acre bounty in Bastrop County for service from March 7 to June 7, 1836.

Walker, Daniel, Co. K. **Daniel Walker** was a "Three-Month Volunteer" in 1836.

****Waters, William,** deserted Co. C, U.S. 6th Infantry Regiment, August 22, 1836. **William Waters** served in Capt. William J.E.Heard's Company, Burleson's Command, at San Jacinto. **William Waters** received a 640-acre donation in Mason County for service at San Jacinto.

Welch, John, Co. D. **John Welch** was granted a 320-acre bounty in Parker County for service from June 4 to September 4, 1836.

****Williams, Sgt. Edward W.,** remained on the roster of Co. G. **Edward Williams** received a bounty of 320 acres in Rusk County for service from March 18 to July 23, 1836. He was issued another 640 acres in Denton County as a donation for his service guarding baggage at Harrisburg during the Battle of San

Jacinto.

Williamson, William, Co. K. **William Williamson** served with Lt. H.D. Chamberlain's Company. On September 6, 1836, he was "Confined for Mutiny."

****Young, Jacob,** discharged from Co. G March 13, 1834, reenlisted in Co. A July 8, 1834. **Jacob Young** enlisted in Capt. John Hart's Company at Velasco January 30, 1836.

Names of deserters and men discharged from the U.S. 4th Infantry Regiment at Baton Rouge, Louisiana:

****Moore, Samuel,** deserted Co. A, December 3, 1835. Samuel Moore enlisted in the Texas Army April 9, 1836, and earned a 640-acre donation in Milam County for fighting in the Battle of San Jacinto and a 1,280-acre grant in Navarro County for service until October 1837. **Moore,** no first name, was listed as a Regular in Capt. Amasa Turner's Company, Millard's Command, at San Jacinto.

****Moss, Sgt. John,** was discharged from Co. F, December 3, 1835. **John Moss** served under Capt. Hayden Arnold in Colonel Burleson's Command at San Jacinto and was awarded a 640-acre donation in Erath County.

****O'Niel, John D,** deserted Co. G, November 30, 1835. John O'Neil received a 640-acre donation in Hays County for serving at San Jacinto. He enlisted in Capt. Henry Teal's Company January 20, 1836. **John O'Neil** received a 1,280-acre warrant in Smith and Jack counties for service to January 1839.

****Richardson, John,** Musician, was discharged from Co. D, November 28, 1835. **John Richardson** received a 640-acre bounty in Bosque County for fighting at San Jacinto and a 320-acre bounty in Bosque County for service from March 1 to December 13, 1836.

****Scott, William,** was discharged from Co. G, August 2, 1835. **W.P. Scott** received a 640-acre donation in Taylor County for fighting at San Jacinto and a 320-acre bounty in Refugio County for service from March 15 to May 5, 1836.

Appendix B
Tejanos

Here is a partial list of Tejanos, native-born Texians, who served in the Texas Army during the 1835-1836 Revolution. The list has been compiled from available rosters and from lists of persons receiving land grants for revolutionary service. It is not complete, for Frank W. Johnson did not credit most of the Tejanos who served during the Siege and Storming of Bexar, and Juan Seguín's men sent to escort civilians to safety in April 1836 also did not receive credit for their service.

Alameda, José—Bexar
Aldrete, José Miguel—Bexar
Arocha, José María—San Jacinto
Arocha, Juan José—Bexar
Arocha, Manuel—San Jacinto
Arreola, Simon—San Jacinto
Badillo, Juan Andres—Bexar
Badillo, Juan Antonio—died in the Alamo
Ballí, Antonio—Bexar
Barbo, Juan J.E.—Bexar
Barbo, Juan J.J.—Bexar
Barcenas, Andre—San Jacinto
Benavides, Placido—Bexar
Becerra, José María—Bexar headright
Berzan, Ansel M.—Bexar
Bueno, Manuel—Bexar
Bustillos, Clemente—Bexar
Cabasas, Albino—Bexar
Carbajal, José María Jesus
Carbajal, Manuel—Bexar
Carbajal, Mariano—died with Fannin
Cardenas, Francisco—Bexar
Carmona, Caesario—San Jacinto
Casias, Gruviel—San Jacinto
Casillas, Juan—Bexar
Casillas, Mateo—Bexar
Casillas, Pablo—Bexar
Castanon, Luis—Bexar
Cervantes, Agapito—Bexar
Chacon, Carlos—Bexar
Chirino, José María—Bexar headright
Cilba, Miguel—Bexar
Conti, Circaco—Bexar
Conti, Julian—Bexar
Cruz y Arocha, Antonio—Bexar
Curvier, Antonio—Bexar, San Jacinto
Curvier, Fernando—Bexar
Curvier, Matías—Bexar
de la Garza, Alejandro—Bexar
de la Garza, Ana María—Bexar headright
de la Garza, José María—Bexar
de la Garza, Marcelino—Bexar
de la Garza, Paulino—Bexar
Diaz, Domingo—Bexar
Diaz, Francisco—Bexar
Duran, Blas—Bexar headright
Enriquez, Lucio—San Jacinto
Escalero, Manuel—Bexar
Espalier, Carlos—died in the Alamo
Esparza, Gregorio—Bexar, died in the Alamo
Espinosa, Jose María—died in the service
Espinoza, Ignacio—Bexar
Flores, Manuel—Bexar, San Jacinto
Flores, Manuel María—Bexar, San Jacinto
Flores, Martín
Flores, Nepomencino—San Jacinto
Flores, Salvador—Bexar
Franco, Miguel—one of Santa Anna's soldiers, Bexar headright
Francois, Sebastian

Fuentes, Antonio–Bexar, died in the Alamo
Gallardo, Manuel
Gaona, Pedro–Bexar
Garcia, Casimiro–Bexar
Garcia, Clemente–Bexar
Garcia, Francisco–fought at Coleto
Garcia, Guadalupe–Bexar
Garcia, Jesús–Bexar
Gayton, Agapito–Bexar
Gomez, Francisco–Bexar
Gomez, Jesús–Bexar
Gomez, Maximo–Bexar
Gonzales, Simón
Gonzalez, Gabriel–Bexar
Guano, Pedro–Bexar
Guardo, Manuel–Bexar
Guerra, Ygnacio
Guerrero, Brigido–survived the Alamo
Guerrero, José María–Bexar
Guerrero, Trinidad–Bexar headright
Hernandez, Antonio–Bexar
Hernandez, Eduardo–Bexar
Hernandez, Gregorio–Bexar
Herrera, Guadalupe–Bexar headright
Herrera, Pedro–Bexar, San Jacinto
Herrera, Toríbio–Bexar
Huizar, Carlos–Bexar headright
Jiminez, Juan–Bexar
Laso, Carlos–Bexar
Lavina, José Palonia
Leal, Manuel–Bexar
Losoya, José Domingo–Bexar
Losoya, Toríbio–Bexar, died in the Alamo
Maldonado, — –Bexar headright
Maldonado, Tomás–San Jacinto
Malona, José–San Jacinto
Mancha, Jose María–(Austin Colonist)–Bexar headright
Mancha, Nazario–Bexar headright
Mansolo, Pablo–Bexar
Mata, Miguel–Bexar
Menchaca, Antonio–San Jacinto
Mirando, Francisco–Bexar
Mora, Esteban
Moran, Martín–served under Fannin
Nava, Andres–died in the Alamo
Nava, Antonio–Bexar
Navarro, Nepomuceno–Bexar
Palacios, Juan José–Bexar
Pena, Jacinto–San Jacinto
Piñeda, José–Bexar headright
Pru, Anselmo–Bexar headright
Ramirez, Eduardo–Bexar, San Jacinto
Ramos, María Luísa–Bexar headright
Ramos, Vicente–Bexar
Rendón, José–Bexar
Rocha, José María–San Jacinto
Rodriguez, Ambrosio–Bexar, San Jacinto
Rodriguez, José de Jesús–Bexar
Rodriguez, Justo–Bexar
Rubio, Ramón–Bexar
Ruiz, Antonio–Bexar
Ruiz, Esmergaldo–Bexar
Salinas, Nicolas–Bexar headright
Salinas, Francisco–Bexar
Salinas, Miguel–Bexar
Salinas, Pablo–Bexar
Seguín, Juan N.–Bexar, San Jacinto
Silva, Manuel–Bexar
Tarin, Manuel–San Jacinto
Tejado, Agapito–Bexar
Travieso, Justo–Bexar
Trevino, Antonio–San Jacinto
Valdez, Francisco–Bexar
Valta, Gaetano
Villanueva, Juan
Villarreal, Esteban–Bexar
Ximenes, Damacio–died in the Alamo
Ybarbo, Jesus–Bexar headright
Zepeda, Vicente–Bexar
Zambrano, José–Bexar
Zambrano, Juan M.
Zuniga, José–Bexar

These Tejanos from Goliad, Refugio, and Victoria were mentioned by Refugio Historian Hobart Huson as serving as scouts, spies, guides, couriers, carters, wagoneers and provisioners for the Texian forces:

Albin, Jaimie
Arce, Juan
Castro, Ignacio
de la Garza, Carlos
Galan, ——
Guzman, Andres
Hernandez, Jose Maria
Lopez, ——
Mendez, Gertrudis
Pobedando, ——
Portilla, Felipe Roque
Ramon, B.
Ramon, Francisco
Reojas, ——
Rios, Florentin
Rios, ——
Trevino, ——
Vasquez, Encarnacion

Roster of Mexican Troops at Fort Lipantitlán, October 1835
Source: Bexar Archives
2nd Company of Cavalry, Active, of Tamaulipas:

Two rosters, drawn the month before the garrison was attacked by Texian Volunteers on November 5, 1835, were apparently written by Marcelino Garcia, ensign second class, who acted as company clerk, for he signed the reports along with Nicolas Rodriguez, first lieutenant and commanding officer in the absence of Capt. Enrique Villarreal, who was in Matamoros and avoided all the action at the fort. The reports, in recapitulation, list one captain, one teniente or lieutenant, one ensign or possibly second lieutenant, four sergeants, one sub sergeant, five corporals, one bugler or clarin, and seventy common soldiers.

Officers

1. **Capt. Enrique Villarreal** (In Matamoros)
2. **1st Lt. Nicolas Rodriguez**
3. **2nd Lt.** Vacant
4. **2nd Lt. Marcelino Garcia**

Noncommissioned Officers

5. **Sgt. Rafael Aceves**
6. **Ysabel Longoria** (detached to Goliad)
7. **Rogero Trevino**
8. **Antonio Aceves** (Bugler)
9. **Roman Perez** (In Matamoros)
10. **Lorenso Hernandez** (To Goliad)
11. **Jose Maria Loya**
12. **Juan Villarreal**
13. **Francisco DeLeon**

Soldiers

14. **Ysidro Pena** (To Goliad)
15. **Cornelio Espinosa**
16. **Jose M. Paredes** (In Matamoros)
17. **Segundo Garcia**
18. **Santos Hernandes**
19. **Antonio Villarreal**
20. **Jose Maria Moya**
21. **Capetano Flores**
22. **Tomas Cabera**
23. **Jacabo Barrera**
24. **Nepomucena Garcia**
25. **Garcia, Marcelino** (To Goliad)
26. **Manuel Cavasos**
27. **Pedro Garibayo** (To Goliad)
28. **Ascensio Sifuentes**
29. **Pablo Flores** (To Goliad)
30. **Pedro Munguia**
31. **Claudio Longoria**
32. **Anicito Tijerina**
33. **Juan Jose Rios**
34. **Francisco DeLuna**
35. **Jesus Vasquez** (To Goliad)
36. **Cavisias Bela** (Ill)
37. **Juan Garcia**
38. **Felipe Garcia** (To Goliad)
39. **Antonio Espinosa**
40. **Santiago Sanchez**
41. **Francisco Flores** (To Goliad)
42. **José María Garcia**
43. **Esteban Barrera** (To Goliad)
44. **Yldefonso Flores**
45. **José María Flores**
46. **Clemeno Barrera**
47. **Fiburcio Diaz**
48. **Juan Soliz** (To Goliad)
49. **Ygnacio Longoria**
50. **Juan Longori**
51. **Rumaldo Chapa**
52. **Antonio Amaya** (To Goliad)
53. **Mateos De Los Santos**
54. **Ygnacio Trevino**
55. **Bernardo Loya**
56. **Jesús Pena**
57. **Andres Cabasos**
58. **Francisco Cantu** (To Goliad)
59. **Benito Munguia**
60. **Miguel Ramerina**
61. **Miguel Longoria** (In Matamoros)
62. **Andres Relles** (To Goliad)
63. **Lino Salinas**
64. **Panifilo Garza**
65. **Rafael Peña**
66. **Cecilio Fernandez** (To Goliad)
67. **Eligio Sosa**
68. **Jose Maria Balensuela** (To Goliad)
69. **Luis Bargos**
70. **Jesus Martinez**
71. **Balentino Leal** (In Matamoros)
72. **Benito Balensuela**
73. **Cisto Lopez**
74. **Guillermo Yanez**
75. **Pedro Garza**
76. **Juan Zamora** (To Goliad)
77. **Florintino Quesado**
78. **Martin Ramirez** (Ill)
79. **Pedro Flores** (To Goliad)
80. **Gil Trevino** (Matamoros)
81. **José María Davila** (Ill)
82. **Bernaldo Martinez** (To Goliad)
83. **Juan De Abarco** (To Goliad)
84. **Bacilio Gonzales**
85. **Marcelino Hernandez** (To Goliad)
86. **Juan Villarreal**
87. **Juan de Abrego**
88. **Rafael Garcia**
89. **Francisco Garcia**
90. **José María Marriquin** (In Matamoros)
91. **Sgt. Hilario Garza** (Confined to Camp)

Sources

American Military History, 1607-1958. Department of the Army ROTC Training Manual 145-20. Washington, D.C.: Department of the Army, 1959.

Ashford, Gerald. *Spanish Texas, Yesterday and Today.* Austin & New York: Jenkins Publishing Co., 1971.

Bancroft, Hubert Howe. *History of the North Mexican States and Texas.* San Francisco: 1899.

Barker, Eugene, editor. *The Austin Papers.* Washington, D.C.: Government Printing Office, 1924-1928.

Barragy, Terrence J., and Harry Russell Huebel. *From Colony to Republic: Readings in American History to 1877.* Houston: Cayo Del Grullo Press, 1983.

Bass, Ferris A., Jr., and B.R. Brunson, editors. *Fragile Empires: The Texas Correspondence of Samuel Swartwout and James Morgan, 1836-1856.* Austin: Shoal Creek Publishers, Inc., 1978.

Bassett, John Spencer, editor. *Correspondence of Andrew Jackson, Vol. V.* Washington, D.C.: Carnegie Institution of Washington, 1926-1935.

Becerra, Francisco. *A Mexican Sergeant's Recollections of the Alamo & San Jacinto.* Austin: Jenkins Publishing Co., 1980.

Bradfield, Jane. *Take One Cannon.* Shiner, Texas: Patrick J. Wagner Research & Publishing Co., 1981.

Briscoe, Eugenia Reynolds. *City by the Sea, A History of Corpus Christi, Texas, 1519-1875.* New York: Vantage Press, 1985.

Brown, John Henry. *History of Texas from 1685 to 1892.* Austin: Jenkins Publishing Co., 1970.

——. *Life and Times of Henry Smith.* Dallas: A.D. Aldridge & Co., 1887.

Casey, Powell A. *Louisiana in the War of 1812.* 1963.

Castañeda, Carlos Eduardo. *The Mexican Side of the Texas Revolution.* Austin: Graphic Ideas, Inc., 1970.

——. *Our Catholic Heritage in Texas 1519-1936.* Austin: Van Boeckman-Jones Co., 1936.

Chabot, Frederick Charles. *With the Makers of San Antonio.* San Antonio: Privately published, 1937.

Clark, Mary Whatley. *David G. Burnet, First President of Texas.* Austin & New York: The Pemberton Press, 1969.

Coalson, George O. "Texas Mexicans in the Texas Revolution." Essay published in *The American West*. Toledo: University of Toledo Press, 1980.

Conner, John Edwin, Jack Edward Conner, and Robbie C. Harper. *The Flags of Texas*. Norman, Oklahoma: Harlow Publishing Corporation, 1964.

Cox, Mamie Wynne. *The Romantic Flags of Texas*. Dallas: Banks Upshaw & Company, 1936.

Crane, William Carey. *Life and Literary Remains of Sam Houston of Texas*. Dallas: W.G. Scarff, 1884.

Daughters of the Republic of Texas. *Muster Rolls of the Texas Revolution*. Austin: 1986.

—–. *Defenders of the Republic of Texas, Vol. I, Texas Army Muster Rolls, Receipt Rolls and Other Rolls, 1836-1841*. Austin: Laurel House Press, 1989.

Davis, Joe Tom. *Legendary Texians*. Austin: Eakin Press, 1985.

Davis, John L. *Treasure, People, Ships, and Dreams, A Spanish Shipwreck on the Texas Coast*. San Antonio: Texas Antiquities Committee, 1977.

Day, Donald, and Harry Herbert Ullom. *The Autobiography of Sam Houston*. Norman, Oklahoma: University of Oklahoma Press, 1954.

DeGolyer, E. *Across Aboriginal America, Journeying Through Texas in 1568*. El Paso: Perapatetic Press, 1947.

de la Peña, José Enrique. *With Santa Anna in Texas, A Personal Narrative of the Revolution*, translated and edited by Carmen Perry. College Station, Texas: Texas A&M University Press, 1975.

Dewees, William B. *Letters from an Early Settler of Texas*. Waco: Texian Press, 1968.

Dixon, Sam Houston, and Louis Wiltz Kemp. *The Heroes of San Jacinto*. Houston: The Anson Jones Press, 1932.

Dobie, J. Frank, Mody C. Boatright, and Harry H. Ransom. *In the Shadow of History*. Austin: Folklore Society, 1939.

Ehrenberg, Herman. *With Milam and Fannin, The Adventures of a German Boy in Texas' Revolution*. Translated by Charlotte Churchill. Austin: The Pemberton Press, 1968.

Fehrenbach, T.R. *Lone Star: A History of Texas and the Texans*. New York: Macmillan Publishing Co., Inc., 1968.

——. *Fire and Blood: A Bold and Definitive Modern Chronicle of Mexico*. New York: Bonanza Books, 1985.

Filisola, Vicente. *Memorias para la Historia de la Guerra de Tejas*, translated by Wallace Woolsey. Austin: Eakin Press, 1987.

Foote, Henry Stuart. *Texas and the Texans*. Austin, The Steck Co., 1935.

Frantz, Joe B. *The Alamo in the Battles of Texas*. Waco: Texian Press, 1967.

Friend, Llerena B. *Sam Houston, The Great Designer*. Austin: University of Texas Press, 1954.

Gambrell, Herbert. *Anson Jones, The Last President of Texas*. Austin, University of Texas Press, 1988.

Gambrell, Herbert, and Virginia Gambrell. *A Pictorial History of Texas*. New York: E.P. Dutton & Co., Inc., 1960.

Garrett, Julia Kathryn. *Green Flag Over Texas. The Story of the First War of Independence in Texas. The Last Years of Spain in Texas*. Austin & New York: Pemberton Press, 1969.

Gray, William Fairfax. *Diary of Col. Wm. F. Gray Giving Details of His Journey to Texas and Returns in 1835-1836*. Houston: Fletcher Young, 1965.

Green, Rena Maverick, editor. *Samuel Maverick, Texan: 1803-1870. A Collection of Letters, Journals and Memoirs*. San Antonio: Privately printed, 1952.

Gregory, Jack, and Rennard Strickland. *Sam Houston With the Cherokees, 1829-1833*. Austin: University of Texas Press, 1976.

Groneman, Bill. *Alamo Defenders*. Austin: Eakin Press, 1990.

Hakluyt, Richard. *The Principal Navigations, Voiages and Discoveries of the English Nation*. New York: Viking Press, 1965.

Handbook of Texas. 2 vols. Edited by Walter Prescott Webb. Austin: Texas State Historical Association, 1952.

——. *A Supplement*. Vol. 3. Edited by Eldon Stephen Branda. Austin: Texas State Historical Association, 1976.

Hatcher, Mattie Austin. *The Opening of Texas to Foreign Settlement, 1801-1821*. Austin: The University of Texas, 1927.

Hebert, Rachel Bluntzer. *The Forgotten Colony, San Patricio de Hibernia*. Burnet, Texas: Eakin Press, 1981.

Hodge, F.W., and T.H. Lewis, editors. *Spanish Explorers in the Southern United States, 1528-1543, Original Narratives of Early American History*. New York: Barnes & Noble, Inc., 1971.

Holley, Mary Austin. *Texas*. Austin: Texas State Historical Association, 1985.

Horgan, Paul. *Great River, The Rio Grande in North American History, Volume One, Indians and Spain*. New York & Toronto: Rinehart & Company, Inc., 1954.

Houston, Andrew Jackson. *Texas Independence*. Houston: A. Jones, 1938.

Huson, Hobart. *Captain Phillip Dimmitt's Commandancy of Goliad, October 15, 1835-January 17, 1836*. Austin: Von Boeckman-Jones Co., 1974.

——. *El Copano: Ancient Port of La Bahia and Bexar*. Refugio, Texas: Refugio timely remarks, 1935.

——. *Refugio: A Comprehensive History of Refugio County*, 2 vols. Woodsboro, Texas: Rooke Foundation, 1953-55.

——. *Dr. J.H. Barnard's Journal*. Goliad: H. Huson, 1949.

Irion Family. *Ever Thine Truly*. Letters of Sam Houston and Anna Raguet. Austin: Jenkins-Garrett Press, 1975.

Jackson, Jack. *Los Mesteños, Spanish Ranching in Texas*. College Station: Texas A&M University Press, 1986.

James, Marquis. *Andrew Jackson, The Border Captain*. New York: Grosset & Dunlap, 1933.

——. *The Raven, A Biography of Sam Houston*. Indianapolis: Bobbs-Merrill, 1929.

Jenkins, John H. *The Papers of the Texas Revolution*. 10 vols. Austin: Presidial Press, 1973.

Johnson, Frank W. *A History of Texas and Texans*. Chicago: American Historical Society, 1914.

Jones, Anson. *Memoranda and Official Correspondence Relating to the Republic of Texas, Its History and Annexation, Including a Brief Autobiography of the Author*. Chicago: Rio Grande Press, 1966.

Kemp, Louis Wiltz. *The Signers of the Texas Declaration of Independence*. Salado: Anson Jones Press, 1959.

Kendall, Dorothy Steinbomer, with Carmen Perry. *Gentilz, Artist of the Old Southwest*. Austin: University of Texas Press, 1974.

Kennedy, William. *Texas: The Rise, Progress, and Prospects of the Republic of Texas*. Fort Worth: The Molyneaux Craftsmen, 1925.

Kilgore, Dan. *How Did Davy Die?* College Station: Texas A&M University Press,

1978.

King, C. Richard. *Susanna Dickinson: Messenger of the Alamo.* Austin: Shoal Creek Publishers, Inc., 1976.

Lamar, Mirabeau B. *The Papers of Mirabeau Buonaparte Lamar.* Edited by Charles Adams Gulick, Jr., Winnie Allen, Katherine Elliott, and Harriet Smither. Austin: Pemberton Press, 1968.

Lay, Bennett. *The Lives of Ellis P. Bean.* Austin: University of Texas Press, 1960.

Linn, John J. *Reminiscences of Fifty Years in Texas.* Austin: State House Press, 1986.

Long, Jeff. *Duel of Eagles.* New York: William Morrow and Co., Inc., 1990.

Lord, Walter. *A Time to Stand.* New York: Harper & Brothers, 1961.

Lozano, Ruben Rendon. *Viva Tejas, The Story of the Tejanos, the Mexican-born Patriots of the Texas Revolution.* San Antonio: Alamo Press, 1985.

Mahan, William. *Padre Island, Treasure Kingdom of the World.* Waco: Texian Press, 1967.

McDonald, Archie P. *William Barret Travis, A Biography.* Austin: Eakin Press, 1976.

McDonlay, David, translator; Barto, J. Arnold III, State Marine Archaeologist. *Documentary Sources for the Wreck of the New Spain Fleet of 1554.* Austin: Texas Antiquities Commission, 1979.

Marshall, Thomas M. *A History of the Western Boundary of the Louisiana Purchase 1819-1841.* Berkeley: University of California Press, 1914.

Menchaca, Antonio. *Memoirs.* Edited by Frederick C. Chabot. San Antonio: Yanaguana Society, 1937.

Miller, Thomas Lloyd. *Bounty and Donation Land Grants of Texas, 1835-1888.* Austin: University of Texas Press, 1967.

Morison, Samuel Eliot. *The Oxford History of the American People.* New York: Oxford University Press, 1965.

Nance, Joseph Milton. *After San Jacinto: The Texas-Mexican Frontier, 1836-1841.* Austin: University of Texas Press, 1963.

——. *Attack and Counterattack: The Texas-Mexican Frontier.* Austin: University of Texas Press, 1964.

Newcomb, W.W., Jr. *The Indians of Texas from Prehistoric to Modern Times.* Austin: University of Texas Press, 1961.

Nixon, Pat Ireland. *The Medical Story of Early Texas, 1512-1853.* Lancaster, Pennsylvania: 1946.

Nueces County Historical Society. *The History of Nueces County.* Austin: Jenkins Publishing Co., 1972.

Oates, Stephen B., editor. *The Republic of Texas.* Austin: Texas State Historical Society, 1968.

Oberste, Msgr. William H. *Texan Irish Empresarios and Their Colonies, Power & Hewetson; Mullen & McGloin.* Austin: Von Boeckman-Jones, 1953.

O'Connor, Kathryn Stoner. *The Presidio La Bahia del Espiritu Santo de Zuniga, 1701-1846.* Austin: Privately printed, 1966.

Parkes, Henry Bamford. *A History of Mexico.* Boston: Houghton-Mifflin Co., 1960.

Pennybacker, Mrs. Anna M.J. *A New History of Texas for Schools, Also for Teachers Preparing for Examinations.* Palestine, Texas: P.V. Pennybacker, 1895.

Potter, Reuben Marmaduke. *The Fall of the Alamo.* Hillsdale, New Jersey: Otterden Press, 1977.

Richardson, Rupert N. *Texas, The Lone Star State.* New York: Prentice-Hall, Inc., 1953.

Rose, Victor M. *Victor Rose's History of Victoria.* Edited by J.W. Petty, Jr. Victoria, Texas: Book Mart, 1961.

Santos, Richard G. *Santa Anna's Campaign Against Texas, 1835-1836.* Waco: Texian Press, 1970.

Sanchez Lamego, Gen. Miguel A. *The Siege & Taking of the Alamo.* Santa Fe, New Mexico: Press of the Territorian, 1968.

Schoelwer, Susan Prendergast, editor. *Alamo Images, Changing Perceptions of a Texas Experience.* Dallas: DeGolyer Library and Southern Methodist University Press, 1985.

Schwarz, Ted. *Forgotten Battlefield of the First Texas Revolution.* Edited by Robert H. Thonhoff. Austin: Eakin Press, 1985.

Seguín, Juan N. *A Revolution Remembered: The Memoirs and Selected Correspondence of Juan N. Seguin.* Edited by Jesus F. de la Teja. Austin: State House Press, 1991.

Sibley, Marilyn McAdams. *Travelers in Texas, 1761-1860.* Austin & London: University of Texas Press, 1967.

Smithwick, Noah. *The Evolution of a State or Recollections of Old Texas Days.* Austin: University of Texas Press, 1983.

Thrall, H.S. *History of Texas.* New York: University Publishing Co., 1885.

Tinkle, Lon. *13 Days to Glory.* New York: McGraw-Hill Book Company, Inc., 1958.

Tolbert, Frank X. *The Day of San Jacinto.* New York, Toronto, London: McGraw-Hill Book Company, Inc., 1959.

Travis, William Barret. *Diary of William Barret Travis.* Edited by Robert E. Davis. Waco: Texian Press, 1966.

Unwin, Rayner. *The Defeat of John Hawkins, A Biography of His Third Slaving Voyage.* New York: Macmillan, 1960.

Wallace, Ernest, and David M. Vigness. *Documents of Texas History.* Austin: The Steck Company, 1963.

Williams, Amelia W., and Eugene C. Barker. *Writings of Sam Houston.* Austin: Jenkins Publishing Company, 1970.

Woodman, Lyman L. *Cortina: The Rogue of the Rio Grande.* San Antonio: Naylor Company, 1950.

Wooten, Dudley Goodall. *A Comprehensive History of Texas, 1685-1879.* Dallas: The Texas History Company, 1899.

Wortham, Louis J. *A History of Texas.* Fort Worth: Wortham-Molyneux Company, 1924.

Yoakum, Henderson K. *History of Texas, 1685-1846.* New York: Redfield Company, 1855.

Young, Kevin R. *Texas Forgotten Heroes.* Goliad: Goliad County Historical Commission, 1986.

Periodicals

Dobie, J. Frank. "No Help for the Alamo." *True West,* Vol. 6, No. 5, May-June, 1959.

Duewall, L.A. "The Story of Monument Hill." *La Grange Journal.*

Hunter, John Warren. "Autobiography of Carlos Beltran." *Frontier Times*, De-

cember 1940.
Hutton, Paul Andrew. "Davy Crockett, Still King of the Wild Frontier and a Hell of a Nice Guy Besides." *Texas Monthly*, November 1986.
Ivy, James. *Alamo Lore and Myth Organization Newsletter*.
Mercurio de Matamoros, Archdiocese Library, Austin.
National Geographic, March 1986.
Potter, Rueben M. "The Prisoners of Matamoros." *The Alamo Magazine*, March 1915.
Southwestern Historical Quarterly.
Texana Magazine, Vol. 11, No. 1.
Texas Almanac. 1858.
Texas Historical Quarterly.
Wade, Houston. "The Dawson Men of Fayette County." *La Grange Journal*, 1936.

Unpublished Documents

3rd U.S. Infantry Regiment Monthly Returns, 1834–1837. National Archives.
3rd U.S. Infantry Regiment Rosters, 1832–1837. National Archives.
4th U.S. Infantry Post Returns. National Archives.
6th U.S. Infantry Regiment Monthly Returns, 1834–1837. National Archives.
Andrew Jackson Houston Collection, Texas State Archives.
Baugh, Adj. J.J., report from the Alamo. Note on file at the Daughters of the Republic of Texas Alamo Library.
Baylor family papers, Baylor University Archives.
Bowie, James, note. Daughters of the Republic of Texas Alamo Library.
"Capt. Juan N. Seguín's soldiers," transcripted by Etna P. Scott. Cassiano Collection, Daughters of the Republic of Texas Alamo Library.
Davenport, Harbert. Papers. Texas State Archives.
Fort Lipantitlan Mexican Army Rosters, October 1835. Bexar Archives.
Giddings, Giles A., Letter to his parents, April 10, 1836. Copy from Giddings family.
Huson, Hobart. "Lipantitlan." Dawgwood Library, Refugio, Texas.
——. "The Republic of the Rio Grande." Dawgwood Library, Refugio, Texas.
——. "Iron Men: A History of the Texian Participation in the Mexican Federalist Wars 1838-1842." Dawgwood Library, Refugio, Texas.
——. "History in the Schools and Colleges, Address to South Texas Historical Society, May 8, 1971." Dawgwood Library, Refugio, Texas.
——. "San Patricio and Agua Dulce." Dawgwood Library, Refugio, Texas.
——. "The Matamoros Expedition." Dawgwood Library, Refugio, Texas.
Oberste, Msgr. William. "Goliad" (manuscript).
Priour, Rosalie B. Hart. "The Adventures of a Family of Emmigrants Who Emmigrated to Texas in 1834, An Autobiography by Rosalie B. Hart Priour" (manuscript). Corpus Christi Public Library.
U.S. Military Academy Disciplinary Records, November and December 1834.
Williams, Amelia. "A Critical Study of the Siege of the Alamo and the Personnel of Some of Its Defenders."

Index

B

D

E

F

G

J

K

L

Q

R

T

U

V

W

Y

Z